HOW TO HAVE AN ELEGANT WEDDING
FOR $5,000 OR LESS

JAN WILSON ❧ BETH WILSON HICKMAN

HOW TO HAVE AN
ELEGANT
WEDDING

FOR $5,000 OR LESS

Achieving Beautiful Simplicity Without
Mortgaging Your Future

THREE RIVERS PRESS · NEW YORK

Published by Three Rivers Press, New York, New York.
Member of the Crown Publishing Group, a division of Random House, Inc.
www.crownpublishing.com

THREE RIVERS PRESS and the Tugboat design are registered trademarks of Random House, Inc.

Originally published by Prima Publishing, Roseville, California, in 1999.

WARNING—DISCLAIMER
Certain suggestions are made in this book. While these are intended to be helpful to the reader, the reader must assume all risk associated with following any particular suggestion. Therefore, in purchasing this book, the reader agrees that the authors and publisher are not liable or responsible for any injury or damage caused by the use of any information contained herein.

All of the characters in this book are based on real persons, but in some cases, names have been omitted or changed to protect the privacy of the people involved. Therefore, any resemblance to actual persons, living or dead, is purely coincidental, unless authorized by the actual person mentioned.

Printed in the United States of America

Interior illustrations by Andrew Vallas

Library of Congress Cataloging-in-Publication Data

Wilson, Jan.
    How to have an elegant wedding for $5,000 or less : achieving beautiful simplicity without mortgaging your future / Jan Wilson and Beth Wilson Hickman.
        p. cm.
    Includes index.
    1. Weddings—United States—Planning. 2. Weddings—United States—Costs. 3. Shopping—United States. 4. Consumer education—United States. I. Title.
HQ745.W55   1998
395.2'2—dc21   98-50842
                                                            CIP

ISBN 0-7615-1804-5

10 9 8

First Edition

CONTENTS

4. WEDDING ATTIRE ❧ 57
DRESSING FOR THE DAY OF A LIFETIME

5. THE RECEPTION AND CATERING ❧ 81
CELEBRATING WITH FOOD AND DRINK

6. PHOTOGRAPHY AND VIDEOGRAPHY ❧ 107
PRESERVING MEMORIES OF YOUR WEDDING ON FILM

7. MUSIC ❧ 125
CREATING AND ADDING PERFECT HARMONY

8. FLOWERS ❧ 139
ADDING JUST THE RIGHT TOUCH TO YOUR DAY

9. DECORATIONS ❧ 155
PICKING THE PERFECT ACCENTS

10. THE CAKE   ❧   173
SELECTING A MAGNIFICENT EDIBLE SHOWPIECE

11. INVITATIONS   ❧   185
ASKING FRIENDS AND FAMILY TO SHARE IN YOUR SPECIAL DAY

12. TRANSPORTATION ❧ 205
ARRIVING IN STYLE AND ON TIME

13. A PERSONALIZED CEREMONY ❧ 215
INDIVIDUALIZING THE WEDDING RITUAL

14. DETAILS, DETAILS, DETAILS ❧ 231
TYING THE LOOSE ENDS TOGETHER FOR A
FUN AND ORGANIZED WEDDING DAY

15. THE FINISHING TOUCHES   261
SCHEDULING AND REHEARSING THE DETAILS

16. THE DAY YOU'VE BEEN WAITING FOR   275
MAKING YOUR DREAM COME TRUE

ACKNOWLEDGMENTS

FROM BOTH OF US

We would like to thank Kim, who lovingly critiqued our book and went above and beyond the little sis/daughter call of duty. And to our brides and grooms and wedding professionals, who enthusiastically participated in this book: Thank you for all your ideas and support.

FROM JAN

I would like to thank Gary, my "favorite" husband, who lent much love, encouragement, and support (he even vacuumed!). I am so lucky to have had you for thirty-five years!

I also want to thank Beth—my daughter, business partner, co-author, and friend. What's next, honey? Much love, Liebs

FROM BETH

I'd like to thank my husband, Jeff, for always believing in me and for continuing to be our greatest fan. I look forward to many more years of wedded bliss with you.

And to my mom, I am so fortunate to have a mother that I enjoy doing so many things with! Thank you for all your love and support, always. You and I planning Jeff's and my dream wedding (on a budget) was the beginning of many great things!

INTRODUCTION

YOU ARE ENGAGED! What an exciting time! Every couple hopes their wedding will be a beautiful and memorable occasion. You have probably dreamed of your wedding day for many years. Creating a day as special as your dreams requires much planning and organization. We have designed our book to be your guide as you start your planning, to be by your side as you make a number of important decisions along the way and through the end of your special day.

Most couples envision their perfect wedding, but actually planning the big day can seem like quite a daunting task. Perhaps even more overwhelming than the planning is the thought of trying to afford this perfect day without breaking the bank. Everyone would like to achieve the wedding of their dreams, but many fear they can't afford it. We feel dreams can be realized within a reasonable budget, even for under $5,000, through careful planning and prioritizing. Good organization is crucial to the success of a wedding. Not only can it lessen the possibility of costly mistakes, but it can also eliminate the stress and anxiety. Our book will help you be organized and knowledgeable so you can get hitched without a hitch!

How Did We Get Our Start?

WHILE planning Beth and her husband Jeff's wedding, we experienced firsthand that it is possible to have a lovely wedding while remaining on a budget. We spent hours, days, weeks, and months reaching our goal of a simply elegant yet affordable wedding. We were inexperienced ten years ago and would have appreciated a book like this to guide us in a more organized way. The wedding day turned out to be extremely memorable and beautiful. It was everything we had dreamed of. "Hey," we thought, "we are good at this!"

Soon after the wedding, a guest contacted us to ask for advice with her daughter's wedding. We were pleased to share what we had learned. We found we had many money-saving and organizing ideas. After successfully assisting them, we formed our mother–daughter wedding-coordinating business and have coordinated dozens of weddings since.

When we planned Beth's wedding, we were not aware that wedding coordinators existed. In case you aren't sure what a wedding coordinator's role is, we assist couples with everything from the beginning stages of planning through waving goodbye to the newly betrothed couple at the end of the big day, and everything in between. Coordinators also give advice and act as a liaison between the bride and the wedding vendors such as the caterer and disc jockey. We often receive requests for our services when the panicked bride realizes thirty days before her wedding that she cannot be both posing for pictures and checking on the caterers at the same time. Thorough communication and organization ahead of time can help eliminate these worries.

We have planned weddings with budgets ranging from shoestring to quite extravagant during the past eight years of being in business, and we have found we really enjoy the challenges a wedding on a small budget brings. We often hear guests say, "Everything went so smoothly. It was such a lovely occasion." It is often the well-orchestrated wedding that impresses guests more than how much money was spent. We would like to help you achieve a well-coordinated wedding. Not everyone can afford the luxury of hiring a professional wedding coordinator, so we have written our book to teach you how to have a wedding that appears to have been professionally planned. We are pleased to share our wedding-coordinating strategies with you.

How to Use This Book

OUR book is designed to be the only book you will need. By following our guidelines, your wedding will run as smoothly as it would if it were professionally coordinated by us. We have arranged the chapters in the order that we feel you should accomplish each step. For instance, it is important to determine your wedding date and location first because style, time of day, and vendor availability will be based on this. It is also more imperative to find a reputable photographer whose work you like than it is to taste cakes. Good photographers are booked well in advance, and you cannot duplicate them, whereas bakeries can create many cakes in one day. Of course, since all weddings are different, all the information in this book will not necessarily apply or appeal to you.

Although you may have already decided on some parts of your wedding, we encourage you to read each clearly marked chapter, as you may learn of some details that you can incorporate into your special event.

Throughout each chapter we share our experiences and expertise. We offer help and ideas on how to achieve what you want within the guidelines of your budget. The sidebars offer our advice, suggestions from professionals, and thoughts from former brides on how to make your wedding day more perfect. We cover tips on choosing your attendants; keeping costs low in all areas; finding the perfect location; selecting music, flowers, and attire; questioning professionals you may hire; deciding what family and friends can help you with; and much more. We also share with you our organization system and remind you at the end of chapters what to do to remain organized. With the help of our time-saving suggestions, rehearsal information, and sample schedules, we can ensure your entire wedding day will go smoothly.

Your engagement should be a time for romance and visions of your new life together, not a time for worrying about impending wedding bills. Let us help you achieve a simply elegant wedding while staying within your budget.

FIRST THINGS FIRST

PLANNING TO MAKE YOUR DREAM WEDDING A REALITY

Most couples wonder where they should begin. Sharing the news with your family and friends is a lot of fun and, of course, at the top of your list. If your families have not met, you may want to arrange a gathering so they can get to know each other.

After your engagement, anyone may give a party in your honor. The first party is traditionally hosted by the parents of the bride, with the formal announcement of your engagement made during a toast given by the bride's father. The groom's family may then also wish to give a party to introduce their friends and extended family to the bride. The formal announcement may be sent to your local newspaper as well as to the paper in your groom's hometown. Most big-city newspapers are no longer able to print this information. Call the papers in which you are interested in having your announcement appear and inquire about their policies and format requirements.

Of Utmost Importance

During the wedding-planning process, don't lose sight of what this event is really about. Of utmost importance is the fact that you will be taking vows to love and cherish each other and will promise to spend the rest of your lives together. When a problem arises with some part of the planning procedure (and it will!), stop and remember the reason for the celebration is what is most important, not the color of the ribbons, the style of the cake, or the type of flower in Mom's corsage.

Let's Dream

LET'S start at the beginning and have fun planning! Planning a wedding can be very exciting. This is a big celebration when your friends and families gather together, and most couples want it to be very memorable. This event is possibly a bigger function than you have ever planned and probably something you know very little about. Conduct your planning as you would a business. Be very organized and enjoy this time!

Let's do some dreaming. What do you envision as the ideal day? Have you always dreamed of having a horse and carriage? Have you had your eyes on a particular location? Are flowers really important to you? Have you looked through bridal magazines and cut out a picture of the "have to have it" cake? Does your fiancé want the wedding to be held outdoors? Have you thought you would like a candlelight ceremony? Will you have a religious or nonsectarian ceremony? Is your idea of the perfect reception romantic, lively, intimate, family oriented, casual, or formal?

If money were no object, what would you plan? Perhaps you and your fiancé attended a beautiful wedding several years ago that really stayed in your mind. What was it that you remember? Was it the location? Was it the food? Did it capture the bride's and groom's personalities? These questions may seem overwhelming, but it is important to remember that they are all part of a *fun* process. You don't have to let your dreams go unfulfilled. Decide what is really important to include on your special day and make that a priority. Know what is right for the two of you. Your wedding day should reflect that.

JEFF AND BETH'S STORY

When Beth started planning her wedding, we were flying to visit relatives. She had a bridal magazine on her lap, and we were looking at pictures of lovely gowns. She was just newly engaged, her fiancé and she were college students, their wedding was still more than a year and a half away, and we had done nothing at this point. We started talking about what she would like for a location. She got real dreamy and said she had always pictured herself in a beautiful dress walking next to marble columns. Mom saw dollar signs! But it was fun dreaming. After our trip, we asked her fiancé, Jeff, what he envisioned for his wedding, and he said he wanted to be married outdoors, on a mountaintop. This couple was not on the same wavelength! However, several months later when we actually started working on their wedding, Beth's parents remembered a wedding they had attended perhaps five years earlier. The ceremony was held outdoors on the lawn of a gorgeous old mansion, which had large marble columns at the entrance. We couldn't remember exactly where the mansion was located or its name, but we did some sleuthing and the four of us (Jeff, Beth, my husband, and I) took a drive to check it out. When we pulled into the circular driveway, Beth said, "This is it! I love it!" We were afraid we would not be able to afford it, but after meeting with the staff and discussing pricing, our fears were allayed. Jeff had his outdoor ceremony on the lawn of this beautiful mansion and Beth had her marble columns. We had found their perfect wedding location, and it was also very affordable. Because the mansion was quite a drive out of town, the prices were lower, and we chose to have an 11:00 A.M. ceremony followed by a lunch reception, which kept our food costs down. After the ceremony, as guests walked from the lawn toward the mansion, they were met by servers who carried trays of champagne and hors d'oeuvres. This was such a nice touch and something that caught the guests by surprise.

The buffet was held inside the mansion on the main floor; the only drawback was that our guests were not all in the same room for the meal but divided among the parlors, conservatory, and dining room. We then all adjourned to the ballroom on the lower level for the cake cutting and dancing. A lovely wedding and much fun! We even got several thank-you notes from guests saying what a wonderful time they had.

Because of our personal experience, we are real believers in dreaming. Set your goals as high as you want, and figure out what you can accomplish with whatever you have to work with. Remember, fortunately Beth didn't specify what the marble columns had to be attached to, and Jeff really just wanted to be outdoors!

Back to Reality

BEGIN with your dreaming and then be realistic. You need to factor in time, money, location, and guests. Even if what you have in mind is simple, you will be amazed at how much time is spent planning your big day. Careful planning and organization, both of which we will help you with, create the feeling of the perfect wedding. Fortunately, a wedding's success does not depend on a large budget but a good plan.

Let's Get Started

IT is important to get started as soon as possible. Planning well in advance gives you many more options. You will have first choice at any great yet inexpensive locations, and you will be able to choose the date and time you want.

We recently received a call from a bride who wanted us to help her plan her wedding for a date only two months in advance. She could only be married at that time because she was teaching summer school and had a short break between two school sessions. In this case, she was only able to choose from what was still available and it had to be relatively inexpensive. Her choices, therefore, were very limited.

THE GUEST LIST

It is very important to understand that limiting your guest list is the biggest factor in saving money. Do you come from very large families where everyone is invited to a wedding? Do you have small families and wish to invite only an intimate number of friends? These are decisions for you both to make early in your planning session.

If you wish to include many people on your guest list but still keep costs down, consider planning your ceremony and reception at a time when lighter fare can be

Wedding Day Reflections

Planning *early reduces stress later.*
—Jill and Steve

served. The lower cost of this type of meal will help you stay within your budget. Perhaps a garden wedding with a cake and champagne reception would be the perfect answer. If you envision an evening wedding with a sit-down dinner, which tends to be very expensive, a list with fewer guests would be a priority.

Once you have an idea of how many people you will be able to invite to your ceremony and reception, decide how many each set of parents can invite and how many each of you can include. We suggest each of you compile your own list and combine them for your master list. We will give you easy ways to keep your guest list organized in chapter 11, "Invitations."

THE CEREMONY

Deciding whether you will have a clergyperson or judge perform your ceremony goes hand in hand with whether your ceremony will be held in a house of worship or elsewhere. These decisions are based on the couple's religious background, whether they both attend a church of a particular denomination, and what they are comfortable with at this point in their lives. Some rabbis, judges, and Protestant ministers make themselves available to perform wedding ceremonies at any site. These ceremonies can be especially meaningful, as the couples are more at liberty to add their own touches. We work with several judges who have a selection of ceremonies from which the couple can choose. They also stress that the couple is welcome to make any changes or additions they would like. Most couples will add a reading or a poem. Several have written and memorized their vows to each other.

?

May I have a male bridesmaid?

Yes, *and a groom may choose a female "groomsman." As long as your fiancé feels this is okay, there is no reason not to. We suggest asking this opposite-gender attendant to wear the appropriate attire (dresses for females, suits or tuxes for males). They may stand on whichever side of the altar you wish.*

THE ATTENDANTS

Once you have shared the news with your families, it is appropriate to choose your attendants. Be very careful and give this much thought. Select only close friends and family members who are very special to you. You would be amazed at how many calls we get from a bride lamenting about an attendant, very upset with her choice and seeking help in solving the problem. Recently we heard from a bride who said one of her attendants wasn't speaking to her. We advised the bride to contact this attendant and suggest that maybe she would prefer not to be in the wedding party, as she seemed to be unhappy about something. So, please give each member of your wedding party very careful consideration.

A word to the wise: having fewer attendants costs less. Some of the expenses involved are flowers (bouquets and boutonnieres), gifts, transportation and accommodations for out-of-town attendants, and food. Also, keep in mind you should not ask someone to be your attendant when you know it will be a financial burden to that person. The attendants have expenses such as their gowns, tuxedo rentals, travel, and perhaps even time off work. So again, choose wisely. Select only those people who are really special to you and vice versa.

We are often asked whether the bride and groom need to have the same number of attendants. The answer is no.

TONY AND LISA'S STORY

Several years ago we were working with a darling couple, Tony and Lisa, who said they were having a lot of trouble with their plans and arguing a lot. Although we were afraid we were walking into the middle of a big problem, we hesitantly asked what they were having trouble with. Lisa said Tony wanted to have five groomsmen, while she had only four bridesmaids and he wouldn't give in. We breathed a collective sigh of relief and said the only place it would really be noticeable would be during the recessional (when the attendants leave the church after the ceremony), but we had an easy solution and drew it out for them as follows:

BRIDE
GROOM
MH - MAID OF HONOR
BM - BEST MAN
G – GROOMSMAN
B – BRIDESMAID

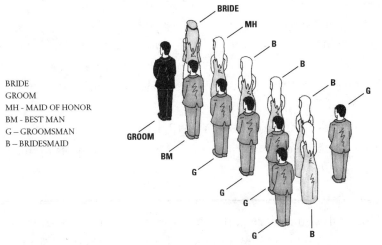

A lucky bridesmaid escorted by two men! Of course, this setup could be reversed should you have more bridesmaids than groomsmen. Tony and Lisa now both went about their planning with renewed optimism that there was a solution for any problem.

Choosing Your Attendants

❧

In deciding on your attendants, there are many factors to consider, and personality types must suit their respective roles. The following list of duties for your attendants may help you with your decisions.

YOUR MAID OF HONOR

- Helps with the pre-wedding plans
- Assists with the choice of the bridesmaids' gowns
- Gets fitted for and purchases her own gown
- May help address invitations
- Plans a shower for the bride (unless she is a member of immediate family)
- Attends the rehearsal and the rehearsal dinner
- Makes sure the bridesmaids are where they are supposed to be before the ceremony
- Assists the bride with dressing before the ceremony
- Holds the bridal bouquet and the groom's ring at the altar
- Arranges the bride's train and veil
- Signs the wedding certificate
- Stands in the receiving line if asked
- Offers a toast to the couple
- Helps the bride change into her going-away outfit

YOUR BEST MAN

- Makes arrangements for the bachelor party

Although you may read that it is appropriate to have more attendants for a formal wedding and fewer for an informal or casual wedding, we don't feel you need to have this constraint. Several years ago we assisted with a lovely wedding held in a meadow in Yosemite National Park in California. There were eight bridesmaids including the maid of honor. They wore sandals, blue flowered sundresses, and straw hats with ribbons tied around the crown that hung down their backs. The eight male attendants wore khaki pants and matching blue

- Gets fitted for his own tux
- Helps make sure the groomsmen have been measured for their tuxes
- Oversees all the men picking up their tuxes the day before the wedding
- Attends the rehearsal and the rehearsal dinner
- Provides transportation for the groom to the ceremony
- Helps the groom dress
- Gives the honorarium fee to the officiant (priest, judge, minister, or pastor)
- Holds the bride's ring
- Signs the wedding certificate
- Offers the first toast to the couple at the reception
- Returns all the tuxes after the reception

YOUR BRIDESMAIDS

- Help with addressing the invitations or other details such as decorations
- Participate in the bridal shower
- Get fitted for and purchase their gowns
- Attend the rehearsal and the rehearsal dinner
- Circulate during the reception
- Dance with the groomsmen at the reception

YOUR GROOMSMEN

- Help with the bachelor party
- Get fitted for and rent their tuxes
- Attend the rehearsal and the rehearsal dinner
- Escort guests to their seats
- Ask the bridesmaids to dance at the reception

shirts. This was a very casual setting, and the large wedding party was most appropriate.

Another example was a very large formal wedding held at a local cathedral. The bride had two sisters, one of whom was married, and a younger sister who was finishing her last year of college. She was very close to both of her sisters and wanted no other attendants, but she had read that for a formal wedding, she should have a larger number of participants. We suggested she have only the two sisters—both serving as honor attendants—a matron of honor, and a maid of honor. They shared duties: the maid of honor carried the ring and held the bride's bouquet, while the matron of honor stood next to the bride, straightened her veil and train at the altar, and signed the marriage certificate after the ceremony. The maid of honor juggled all three bouquets during the ceremony, placing her own on the railing in front of her and holding both sisters' bouquets to free up the matron of honor's hands.

The groom also had two honor attendants, his best men. Again, one carried the ring and one signed the certificate. They both hosted the bachelor party and were most attentive to everything going on. They each gave a beautiful toast at the reception.

YOUR OTHER ATTENDANTS If you decide to have just a couple of attendants each and a rather large guest list, ask several men to be ushers for you. You should have at least one usher per every fifty guests. These men would not stand at the altar with you and would not need to rent a tuxedo but rather would wear their own suit. They should be honored with a boutonniere and included at the rehearsal and rehearsal dinner and any other festivities.

Other tasks that can be filled by friends or relatives in honored positions include the following:

♦ **Program Distributors** This also could be done by the ushers, but this is a wonderful job for small children. They can be positioned at the doors and feel very important.

♦ **Candle Lighters** Best done in pairs. They would go together to the altar and light candles there. They could also light pew candles.

Wedding Day Reflections

My advice is to keep a positive attitude and remain flexible. We planned a small ceremony for family and a couple of friends, outdoors at a park. It poured down rain all day, so we called everyone to tell them of the necessary location change. We just moved the coffee table and had the ceremony in the living room!

—Lucianna and Phil

◆ **Readers** During the ceremony, they would read from the Scriptures or recite a poem.

◆ **Guest Book Attendant** This person would stand next to the guest book and greet guests before the ceremony and again at the early part of the reception and make sure that no pages in the book are skipped and that everyone signs their names as they go past.

◆ **Seaters at the Reception** If you choose to have assigned seating at the reception, it is a good idea to have people at the entrance to guide guests to their seats.

◆ **Gift Taker** This person would stand near the entrance of the reception to assist guests with their packages and ensure that they are neatly arranged on the gift table. They could also tape the cards to the gift boxes.

◆ **Favors** Favors can be placed in baskets, carried through the reception hall, and passed out—another role handled well by children.

CHILDREN IN THE WEDDING PARTY

Small children are a delight, but keep in mind that they can be a lot of work.

TODD AND CHERYL'S STORY

At Todd and Cheryl's wedding, the ring bearer was the son of the matron of honor. A delightful three-year-old, he practiced carrying the ring pillow at home for several weeks. He did well at the rehearsal although he was a little hesitant. However, when it was his turn to precede the bride and her dad down the aisle during the ceremony, while walking he alternated between carrying the pillow by one corner and swinging it and putting it on his head. He did make it down the long aisle and only dropped the pillow twice. Fortunately, one of the best men had the real ring safely in his pocket, just in case the pillow had not made the entire journey to the altar. We had positioned the boy's father on the aisle in the second row and after the processional the boy went to sit with his dad. He ended up being taken out before the ceremony was over as he was fidgeting and asking questions in a loud whisper. He rejoined the party for pictures after the ceremony and he was an angel. His parents very wisely had a babysitter reserved for that evening. They were able to enjoy themselves at the reception, and after the excitement of the day, the little boy was much happier going to sleep at his normal time in his own bed. Before going to bed, he showed the babysitter how he carried the pillow and he held it level in front of him—not swinging by the corner or on his head. The perfect ring bearer!

As this story illustrates, small children are a delight and usually add some unexpected twists to a wedding. However, predicting their behavior is almost impossible. It is certainly not appropriate to expect a child any younger than four to perform the duties of a flower girl or ring bearer. If you're striving for perfection, we suggest you don't choose to have children participate of any age.

Another wedding in which children "stole the show" began at the rehearsal when two adorable children about four years old were the flower girl and ring bearer. They were very well behaved and really seemed to listen to our instructions. After we had completed the rehearsal, the white linen aisle runner was being laid in preparation for the ceremony the next morning. The inquisitive pair was quite intrigued with it, and their mother admonished them to not walk on it, as they would get it dirty. You guessed it! On the actual wedding day they wouldn't walk on the runner. When it came their time to walk down the aisle they followed each other on the right side of the aisle tippy-toed, making sure neither one touched the white runner so they wouldn't get it dirty! We figured out immediately why they were doing what they were doing, but they were too far away from the back doors of the church for us to correct them. They proceeded very nicely with big grins on their faces in response to the guests' laughter. Absolutely delightful!

You Will Need Help

PUTTING together a lovely wedding takes a great deal of planning in the early stages and then coordination to make it all happen. We strongly suggest you ask a friend or relative to be a "coordinator" for you. This person should want to be involved in the planning of your wedding and be willing to be in charge of the last-minute details and choreography. These chores could be shared by two or more people. See chapter 14, "Details, Details, Details" and chapter 15, "The Finishing Touches," for more information.

Please do not have yourself, your fiancé, parents, or members of your bridal party be in charge of any details on the day of the wedding. Your family and wedding party will be posing for photos and visiting with guests and should be free to enjoy the day you have worked so hard to ensure is perfect. Friends or relatives who have recently been brides themselves, or who offer their help, can be of invaluable assistance to you. They can check on details, find the missing groomsmen for pictures, pass on messages to DJs, and so forth, to help the bride and groom feel more at ease. Everyone agrees that the couple should enjoy their big day,

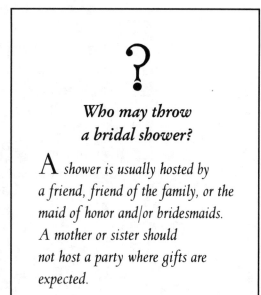

?

***Who may throw
a bridal shower?***

A *shower is usually hosted by
a friend, friend of the family, or the
maid of honor and/or bridesmaids.
A mother or sister should
not host a party where gifts are
expected.*

and most friends would feel honored to help ensure this. These assistants can serve as your wedding coordinators for the day, and with the help of our guidelines later in the book, they can make the ceremony and reception appear as if they were professionally planned.

Your Own Personal Checklist— From Beginning to End

We have created a checklist to help you realize what has to be done and when. Of course, not every item will be pertinent to all weddings.

After the Engagement (ideally twelve months before the wedding)

____ Share the news first with your families and then with friends.

____ Announce your engagement in the newspapers.

____ The parents of the bride might wish to have an engagement party.

____ Determine the type and size of wedding you want, degree of formality, and setting.

____ Determine the number of guests you will be able to invite.

____ Start your guest lists.

____ Select wedding attendants.

____ Plan your wedding budget.

____ Select a tentative wedding date and time. (These may depend on the availability of the wedding site.)

____ Research, select, and reserve the ceremony site.

____ Research, select, and reserve the reception site.

____ Determine who will officiate at the ceremony.

____ Select your gown and headpiece.

____ Select the bridesmaids' gowns with the help of your honor attendant.

____ Interview, select, and reserve the caterer.

____ Interview, select, and reserve the photographer.

____ Interview, select, and reserve the videographer.

____ Interview, select, and reserve the musician(s) for the ceremony.

____ Interview, select, and reserve the DJ or band for the reception.

____ Interview, select, and reserve the florist.

____ Discuss honeymoon plans.

____ Determine decorations for both the ceremony and reception.

Four to Six Months Before the Wedding

____ Ask a best friend (or two) to be your coordinator(s).

____ Interview, taste, select, and reserve the bakery.

____ Determine what is needed from a rental company and reserve.

____ Make sure all deposits are paid and contracts signed.

____ Send letters of confirmation to each vendor involved with your wedding. (This helps remind them of the date, time, and location.)

____ Make an appointment with a clergyperson for pre-marriage counseling.

____ Determine the requirements for a marriage license.

____ Complete your guest list with current addresses.

____ Order invitations, announcements, and personal stationery.

____ Determine and reserve transportation for the day of the wedding.

____ Have both mothers coordinate and select their dresses.

____ Choose men's wedding attire.

____ Arrange for all groomsmen to get fitted for their tuxes.

____ Make accommodations for out-of-town attendants and guests.

____ Prepare an accommodation list and maps for out-of-town guests.

____ Have an engagement picture taken.

____ Choose people for the guest book attendant and other roles.

____ Determine the date and time for the rehearsal.

____ Make arrangements for the rehearsal dinner (this is usually a task for the groom's parents).

____ Make honeymoon reservations.

____ Register at a bridal registry in the towns of both families.

____ Select wedding rings.

____ Decide on gifts for wedding attendants.

____ Refer to your payment schedule (explained in chapter 2, "The Wedding Budget and Organization") for any payments to be made.

____ Work on your decorations.

Three Months Before the Wedding

____ Check on the status of the wedding and bridesmaids' gowns.

____ Check in with the caterer, florist, and other service providers and determine what still needs to be done.

____ Plan the wedding-day schedule with your coordinator—what will happen when . . . ? (Example shown in Chapter 14, "Details, Details, Details.")

____ Meet with the officiant and finalize plans.

____ Meet with the musician(s) (organist, harpist, etc.) to decide on music for the ceremony.

____ Design the wedding program to be handed out before the ceremony, if desired.

____ Plan going-away outfits, if desired.

____ How are you doing on decorations?

____ Schedule a consultation with your hair and makeup stylists.

Two Months Before the Wedding

____ Purchase pretty "love" stamps for invitations.

____ Address the invitations and announcements.

____ Plan a luncheon for the bridesmaids.

____ Reconfirm honeymoon reservations.

____ Attend showers given in your honor.

____ Schedule blood tests, if required.

____ Tend to any legal details—get necessary forms to change names on Social Security card, driver's license, insurance and medical plans, and bank accounts.

Six Weeks Before the Wedding

____ Put finishing touches on decorations.

____ Mail invitations, including maps and an accommodation list.

____ Let each of your attendants know where they are to be and when, and what attire is appropriate so they have plenty of time to plan.

____ Send thank-you notes for shower gifts.

____ Get any accessories you may still need such as the guest book and the garter.

____ Make appointments with your hairdresser and manicurist.

One Month Before the Wedding

____ Set a date with your fiancé to get the marriage license.

____ Arrange the final fitting on the bridal gown and bridesmaids' dresses.

____ Schedule a formal wedding portrait of the bride, if desired.

____ Plan clothes needed for the honeymoon.

____ Choose music for the reception (first dance, etc.), and discuss it with the DJ or bandleader.

Two Weeks Before the Wedding

____ Contact the guests who have not responded.

____ Give the caterer a final count.

____ Finalize all details with the church, reception location, caterer, rental store, photographer, videographer, musicians, DJ, florist, bakery, and transportation provider.

____ Review your payment schedule. Final payments are due to most vendors about this time.

____ Have a meeting with your coordinator and work out final details for the rehearsal and the wedding day.

____ Confirm the rehearsal and wedding-day plans with officiant and attendants.

____ Confirm the rehearsal dinner arrangements.

____ Confirm honeymoon arrangements.

____ Check on shoes, earrings, and other accessories for yourself, the mothers, and attendants.

____ Have the groom check on accessories for himself, fathers, best man, and ushers.

One Week Before the Wedding

____ Prepare checks for vendors due on the wedding day, put them in envelopes, and give them to your coordinator for distribution.

____ Assemble all toasting goblets, guest book, unity candle, and so forth and give them to your coordinator.

___ Give the bridesmaids' luncheon.

___ Pack for your honeymoon.

___ Obtain cash and traveler's checks for the honeymoon.

One or Two Days Before the Wedding

___ Greet or make arrangements for others to greet out-of-town guests as they arrive.

___ Have your nail appointment the day before the wedding.

___ Make sure you have packed everything for the honeymoon.

___ Make sure you have packed everything you will need at the wedding site. (Refer to the Emergency Kit in Chapter 14, "Details, Details, Details," to ensure you have everything you need.)

___ Give all items for the ceremony and reception to your coordinator.

___ Attend the wedding rehearsal and dinner.

___ Give the marriage license and the honorarium for the officiant to the best man.

Your Wedding Day

___ Be sure to eat!

___ Have your hair appointment; take headpiece and wear a top that buttons.

___ Allow yourself plenty of time to dress and apply makeup.

___ Make sure you have the rings before proceeding to the ceremony.

___ Relax! You have worked hard preparing for this day.

___ Enjoy yourself!

After the Wedding

___ Mail the announcements.

___ Change your name on all necessary documents. Do anything you were unable to do prior to having the marriage license.

___ Complete all thank-you notes as soon as possible.

___ Send the wedding announcement and picture to newspapers.

We hope these lists will give you an idea of when each task should be completed. The next chapter will help you determine how to allocate your money and organize all the "stuff" you will accumulate over the next few months.

2

THE WEDDING BUDGET AND ORGANIZATION

TRACKING AND DECIDING HOW TO SPEND YOUR MONEY

Your BUDGET WILL influence many of the decisions you make during your planning process, so we feel it is crucial to address it at the beginning. Fortunately, as we said before, having a lovely wedding does not depend on the size of your budget as much as it does on your planning and organization. It *is* possible to have a lovely wedding for $5,000 (or less).

Traditionally, the bride's family is responsible for most of the expenses of both the wedding and the reception. Today, however, more and more couples who have been living on their own for several years are contributing to the budget or assuming the entire cost of the wedding themselves. Occasionally, the groom's family will volunteer to help with some of the expenses, such as the cost of the photographer or perhaps the liquor served at the reception. We recently had a wedding in which the bride's family, the groom's family, and the couple each contributed one-third toward the total budget. However you approach your budget, it is most important to determine the amount first and then make specific plans based on that amount.

As you start to lay out your budget, take into account all sources

Who Pays for What?

❧

The following summary lists typical expenses for a wedding and who traditionally is responsible for them:

THE BRIDE AND HER FAMILY

- Engagement party
- Bride's wedding dress and accessories
- Invitations, announcements, reception cards, postage, and so forth
- Rental fee of the church or ceremony location
- Music for the ceremony
- Music for the reception
- Cost of the reception, including food, drinks, and wedding cake
- Decorations for the ceremony and reception locations
- Bridesmaids' bouquets
- Transportation to the ceremony and reception for the wedding party
- Engagement and wedding photography
- Accessories such as the guest book, favors, and so forth
- Gifts for the bride's attendants
- Accommodations for out-of-town bridesmaids
- Wedding ring for the groom

of money, without using credit cards or borrowing. After the wedding, you want to have nothing but great memories of your day—not bills arriving in the mail. We recently received a call from a man who had what he thought was a great idea. He was promoting the new 125% home equity loans/mortgages for refinancing, describing them as a wonderful way for our couples who owned their own home or for the parents of the bride to finance an extra 25% for a fabulous wedding. He was not very happy with us when we expressed that we don't feel it is desirable, or even necessary, to go into debt for a wedding, and it was

THE GROOM AND HIS FAMILY

- The bride's engagement and wedding rings
- Personal wedding attire
- Travel and accommodations for family
- Accommodations for out-of-town groomsmen
- Marriage license
- Fee for the officiant
- Gifts for the best man and groomsmen
- Boutonnieres for the groom, best man, and groomsmen
- The bride's bouquet and going-away corsage
- Corsages for mothers and grandmothers
- Rehearsal dinner

MAID OF HONOR AND BRIDESMAIDS

- Purchase of their dresses and accessories
- Transportation expenses to and from the wedding
- Wedding gift for the couple
- Showers given by the brides-maids

BEST MAN AND GROOMSMEN

- Rental of their tuxedos
- Transportation expenses to and from the wedding
- Wedding gift for the couple
- Shared cost of the bachelor party

not something we would ever propose to our couples no matter how good an idea he thought it was.

Money Decisions

FOR our purposes, we will assume your wedding budget is $5,000. The amount could be less; it doesn't matter as the budgeting process is still the same.

After you have determined what comprises your ideal wedding, decide on one or two things that you definitely want to include.

TED AND CARRIE'S STORY

Ted and Carrie were adamant in their decision to have a horse and carriage. (A number of our couples consider this a must.) We are much in favor of the carriage ride because we feel it gives the couple some time to themselves after the seriousness of the ceremony and before they are surrounded by family and friends at the reception. However, this couple was being married at a church with the reception following next door in the church fellowship hall. They had nowhere to go in the carriage! After the reception, they were going directly to the hotel at the airport, and a horse and carriage would not be a good mode of transportation to that location. If the situation involved needing transportation from the church to the reception spot, it could be rented for just an hour and be worthwhile. After thinking through the pros and cons of the horse and carriage under their circumstances, Ted and Carrie both decided that it just would not work and the money could be better spent elsewhere. (This is a good example of how in planning, you must also be practical.)

Wedding Day Reflections

Do a budget first. This helps to avoid possible conflict with your fiancé. Talk through every detail, so that both partners are aware of what the other one envisions and plans to spend money on.

—Suzanne and Russell

Perhaps you would really like a classic car or a limousine. If you have circumstances that will work well with this, call several companies to get an idea of what the cost would be for an hour or their minimum rental. Is this something you could work into your budget? Should you find that there is a minimum of two hours' rental for the vehicle, perhaps you and your dad could be delivered to the church and then you and your fiancé leave the church after the ceremony on your way to the reception. You may find that the cost for the two hours is $350, which leaves you with $4,650 to spend for the rest of the wedding—a very workable budget.

On the other hand, what are the items incurring very little expense? Does your mother have a friend who owns a bakery and has volunteered to do your cake as her gift to you? Will you be wearing your mother's wedding gown? Do you sew and wish to make your own veil? Does a neighbor have a beautiful Model T and would love to be your chauffeur for the day? Anything like this would greatly ease your budget.

From here you are on your way to working up a budget that will be easy to follow. Of course, the budget can always change, but remember that if you spend a little more in one area, the money then has to come from somewhere else. We have prepared a pie chart (see Figure 2.1) for a budget based on average percentages allocated for a reception with 100 guests.

> ## *Wedding Day Reflections*
>
> When on a budget, couples have to identify what is important to them and what is not. For instance, we thought that we would not spend a lot of money on a dress, and that we would splurge on the cake. Well, then I found a dress I loved for more money than we budgeted, so the dress had to move up in the percentage of budget, and the cake had to move down in percentage of budget."
>
> —Jennifer and Peter

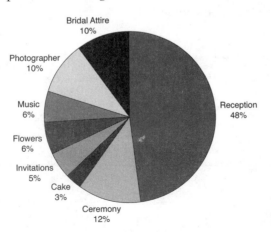

Figure 2.1. Average percentages for a budget based on a guest list of 100

The following wedding estimates (based on 100 guests) may give you an idea of price ranges for various wedding-related items. Keep in mind that the high-end amounts may not fit into a $5,000 budget.

Ceremony

Church/synagogue fee		$ 0–800
Music for ceremony		$ 150–1,000
Marriage license	(approximately)	$ 50
Fee for the officiant		$ 100–250

Reception

Site rental	$ 300–2,000
Caterer/food	$ 1,000–4,000
Alcoholic drinks	$ 800–2,000
Nonalcoholic drinks	$ 100–500
Wedding cake	$ 165–400
Music/DJ	$ 300–1,000
Music/live band	$ 1,000–3,000

Wedding Attire

Bride's dress	$ 400–6,000
Bride's headpiece, accessories	$ 25–400
Bridesmaid's dress	$ 90–500
Groom's tux rental	$ 85–150
Groomsmen's tux rentals	$ 85–150

Other Costs

Flowers for ceremony	$ 300–4,000
Decorations	$ 100–5,000
Photography	$ 500–2,000
Invitations	$ 100–500
Transportation	$ 0–1,000
Videography	$ 0–1,500

As you start to compare locations, pay close attention to what is included with the sites you are considering. What do you need to rent? These items could include chairs and tables. We have prepared a list of rental charges based on the costs in our area. Of course, the costs and availability will vary in different geographic areas. Be sure to inquire whether delivery and pick-up is included.

RENTAL PRICE RANGES

Items for Ceremony

Brass arch	$ 35–50
White lattice arch	$ 35–55*
Wicker arch	$ 50–55
8' white lattice gazebo	$ 120–140
White lattice huppah	$ 120–140*
White wicker flower basket	$ 8–9
Brass kneeling bench	$ 20 per pair

Items for Reception

5–branch candelabra, including dripless candles	$ 8.00–12.50
Dance floor	
4' × 4' sections	$ 16–20*
Tables	
72" × 30" banquet	$ 7–9
96" × 30" banquet	$ 8–10
60" round (8 guests)	$ 8–10
72" round (10 guests)	$ 10–12
Chairs	
White Samsonite	$ 0.85–1.00
White wooden with padded seat	$ 2.00–2.50
Linen tablecloths for banquet tables	
60" × 96"	$ 7–9
60" × 120"	$ 8–10

72" × 144"	$ 15–18
for 60" round–90" (1/2 drop)	$ 9–11
for 120" (to floor)	$12.50–15
for 72" round–102" (1/2 drop)	$ 30–35
Napkins	$ 0.65–1.50
Aisle runner	
Linen, 50'	$ 40–45
Disposable, 50'	$ 25–30
Canopy	
20' × 20'	$ 175–200**
Tents	
For 100 guests at 60" rounds	
Serving dinner only, you would need:	
30' × 40' tent	$ 500–600**
To add a dance floor (20' × 20'), you would need:	
30' × 60' tent	$ 900–1,000**
* Delivery is required at an additional charge.	
** Setup and delivery is an additional charge.	$ 50–100

Budget Samples

BECAUSE not everyone has the same priorities for how their money will be spent, we present here (using Figure 2.2 and Figure 2.3) two budgets from actual weddings to illustrate how two different couples spent their $5,000. (Keep in mind percentages are approximate, not exact.)

Figure 2.2. Budget sample 1 based on a guest list of 100

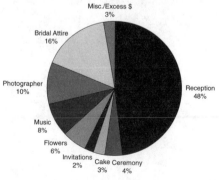

We recently volunteered to help a family friend with a lovely ceremony and brunch reception for 100 guests held in the bride's grandmother's yard. The groom's parents had said they would pay for the last-minute rental of a tent, if necessary, so a backup plan was in place. Fortunately, it wasn't needed. We kept our fingers crossed as the day neared that our weather would be good, and it was perfect.

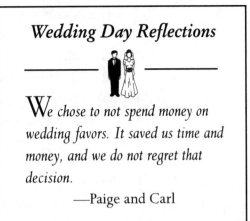

Wedding Day Reflections

W*e chose to not spend money on wedding favors. It saved us time and money, and we do not regret that decision.*

—Paige and Carl

Because everything was taking place at a private home, a number of rentals were needed. That expense turned out to be a large part of our budget. Knowing the couple had $5,000 to work with, we first investigated the rental costs:

White lattice arch	$ 50
100 white wooden chairs: 100 × $2.25	$225
13 round tables, 60": 13 × $9	$117
13 long linen tablecloths: 13 × $13	$169
100 napkins: 100 × $0.65	$ 65
	$626
Tax (applicable tax estimate)	$ 48
Delivery	$ 50
	$724 (or 14%)

The catering for the brunch was $13.50 per person. They served cold lemon chicken, a cheese quiche, fruit salad, and an assortment of rolls. The price also included coffee, juices, nonalcoholic punch, and the dinnerware. The gratuity of 18% would add $243, plus an applicable tax estimate of $105, for a total catering bill of $1,698, or 34% of the couple's budget.

An uncle of the groom gave the couple two cases of champagne for the toast as a gift. So this reception's cost, with catering and rentals, totaled $2,422, which comprises 48% of their pie.

The bride wore a lovely ivory taffeta gown purchased for $600. The alterations were $50. She wore her hair down and decorated with flowers rather than a headpiece. Also, because she would be walking on the lawn, she decided to forego heels and bought ballet-type shoes for $35. The bride's attire totaled $685, which was 14% of the pie. The groom's tux rental was $85, and he decided to wear his own black wing-tip shoes rather than rent a pair, so his costs consumed just 2% of the budget.

The couple bought a four-hour package from a photographer, which was ample time to cover the shots they wanted, since their ceremony and reception were all in one location. They would get the finished proofs several weeks after the reception and could choose to put an album together at a later time. The photography bill was $495, or 10%.

The bride and groom wanted traditional music for their ceremony and dancing at the reception and decided to hire a disc jockey to handle both. The DJ was reserved for four hours at a cost of $400, so music amounted to 8% of the pie.

The groom was computer savvy and wanted to make the invitations. The couple found beautiful card stock paper with a rose border that tied in with their floral plans, pulling their whole theme together. They purchased matching envelopes for the invitations as well as smaller envelopes and cut card stock for their response cards. They estimated the total paper cost at about $60. With 62 envelopes mailed out, their postage expense was about $40 (two stamps each, one on the response card, one on the outer envelope). Thus, their invitation costs were $100, or 2% of the pie.

Because of the lovely setting and the abundance of flowers already in the yard, floral costs were minimal; neighbors volunteered to decorate the arch with ivy and roses picked from their various yards on the morning of the wedding. They also placed roses in bud vases for centerpieces on each table.

The bride and her mother did not want to have any last-minute details to do themselves, so they had all the personal flowers done by their favorite florist, at the following costs:

Bride's bouquet	$125
Maid of honor's bouquet (the only attendant)	$ 50
Two mothers' corsages: $15 each	$ 30
Two grandmothers' corsages: $12 each	$ 24
Guest book attendant corsage	$ 10
Groom's boutonniere	$ 12
Best man's boutonniere	$ 10
Two fathers' boutonnieres: $10 each	$ 20
Grandfather's boutonniere	$ 10
Two ushers' boutonnieres: $7 each	$ 14
	$305 (or 6%)

The couple chose a lovely three-tiered cake done with off-white buttercream frosting. The groom was in charge of picking the flavors for each tier, and the cake was delicious. It was decorated with ten rosebuds from the florist and presented on a patio table covered with a gathered lace cloth. The cost was $1.65 per person, or $165.00—3% of the budget.

The minister from the bride's parents' church was the officiant. His honorarium was $200, or 4%.

The bride used a cake knife and toasting goblets that had been used at her parents' wedding, and she purchased a guest book for $30. The couple decided not to have favors. The last cost they had to figure in was their marriage license at $54. Therefore, their miscellaneous, or excess, costs were $84.

The total expenditures for this couple's wedding added up to $4,941, which is cutting it pretty close to the $5,000 budget. They were proud of themselves nonetheless that they hadn't exceeded their limit, and they felt it was a fun process.

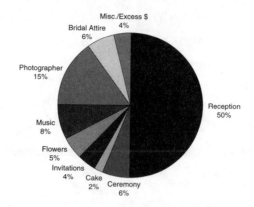

Figure 2.3. Budget sample 2 for a guest list of 50

Another couple had an entirely different idea of how they wanted to work with their $5,000 budget. They envisioned a very elegant sit-down dinner for fifty guests, the Sunday evening prior to Christmas, and wanted to know whether we thought it could be done. We weren't quite sure at first that the Christmas office party rush would be over, but we eventually found an elegant bed-and-breakfast inn with a wonderful restaurant that wasn't booked. The couple was so pleased when this inn was available and thrilled, too, that rooms were available for overnight guests. We reserved a block of rooms at a discounted rate for that evening. (Refer to chapter 14, "Details, Details, Details," for more information on booking rooms.)

The couple immediately ordered lovely invitations and response cards, which came to $178. They had postage costs of $16, for a total invitation cost of $194 (or 4%).

Because it was a small winter wedding, the bride opted to wear a beautiful white wool suit with a very small headpiece and her own

> ## *Wedding Day Reflections*
>
> We are glad we saved money by doing a lot of things ourselves. We made some decorations for the reception site that were grapevine wreaths with silk flower adornments. We also created our own pew bows and ring pillow inexpensively. We also completely designed and printed our programs on our computer, which saved us money in printing costs.
>
> —Tiffany and Ron

shoes. Her suit was $240, the headpiece $45. Her attendant was her sister, who wore a burgundy wool suit. The groom and best man wore dark suits. Wedding attire, then, was just the amount of the bride's outfit: $285, or 6% of the pie.

Both the bride and her attendant carried similar nosegays of white and burgundy flowers; the bride's was $55, and her attendant's was $50. There were four boutonnieres at $12 each and five corsages at $15 each. Candelabras belonging to the inn were used on the tables and were supplemented only with some pine boughs and burgundy balls (or ornaments). The groom's mother arranged the decorations after she was dressed and just before the pictures were taken before the ceremony. Thus, the florist bill was only $228, or 5%.

The parlor of the bed-and-breakfast was the perfect spot for the ceremony. This room boasted a beautiful fireplace and an antique mantel, and we decided the ceremony would be held in front of it with a small fire crackling. The room had a large Christmas tree in one corner to the left of the mantle that added to the warmth and ambiance. To balance this arrangement, we had the harpist stand her lovely gold harp on the right side of the mantle. Once the fifty chairs were placed in the room, the only decoration we felt was necessary was a pine bough arrangement with three candles for the mantle. The center candle was the unity candle used in the ceremony. The cost to use the room was $200, which included the chairs. The couple did not have a church affiliation and decided they would be most comfortable with a judge. His fee was $100. Thus, the total cost for the ceremony was $300, or 6%.

After the ceremony, the guests adjourned to a room where light hors d'oeuvres were being passed and wine and champagne poured. The harpist was hired for four hours, and she moved from room to room as the reception progressed. Her cost was $400, or 8%. Pictures of the couple were taken quickly so they could join the others. The photographer, who had come highly recommended by a coworker, offered a very nice package that included a leather album. Because it was a Sunday, he discounted his fee to $750, or 15% of the budget.

After hors d'oeuvres, everyone went to the dining room where salads were waiting, followed by a lovely chicken marsala dinner. Wine was served at the table. Because the group was small, there was much visiting between tables and a real feeling of camaraderie among guests. Finally the beautiful cake was cut and coffee was served. The cake was $2.10 per slice, which totaled $105.00, or 2%. The tab for dinner came to $4 per person for the hors d'oeuvres, $22 per person for

Create a Payment Schedule

❧

As you engage the various vendors you are using, create a payment schedule. We have compiled a sample here for you to refer to when setting up your own payment schedule. Make a note of what deposits you have made and to whom. Read the contracts as to when the next and final payments are due. Transfer that information to your payment schedule as pictured. Then, at a glance, you can know when your next payments need to be made.

PAYMENT SCHEDULE FOR KIM & MATT'S WEDDING
Wedding Date: June 28

$ Due Now

$100 (deposit)	Mary's Flower Shoppe
$500 (deposit)	Linda's Catering Service

April 10

$300 (second payment)	Mike's Photography Shop

May 28

$250 (balance due)	Pioneer Church
$350 (balance due)	House of Wedding Dresses

dinner, and approximately $14 per person for the drinks, totaling $40 per person or $2,000, plus gratuity and tax for a grand total of $2,515, or about 50% of the pie. There were no extra charges for tables, chairs, or linens.

Other expenses were minimal. The couple used a cake knife and toasting goblets they owned. Instead of a guest book, they framed and matted a picture of themselves when they were in Europe the previous

June 18

 $1,300 (balance due & final count) Linda's Catering Service

 $220 (balance due) Mary's Flower Shoppe

June 27

 $200 (give to best man) Pastor Smith

June 28

 $300 (final payment) Bill's DJ Company

(When proofs are done)

 $300 (final payment) Mike's Photography Shop

Already Paid

 $100 Deposit to church

 $100 DJ

 $350 Dress

 $300 Photographer

Still Need to Add to Budget

 Invitations

 Favors

 Decorations

summer and had their guests sign the matting. The special matting cost $15. They had the photographer take a picture of them with all their guests, and eventually they were going to put that picture in the frame as a memento of their day. The marriage license was $54, bringing their miscellaneous, or excess, items to $69 and their total expenditures to $4,846. What a wonderful evening! When the actual reception was over, the guests retired to the parlors to have after-dinner drinks before returning to their beautiful rooms on the second and third floors. This was truly a very special wedding.

We hope you can see from these two examples how it is possible to have an elegant wedding within a reasonable budget. Each of these couples was able to create their dream day without breaking the bank.

Subsequent chapters will describe specific ways to save money so that all the elements of your dream wedding fit into your budget.

Keeping Organized

GOING hand in hand with budgeting (which is basically organizing your money) is the organization of your paperwork, pictures, samples of fabric, swatches of ribbons, and so forth. With a project of this nature, you will accumulate many different pieces of information you will want to refer to from time to time.

We have witnessed many frustrated brides and their mothers digging through a whole box of magazine pictures and contracts unable to find what they're looking for. To save time and aggravation, we suggest that you set up a filing system with dividers or manila folders, labeled for each category. We use this approach to keep everything straight in our office, and we work on multiple weddings at one time.

Wedding Day Reflections

We tried to start with a budget, but we had no idea how much anything cost, so we did not know where to begin.

—Brandon and Julie

Buy a packet of manila folders—you will probably need about twelve. You can create as many folders as you like.

HOW TO USE THE FILING SYSTEM

These sections should give you a good idea of how to organize all of your wedding information.

CEREMONY   After visiting with your priest, rabbi, or minister, start a file with requirements of classes, when and how often you will meet with him or her, what the different rules of the church or other establishment are, and what music choices you can make.

RECEPTION LOCATION   Chances are you will look at quite a few places to make sure you get just the right one. Most places will provide literature containing the price for their facility, their rules and regulations, and other details. Keep all of this in your file until you have chosen your location; then the file can be thinned to contain only information on the site you booked.

MUSIC FOR CEREMONY   After you and your fiancé decide what type of music you want for your ceremony, jot it down in your folder. Chances are, you will hear lots of music suggestions from people. As you do, keep notes on good singers, CDs, or songs so when it comes time to book or purchase these sources, you won't need to rack your brain trying to remember the name of that CD so-and-so told you about the other day.

MUSIC FOR RECEPTION   Again, discuss with your fiancé, and then note in your file, the various types of music you both like. Then decide on your source of music—for example, a live band, a DJ, or your own collection of CDs. With this file, you'll find it much easier to explain to a prospective DJ or musician what you're looking for.

FLORIST   Cut out pictures of bouquets, boutonnieres, and other flowers that catch your eye and put them in your file. Then your florist will know exactly what your tastes are and all you need to supply is your desired price range.

CAKE　Clip pictures of cakes you find particularly beautiful and note flavors you would like to include, and keep them in this file for when you start your cake search. Cakes are discussed in detail in chapter 10, "The Cake," so you will know how to compare bakeries and what notes to take.

INVITATIONS　As you start getting ideas for sayings, designs, and colors for your invitations, put them in your file. This will help you tremendously when you are faced with the hundreds of different options available.

PHOTOGRAPHER　As people start offering names of photographers, write them down, and as you start running across advertisements, cut them out. Place all this in your file so when you hear about the not-so-good photographers, you can remove them, and follow up on the good ones.

TRANSPORTATION　Get an idea of what type of transportation you want—from an old classic convertible to a stretch limousine—and write the ideas in your file. Again, your final decision is easier to make when you have an idea of what you really want.

WEDDING GOWN　Put pictures of the gowns you really like and gowns you've tried on, the paperwork on the gown you choose, and so on, in this file. It is helpful to the florist to have a picture of your wedding gown. Staple a business card of the bridal store on the inside front cover of the file, or write out the address and phone

---

Professionally Speaking

One way to save money is to hire a company that offers a couple of services. Our company specializes in weddings and offers photography, videography, and a DJ service at a considerable discount when hired as a package.

—Ray Johnston, Events DJ, Videography, Photography

number there for easy locating. When you visit the bridal store, take this file with you so you have everything at your fingertips.

BRIDESMAIDS' DRESSES/WOMEN'S WEAR Keep a picture of the dress chosen by your attendants along with a record of the sizes, the date the dresses were ordered, when they are expected, a swatch of material, and other such details. Be sure to take both these files with you to the florist so he or she can see the style and colors of the dresses.

MEN'S WEAR Place photos of tuxedos you and your fiancé like, sizes for him as well as the groomsmen and other male attendants, rental and fitting information, and so forth, in this file for easy access.

VENDORS AND VOLUNTEERS Keep notes of everything that is said when you talk to each of your vendors (e.g., caterers, florists, etc.). Note the date and to whom you spoke. We also suggest you send a letter of confirmation to each vendor. This way you will reaffirm what was agreed on—dates, times, costs, and so forth. Write a letter, too, confirming any arrangements made with your volunteers. See chapter 14, "Details, Details, Details," for sample letters. These notes and copies of the letters should then be included in your files.

As you consider different vendors, don't be afraid to hire people who work from their homes. Many people in this field choose to do so as a way to keep overhead costs down. These savings are then passed on to you.

We have found the two best sources of information on vendors are from friends, relatives, neighbors, or coworkers who have recently married or know someone who has, and recommendations from other vendors. Some time ago we had a bride who asked her photographer whether he knew of a good florist. He referred her to a woman whose work he had just recently photographed. We and our client were very impressed with the florist's work and her prices. We now suggest this florist to a number of our brides. In short, don't be afraid to ask.

3

CEREMONY AND RECEPTION LOCATIONS

SETTING THE STAGE FOR YOUR WEDDING DAY

THE HEAVY OAK doors of the church are propped open, and the pew candles are casting a warm glow inside. Friends are mingling in the foyer, the tuxedo-attired ushers stand ready to seat guests, and the organist plays in the background. Is this how you picture your ceremony? If so, you may want to visit churches in your area within your denomination.

Perhaps you envision crisp, white table linens arranged perfectly, china glistening in the filtered sunlight, and the flowers of the table arrangements standing out against a manicured green lawn. If so, you may want to consider renting the grounds of a mansion or inn or using a friend's backyard or a park.

This chapter is designed to help you with your search for the ideal ceremony and reception locations, whether you know exactly what you want or are still undecided. We will discuss types of ceremonies and locations, examples, and money-saving ideas, and even provide a list of questions to ask and specifics you will need to consider before booking your site.

Ceremonies to Choose From

DEPENDING on your personal preferences, you may be married in a church, temple, cathedral, or small chapel. You may also choose a hall, your home, a friend's home, a garden, or another outside location. You may even choose a hotel or a judge's chambers. Your ceremony will be the foundation for many memories, so try to select a location with some significance to both of you that complements your style.

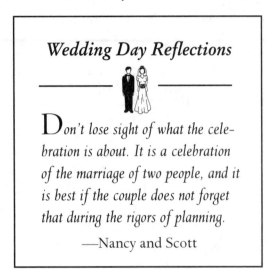

Wedding Day Reflections

Don't lose sight of what the celebration is about. It is a celebration of the marriage of two people, and it is best if the couple does not forget that during the rigors of planning.

—Nancy and Scott

RELIGIOUS CEREMONIES

If you are planning a church wedding, your selection will depend on your affiliation with a particular church or synagogue. Before making any other arrangements, please talk to your clergyperson. Make an appointment with him or her to discuss the service. Most rabbis, priests, and ministers want to meet with the couple at least once. Some churches require you to attend marriage classes, and others invite you to an Engaged Encounter weekend. Our couples who have participated in such events have nothing but wonderful things to say about them.

HOW DOES THIS FIT YOUR SCHEDULE? At your first meeting or when talking with the church secretary, make sure the dates and times you are interested in are available for your ceremony. We were working with a couple who were limited to a 2:00 P.M. ceremony because of their church's schedule. Their reception location did not work well with this timing because it was available only in blocks of time of 11:00 A.M. to 4:00 P.M. and 6:00 P.M. to 11:00 P.M. Therefore, if your church cannot adjust scheduling times, it is essential that your reception site be flexible.

COSTS INVOLVED IN A RELIGIOUS CEREMONY With a church wedding, you can have a large number of guests with little expense, perhaps followed by a simple reception in the church social hall. If you have another location in mind for the reception, it should be within a reasonable distance for your guests' convenience.

The fees for ceremonies vary from church to church. Most churches do not charge members for the use of the facilities. We have found prices for the use of a church for nonmembers to range between $300 and $800. There may be additional fees for soloists or organists. Ask the church secretary for a breakdown of these expenses, including the customary honorarium for the clergy.

VARIOUS RELIGIOUS CEREMONIES TO CHOOSE FROM If your guest list is small, a chapel at the church rather than the large sanctuary would provide a more intimate setting.

Many couples want a religious service in a setting other than a church. Talk with your clergyperson about performing the ceremony at another location. If you are not a member of a church, try contacting a church in which you are interested. Perhaps friends or family members can recommend someone you could talk to.

If you and your fiancé are of different faiths, it is possible to have a minister or rabbi who specializes in interfaith marriages conduct your ceremony. A nondenominational chapel might also be available in your area.

CIVIL CEREMONIES

A civil ceremony is a nonreligious ceremony performed by a judge, justice of the peace, or a county official. This ceremony can take place at the county clerk's office, in a judge's chambers, or almost any location you choose.

> ### Wedding Day Reflections
>
> We recommend finding a location first, and then planning everything around that. Do not get your heart set on one date. We do not think we ever would have found a location if we were not flexible with our wedding date.
>
> —Karen and Mark

Most judges will also travel to locations to perform the ceremony. The couple and two witnesses are all that is necessary. In some areas it is even possible to have a person who is not a member of the clergy or a civil official act as the officiant at your wedding by becoming a deputy marriage commissioner for a day. Check with your local recorder's office for license fees.

One advantage to civil ceremonies is that you have more options for the wording of the vows. Many of our couples choose to personalize their ceremony and write their own vows. During one recent marriage, the couple shared with their guests their thoughts when they first saw each other, how the groom had proposed, and what their dreams were for their life together. It was very touching.

Choosing Your Location and Surroundings

KEEP in mind the following suggestions can be used for both the ceremony and reception or just the reception if you choose a church or synagogue ceremony.

HOME OR PRIVATE GARDEN WEDDINGS

If you or someone close to you has a home or garden suitable for a ceremony and reception, this milieu can make for a very personal and unique wedding. The reception can be either catered or a more casual do-it-yourself (with lots of help) affair. A beautifully decorated fireplace in a living room or a majestic tree or a latticework gazebo in a yard can serve as a focal point for the ceremony. Make sure the available space will accommodate all your guests. This choice can be inexpensive, but be sure to factor in any rental fees you may have. Keep in mind, too, that if you need to landscape a yard, the price increases rapidly.

Couples often choose to have their guests standing during at-home ceremonies; however, chairs should always be made available for older guests. Chairs used at the ceremony can serve double duty by being placed around tables during the reception.

We can't stress enough the need to have a backup plan in case of inclement weather. Yes, it does rain in June! Be prepared to move people inside or have a backup hall reserved. An alternative, since most homes aren't big enough to hold all the guests, is tenting, but that is quite an expensive option.

MANSIONS AND BED-AND-BREAKFAST INNS

If you don't have a suitable home or garden available to you, a bed-and-breakfast or a mansion may fit your needs. Located almost everywhere, inns and renovated mansions have become popular rental spots. These locations usually have beautiful parlors or gardens bordered by hedges and seasonal flowers. A trellis or fountain can act as an altar backdrop. Prices vary depending on what is included and tend to be less expensive in rural areas.

?

Is it possible to "share" chairs between the ceremony and reception areas?

Yes, it just requires some volunteers or hired help and an area for the guests to go while chairs are moved. We find that the officiant making a comment at the end of the ceremony such as "If the guests would please follow me to the deck where refreshments will be served" works well. This remark moves the crowd away from the ceremony site.

One of our most beautiful receptions was held in the garden of a quaint bed-and-breakfast in a small town. A weeping willow hung over a pond that was the backdrop for the area where hors d'oeuvres were served. Umbrella tables had centerpieces of sweet peas picked that morning from the bride's mother's garden. A white lattice gazebo showcased the cake. The setting was so superb that the guests hated to leave at the end of the day.

HOTELS

Hotels have the ability to tailor a banquet room to your desired size, but you are locked into their in-house catering, which can be pricey. Also, be aware that some large hotels reserve the right to bump your reception to a smaller room if the ballroom is needed for a larger party. Such smaller rooms usually leave a lot to be desired and are not worth the big-room rental charge that the ballroom commands. Be sure to ask about the hotel's policy in this regard.

Some of the smaller hotels have wonderful packages for off-season, such as January. Their event room rental rates can be minimal, as low as $250. To stay within your budget, ask whether they can customize an inexpensive per-person menu for you. You will be able to reserve a block of hotel rooms for your guests, and sometimes a complimentary room is provided for you. If you have a number of guests coming from out of town, a hotel can be a wonderful place for everyone to be and make for a great weekend party.

We recently worked with a couple who wanted a wedding where all of their out-of-town friends could gather and spend time together. We suggested a new smaller hotel in our suburb with convenient access for everyone. It has a rose garden, which was perfect for their ceremony, hors d'oeuvres were served on a deck overlooking the pool area, and we had two large rooms that adjoined to accommodate the buffet and indoor seating. A DJ provided music for the ceremony and dancing. The hotel rooms were all occupied by the wedding guests, so the "party" continued on Sunday when all gathered for the hotel's brunch. The couple had a wonderful wedding, and their guests thoroughly enjoyed the surroundings.

RESTAURANTS

Many lovely restaurants have separate banquet rooms that are perfect for receptions and can accommodate modest-size parties very nicely. Banquet rooms provide advantages because they have no setup, cleanup, or rental fees, and small flower arrangements may possibly be included as centerpieces. The cost for a Saturday evening dinner may be formidable, but ask about a brunch, lunch, or a light hors d'oeuvres reception in the early afternoon.

PARK DISTRICTS AND COMMUNITY CENTERS

Providing lovely spots for outdoor ceremonies and receptions, parks range from lush trees surrounded by flowers and scampering chipmunks to ocean or lakeside beaches. These locations often have a clubhouse or pavilion available for use in inclement weather. Find out what is included and whether a fee is charged. It is sometimes only necessary to reserve an area with the governing agency. Some locations require a security guard if alcohol is served, which of course adds to the expense. Your local or regional park districts have a list of suitable sites and their costs.

An example of a park facility we have used is a lovely community center that shares grounds with a library. The center does not showcase the latest decor, but its grounds are beautiful and it is inexpensive. A number of weddings are held outside on the shaded patio with a creek and large oak trees as the backdrop. Because the setting is so lovely, a number of couples choose to set up an arch for their ceremony with this view as their focal point. This year we assisted with a spring wedding there. Because the bride didn't want to use the long rectangular tables and gray metal chairs provided by the center, we rented round tables and white wooden chairs. We planned to have the ceremony outside and tables set up on the patio for the brunch, but a rainy weekend meant we had to move everything inside. We didn't have enough room for chairs positioned for the ceremony as well as tables set and ready for the reception. At the last minute we decided that we would have guests seated at each of the tables for the ceremony. We placed the rented arbor in front of the windows overlooking the patio and allowed space for an "aisle" between the tables. The guests were still able to enjoy the setting, everyone was inside and dry, and it was a wonderful day despite the weather.

ARBORETUMS AND BOTANICAL GARDENS

Some cities are fortunate to have lovely rose gardens, stately groves of towering trees, or other manicured grounds that lend themselves perfectly to a garden wedding. Contact your local chamber of commerce to see whether it has a list of such locations. More than likely you will need to arrange for rental items such as chairs and arbors to be delivered, set up, and then picked up immediately after the ceremony.

HISTORIC GOVERNMENT BUILDINGS

If you live near a state capitol, your capitol building may have a rotunda available for rent. You may have reams of paperwork to complete and need your congressperson's approval, but the out-of-pocket fee will likely be nominal. Other government and historic buildings might also be architectural treasures lending instant ambiance for your special ceremony.

RON AND TIFFANY'S STORY

Probably one of our most fun and unique weddings was that of Ron and Tiffany, a young couple who were married in a lovely Catholic cathedral in our downtown area. Their reception was held in the rotunda of our state capitol building, only a few blocks from their church. Because of limited parking in the city, we determined it would be best to have the guests walk the few blocks to the capitol instead of moving their cars. The couple said they would love to have a processional led by trumpeters. We had recently attended a shopping mall grand opening featuring long herald trumpets, so we called the mall's business office to find out who the musicians were. We hired them to lead the procession from the cathedral to the rotunda. Traffic stopped and waited as the whole wedding entourage followed the trumpeters and bridal couple across two intersections toward the capitol. The rotunda was a lovely setting for their hors d'oeuvres, punch, and cake reception. Ron and Tiffany decided not to serve champagne to keep their expenses down. The cost for renting the rotunda was comparable to other halls; it would have been more expensive—requiring a larger deposit, more insurance, and a state trooper—if any alcohol had been served.

MUSEUMS AND GALLERIES

Some museums have facilities available for receptions at a very nominal rate. An antique automobile museum, for example, could turn out to be the perfect spot for a groom who's a dyed-in-the-wool car buff. Perhaps a combination of a room in the museum and its grounds could be used. Of course, the availability is limited to the hours the museum or gallery is closed to the public.

A museum or gallery may have a list of approved caterers you are required to choose from. This policy is sometimes followed because the staff feels comfortable having these people in their facility based on prior events.

SENIOR CITIZEN COMPLEXES

With more and more beautiful facilities being built for seniors, you may find one that suits your needs. These are often elegant but relaxed settings, with pathways on the grounds for your ceremony and a beautifully appointed hall and patios available for your reception. Make sure adequate parking is available for your guests.

ELKS, GRANGE, AND VETERANS' HALLS

Although these halls are sometimes rather austere buildings, they just might have all the basics you need. More than likely, all of the items necessary for the reception are provided, such as tables and chairs. With a little imagination, some subdued lighting, and a small amount of decorating, you can create the perfect spot. Small lights draped around a room, for instance, can inexpensively add ambiance. Please see chapter 9, "Decorations," for more great ideas.

COLLEGE CAMPUSES

Sometimes these facilities are available only to students or alumni, but they are worth investigating if you live near a college or university. You might discover many wonderful possibilities on campus, from the ivy-covered chapel for your ceremony to the comfortably furnished faculty or alumni house for the reception. A large university near our home has a number of campus locations available to both alumni and the public. The locations include beautiful lawns, creekside settings, and even a barbecue area. All are very conducive to wedding festivities.

BOATS

Some river communities now have historic paddlewheel boats available for rent for private functions. Many are luxurious and climate controlled for year-round cruising. These work especially beautifully for a smaller group. Ask how many people fit easily on one deck, because you will want everyone to view the activities at once. If you have a larger group, it may not be possible for everyone to be able to witness the ceremony or observe the cake cutting.

DESTINATION WEDDINGS

If you have a taste for adventure, holding your wedding in an exotic location can be an exciting option. We know several couples who have traveled to Hawaii, for example, for their weddings. The only drawback to this sort of wedding is that some of your family and friends may have difficulty attending because of their traveling costs. However, most of these affairs are planned with only a small number of guests invited, which keeps the reception costs low. You might consider using part of this savings to help some guests with travel expenses. Because of the lovely surroundings, which can serve as beautiful, natural decorations, other expenses may be limited to your airfare, personal flowers and attire, and food for your few guests. Another big advantage of a destination wedding is the honeymoon begins that much sooner!

Any location may be considered; however, we suggest choosing a resort that specializes in wedding packages. This approach will save you time and money in telephone calls, and the resort staff will do most of the organizing for you. Contact a travel agent or the chamber of commerce in the area in which you are interested, for companies specializing in handling these arrangements.

OTHER FUN YET REALISTIC LOCATIONS

Zoos, libraries, or other nonprofit groups may rent their space as a way to raise funds. Check in your area to see whether such an option is indeed possible. These locations can provide a beautiful and unique reception for a nominal fee. Our local receiving home has a lovely room and tranquil garden for a maximum of seventy-five guests. The staff provides catering, with volunteers preparing and serving the food. It is truly a beautiful spot, and you feel that you are doing something really special with the money you are spending.

For more ideas unique to your particular area, consult your chamber of commerce, department of tourism, visitors' convention bureau, the Yellow Pages under "Wedding Chapels and Locations," and your local newspaper. The resource section of the appendix lists 800 numbers and Web sites that also may prove helpful.

Guest Appeal

After proceeding to the reception site, there was no music, and no food or drinks were being offered. I would have thought we were in the wrong place if I hadn't recognized some people we had seen at the ceremony. My wife and I were ready to leave. I vowed this would never happen at our daughter's wedding.

—Jim Kimberly, wedding guest

Getting More for Your Money

As we stated before, planning far in advance gives you your choice of locations. The beautiful, more elegant, less expensive locations are always in demand and will be booked early. Be flexible with your dates, if at all possible; this can be a big help in finding your perfect place.

The time of year will impact what locations you can consider. For example, if your wedding must take place at semester break in January, a garden wedding would not be an option in most locales. On the other hand, holding a winter wedding can have its benefits. A lovely facility very popular with brides in our area charges $1,500 for room rental for a Saturday wedding in the summer peak season. In the off-season, such as January, the same room rental is $600; additionally, on a Sunday in off-season, that same room rental is only $400. Planning for savings is indeed possible.

The time of day can also play a big part in your decisions. Many locations have two set times for functions, such as 11 A.M. to 4:00 P.M.

and then 6:00 to 11:00 P.M. If this is the case, your ceremony and reception would have to start and end within that time frame if they both were to take place at that location. The earlier time would be less expensive, because a lighter meal could be served. A brunch following a morning ceremony can be lovely. If your reception site does not tie you to a structured time, perhaps you could consider a 2:00 ceremony, followed by light hors d'oeuvres and cake or simply cake and champagne, with a string quartet playing for your guests' entertainment. This sort of reception works very well at this time of day, since guests aren't expecting a heavy meal then. Most important, either of these early-wedding ideas can be achieved at a nominal cost and still be most elegant.

Sites specializing in weddings are often budget pleasers. They usually provide tables, chairs, and china service for a minimal rental rate. On the other hand, a less expensive barn or grassy area with nothing included might seem like a bargain until you take into account the cost of renting chairs, tables, and tablecloths and the extra effort needed for decorating. (Tablecloths are usually necessary on most rental tables due to their plywood surfaces.) For approximate rental charges, please refer to chapter 2, "The Wedding Budget and Organization."

Locations that require you to use their catering may have a required minimum number of guests, such as 100 for a Saturday evening. A reduced guest list wouldn't work here. Perhaps the same location would be available on Friday evening or Sunday afternoon with a lower rental rate and also a lower minimum number of guests. Ask about more reasonable rates on different nights.

Wedding Day Reflections

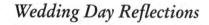

Do what you want, not what your family says you should do! We wanted to have a small group gathered for our nuptials on the anniversary of our first date, and a big reception after we returned from our honeymoon. Lucianna's family tried to talk us out of it because it made the ceremony fall on a Tuesday. We're glad we stuck with our original plan because it made the day even more romantic.

—Lucianna and Phil

We can't stress enough that a backup plan is crucial for outside ceremonies or receptions in case of rain, wind, or weather that is too cool or too hot. For example, at a wedding we recently planned, the wedding day was sunny and clear, but we were unable to have the ceremony in the originally planned location due to weeks of rain. The ground was too wet for guests to be seated in chairs on the lawn without them sinking. Fortunately, we had a backup plan of a rented Astroturf floor and had figured this cost into the budget.

Finding and Booking Your Site

As you visit various locations, keep copious notes for your files to review at a later time. Write down whom you talked to for ease in contacting them later with further questions. We suggest you take along a camera to record the various locations. These photos, along with your notes, will save you many steps.

One question we now ask all locations is whether any redecorating or remodeling is planned. We learned this lesson the hard way when one of our brides selected a lovely country club with muted decor for her reception. Her bridesmaids' dresses and flowers were carefully chosen to match the location. We visited the country club approximately a month before the reception to discuss the menu. The bride walked in and burst into tears when she saw that the soft colors had been replaced by deep royal purple with gold gilding everywhere, and a dark, floral-patterned carpet. The room was beautifully redone, but it was not at all what the poor bride had pictured or planned around. To save the day, we talked to the florist, who introduced deeper mauve and purple shades in the table decorations and the bridesmaids' bouquets that tied in with the new decor and helped the bride feel more comfortable with the colors.

Even churches occasionally remodel, so question them also. We recently heard of a wedding at a lovely old church in our town. The couple arrived at the church for the rehearsal and saw broken fences, piles of concrete where walkways had been broken up, and "Keep

Out" signs where they had envisioned posing for pictures. They had no idea that remodeling was going on, and although the sanctuary was untouched, they had a lot of last-minute arrangements to make as to where the bridal party would dress and where pre-wedding pictures would be taken.

ADDITIONAL POINTS TO CONSIDER

For an outside ceremony, visit the site at the time of your ceremony and do the following:

1. Observe the location of the sun to note where it shines. You don't want yourself or your guests looking directly into the sun.
2. Listen for traffic noise.
3. Check to see whether a playground is located nearby, which also could add unwanted background noise.

For either a ceremony or a reception, double-check the following points:

1. Check for adequate and convenient parking for your guests.
2. Investigate what other events, if any, are going on in the area on your wedding date.
3. Contact someone who has recently had a ceremony or reception there. Find out whether they were happy with the location, whether there is anything they would caution you about, and whether they would have done anything differently.

Remember to Organize

ONCE you have booked your location, you are ready for your first step in organizing. Start two folders, one labeled "Ceremony" and the other "Reception Location," and insert in them contracts and other information you have. If you need to rent tables and/or chairs, you will need a third file labeled "Rentals." Note in each folder what deposits you have made and when the additional dollars are due. Add all amounts due to your payment schedule.

Safeguard Your Plans with Good Questions

❧

Before committing yourself to a location, we suggest you ask a number of questions and also do some research on your own. Don't be timid. Remember, you are doing the planning now so that your wedding day will be problem-free. The following questions cover important areas to address before you choose a location:

1. What are your fees?
2. How many people can you comfortably handle?
3. Are there time restrictions?
4. How many other functions will be going on the day of our wedding?
5. Are tables and chairs included?
6. May we hire outside caterers?
7. Does the music need to be discontinued after a certain time owing to neighbors?
8. May alcohol be served?
9. What decorating may we do?
10. What time is the building accessible for decorating, catering, and so forth?
11. What restrictions are there?
12. Is a place available for the bridal party to dress before the ceremony?
13. Are you planning to do any redecorating or remodeling?
14. May our guests throw birdseed or flower petals as we depart?

Congratulations! With your ceremony and reception locations selected, you have probably the biggest hurdle out of the way. Your other decisions will now revolve around your sites and will seem easier.

4

WEDDING ATTIRE

Dressing for the Day of a Lifetime

Now that you have chosen the time, location, and style of your wedding, you are ready to choose the attire for the bridal party. Selecting your wedding gown, especially, is probably the most exciting part of planning a wedding. No matter how simple or elaborate the dress, when you slip into the right one, you can't help but feel romantic and somehow transformed. Nothing else you might wear is capable of evoking such emotion. This chapter will include points to keep in mind before you go shopping, information about the different styles of gowns and various fabrics, your options on where to shop for gowns, and appropriate attire for the rest of the wedding party.

The Wedding Gown

Choosing your wedding gown is a series of small decisions that together will lead you to the perfect dress. You must settle on a price limit for the gown, including alterations; select a style, fabric, and length that you love and that complement the season and setting of your wedding; and, finally, know where to look. The following sections will give you pointers covering all these details.

WHERE TO SHOP

Today a bride has a variety of options when shopping for a wedding gown. No longer are you limited to having one sewn for you, as once was the custom. Remember, you can find the wedding dress you've

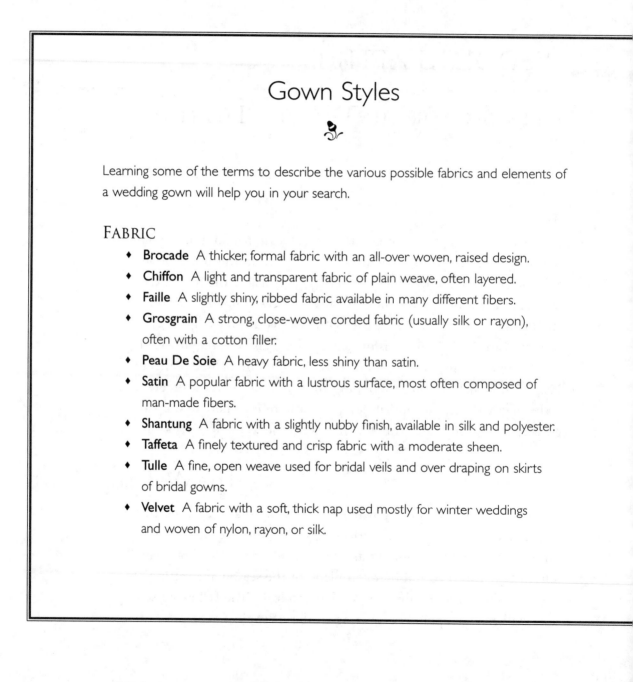

Gown Styles

Learning some of the terms to describe the various possible fabrics and elements of a wedding gown will help you in your search.

FABRIC

- ◆ **Brocade** A thicker, formal fabric with an all-over woven, raised design.
- ◆ **Chiffon** A light and transparent fabric of plain weave, often layered.
- ◆ **Faille** A slightly shiny, ribbed fabric available in many different fibers.
- ◆ **Grosgrain** A strong, close-woven corded fabric (usually silk or rayon), often with a cotton filler.
- ◆ **Peau De Soie** A heavy fabric, less shiny than satin.
- ◆ **Satin** A popular fabric with a lustrous surface, most often composed of man-made fibers.
- ◆ **Shantung** A fabric with a slightly nubby finish, available in silk and polyester.
- ◆ **Taffeta** A finely textured and crisp fabric with a moderate sheen.
- ◆ **Tulle** A fine, open weave used for bridal veils and over draping on skirts of bridal gowns.
- ◆ **Velvet** A fabric with a soft, thick nap used mostly for winter weddings and woven of nylon, rayon, or silk.

always dreamed of without breaking the bank; just know what you're looking for, shop around, be patient, and most of all, have fun!

SILHOUETTES

- **A-Line or Princess** Slim-fitting from shoulder to hem with vertical seams and a gradually flaring skirt.
- **Ball Gown** A low or off-the-shoulder neckline and a very full skirt.
- **Empire** A high waistline stemming from a small bodice with a slim or full skirt.
- **Sheath** A straight dress, often with a detachable train.

HEM LENGTHS

- **Ankle Length** A skirt that reveals the ankles.
- **Tea Length** A hem falling several inches above the ankles.
- **Floor Length** A hem skimming the floor.

SLEEVES

- **Bishop** Full to the cuff, which may be long.
- **Bow** A short sleeve made of looped fabric, worn on or off the shoulder.
- **Cap** A short, fitted sleeve that just covers the top of the arm.
- **Fitted** A long, traditional sleeve.
- **Leg-of-Mutton** Rounded from the shoulder to the elbow with a fitted forearm.
- **Puff** A short sleeve gathered into a puff at the shoulder.

TRAINS

- **Sweep** Barely brushes the floor.
- **Court** Extends approximately one foot past the hemline.
- **Chapel** Extends 1 1/3 to 1 1/2 yards from the hemline.
- **Cathedral** Extends 3 yards from the hemline.

Points to Keep in Mind Before You Shop

❦

1. Look through bridal magazines and choose some pictures that appeal to you. Take a few of these pictures with you when you visit stores so that you can give the bridal-gown consultant an idea of what you like.

2. Choose a style that is becoming to your figure and height, and that reflects your tastes.

3. Keep an open mind toward trying on different gowns. It is not a good idea to "choose" your gown from a magazine picture alone, as this style may not complement your figure. Often the dress a bride ends up loving is not something she would have noticed in a magazine picture.

4. Tell the bridal gown consultant your budget, and do not try on dresses that cost more.

5. Wear or take along shoes similar to the ones you may wear on your wedding day. Everyone stands differently in heels than in sneakers.

6. If you are considering wearing your hair up, put it in barrettes or a bun to give you a better idea of how the dress neckline may look on your wedding day.

7. Before choosing a headpiece or veil, decide how you will wear your hair.

8. Only go shopping with a couple of people, perhaps your mother or your mother and maid of honor or another person whose opinion you trust.

9. Shop on a weekday if at all possible. Most bridal salons and warehouses are extremely busy on weekends. Many require appointments, so please call ahead.

10. Shop early. Some styles take six months to arrive, and then you'll need additional time to complete any alterations.

11. Be very clear as to the bridal store policies before placing an order. Store policies vary greatly. Most deposits are nonrefundable.

12. Is storage included in the price? If not, do you have a safe location to keep the dress?

13. Ask about hidden costs, such as shipping.

BRIDAL SALONS Don't hesitate to visit a full-service bridal salon. They have a wide range of styles and prices to fit all budgets. At better bridal salons you will be treated to good customer service. For best results, a midweek appointment is desirable as the store will be less busy and a consultant will have more time to give you her undivided attention. Fridays and weekends are unbelievably hectic and should be avoided, if at all possible.

At your initial appointment, let your consultant know right away that you have a limited budget or a budget of so many dollars for your gown. Being this up front about cost will eliminate unnecessary trying on for you and unnecessary work for her. She will ask the date of your wedding. Let her know the location of your ceremony and reception so she will have a feel for what would be appropriate. Bridal consultants have the expertise to help you choose the perfect gown.

CLARA'S STORY

One of our brides, Clara, asked us to accompany her to a bridal salon for her initial visit, because her mother and her brides-maids lived out of town and she did not want to go alone. When we met her, she said she had looked through bridal magazines with her fiancé, who said he liked just about any style but really didn't like puffy sleeves. We met with the consultant, who asked all the appropriate questions and then brought out about ten dresses within Clara's budget and similar to the pictures she had brought. They were all lovely, but Clara was not thrilled with any one dress in particular. The consultant then asked the bride-to-be whether she, the consultant, could choose several dresses that were different from the ones Clara had already tried on. The first one the consultant brought out had puffy sleeves, and Clara loved it! We reminded her of what her fiancé had said. "Don't worry. He will just love this," she said. She was right. When he saw her walking down the aisle, all he saw was how beautiful she looked—and he even liked the sleeves!

If a gown you like is shown in silk shantung and is more than you can spend, ask if that same gown could be made in a less expensive material, such as polyester. You might also ask whether the salon has clearance sales, sells their samples, or offers discontinued dresses at a discount. These are possibilities for savings, except they may incur high alteration charges. Most of the dresses the salons stock are in larger sizes so that most brides can try them on. If you are small, a number of alterations will be necessary. Take that into account before buying a bargain.

Don't feel obligated to purchase a gown on your first visit. Most salons will be very happy to keep a card on file of the gowns you like and will save the information for another visit. When you do place your order, most salons require a 50 percent down payment. The final half is due after the dress arrives (usually allow six months for most manufacturers) and before your first fitting. Before you place your order, ask what the charges for all alterations will be. Some salons don't charge extra for common alterations, such as hem lines, when performed by their in-house seamstress. The gown will be pressed and ready to put on when you pick it up. Have the bridal consultant include all agreed-on information on your sales receipt so there are no misunderstandings later. When doing business with a reputable bridal salon, rest assured you will get great service and can feel confident you will have your gown on time.

?

Do I have to wear a white dress?

No, today a bride is not limited to wearing white or even ivory. Traditionally a white wedding dress is associated with purity, but white also symbolizes joy—a most appropriate sentiment for this special day.

BRIDAL WAREHOUSES Stores that stock a large inventory of mostly lower-priced gowns are referred to as bridal warehouses. These stores are popular because you can buy gowns right out of stock, instead of waiting for a custom-ordered dress. A drawback is that the dresses usually are not available in all sizes and most warehouses provide no alteration service. Also, it is possible the gowns will have suffered tears or other damage because they are there for anyone to try on. Pam, a friend of ours, recently bought a gown at a warehouse. She was a size 8 and unfortunately fell in love with a gown that was carried in a size 12. They assured her that alterations could be made, and so she purchased the gown. A seamstress told Pam that because of all the lace and beading and the cut of the gown, it was not possible to alter it. This store did not allow returns, but the staff agreed to take back the gown and only charge the bride a restocking fee of about $100.

If you live a distance from many bridal stores, it might be to your advantage to buy from a bridal warehouse, take the dress, and have alterations done nearer your home. Even though you will be paying for these alterations, it could be less expensive and less time-consuming than making repeated trips to a far-away salon. Before buying a gown from a warehouse, however, we suggest you ask about their return policy in case you find the necessary alterations will be too costly.

DEPARTMENT STORES Your local department store or boutique may have a department of formals and evening wear. This is an excellent area to find a beautiful gown at a fraction of the cost of a bridal gown. Don't look only at white or ivory gowns; if you like the styling of a different-colored dress, it may be available in white or ivory. Ask to speak with the buyer for that department, who can find out whether that same dress is available in other colors.

A number of the dresses carried by department stores are more sophisticated in style, which might suit your tastes better. One of our brides purchased a lovely sheath dress trimmed only with a bow at the waist in the back. Her mother added some beading on both the bow and the bodice, and the dress looked absolutely beautiful.

Department stores are also a great place to shop for more versatile bridesmaids' dresses. The bridesmaids might even truly wear them a second time!

BRIDAL OUTLET STORES   We visited a bridal outlet store several years ago. This shopping trip is not for the weak and weary! To avoid the crowds (we thought), we went early one Saturday morning. A "herd" of people was already lined up, and they all stampeded when the doors opened. By the time we were in, the racks were already in disarray, and several gowns were on the floor. The dressing room (one large open room) was stark, messy, and noisy. On the plus side, some beautiful gowns from well-known designers were offered at great prices.

Here again, you must check the gowns very carefully for damage. We noticed lipstick stains on a number of them. Also, an outlet-bought gown will probably need to be altered and dry-cleaned. At this particular outlet, the gowns could not be returned, since all sales were final.

CONSIGNMENT SHOPS   Consignment shops are gaining in popularity as a wonderful source for wedding and bridesmaids' gowns. One of our brides was able to find a dress for herself and even all her bridesmaids at such a shop! Often you will find gowns of excellent quality, as the shop owners are very careful to accept only dresses of the highest caliber. These dresses may or may not have been worn before and normally cost a fraction of their original cost. Again, alteration costs need to be considered, as do return policies.

Professionally Speaking

I suggest that brides on a budget look at the discontinued rack at bridal salons. It is possible to find dresses that formerly retailed for well over $1,000 offered for under $400. Professional seamstresses employed by better salons can alter size, change sleeves and/or neckline, or add lace to make these dresses into something the bride will love.

—Jenny Vassilian,
House of Fashion bridal store

CLASSIFIED ADS From time to time, ads are placed in newspapers listing a gown at a very low price. It is worth a call to see whether the dress style and fabric is of interest to you. Again, the size is very important. If you decide you do like the dress, inspect it very carefully for stains or other damage before purchasing it.

RENTALS Gowns are now available for rental, just as tuxes are. The difference is that most gown rental shops require you to pay for alterations, and you must have the gown cleaned before returning it. If having a gown to keep after the ceremony is not important to you, this is an option worth considering. You may be able to wear a beautiful, expensive gown at a reasonable cost.

MAIL ORDER We strongly urge you not to buy a dress by mail order. It is very important that you be able to actually see and feel the material in a dress, look at its construction, and try it on before purchasing. Also keep in mind that the bargain price does not include the extra you will have to pay for shipping and handling. These costs could negate any savings.

CUSTOM-MADE GOWNS

Perhaps you have fallen in love with a gown you have seen in a bridal magazine only to learn it is out of your price range. Contact a seamstress who specializes in wedding gowns. Review with her what style and materials you want in your dress. Possibly she could make a similar dress for you within your budget. Be sure to discuss with her what all labor, material, and notion (buttons, zippers, trim, etc.) costs will be.

MAKING YOUR OWN GOWN

We can't imagine tackling such a grand task, but several of our clients and their moms have set out to sew the gown themselves. A large selection of patterns are available at fabric stores, and you can mix and match sleeves, necklines, hemlines, and bodices. This versatility, along with many different choices of fabrics, gives you a truly one-of-a-kind gown.

Professionally Speaking

I suggest to brides who contact me about making their dresses that they try on bridal gowns and really see what style they like on their figures. Then I suggest they choose a pattern or two and we will put pieces together. I really enjoy making their very own personalized wedding dresses.

—Betty Shupe, dressmaker

Only attempt making your gown if you or the volunteer is an accomplished seamstress and you have a lot of time before your wedding date. Most material used in wedding gowns is not easy to work with. A muslin copy should be made first to avoid costly mistakes on the expensive material.

A mother of a bride called our office recently with several etiquette questions. As we talked, she told me about her daughter's upcoming wedding. This mother was making the bridal gown out of white velvet. She was very excited because she had been told that ready-made velvet gowns were $5,000 and up. She estimated the cost of her daughter's gown to be about $500. She had purchased eleven yards of velvet, regularly $22 per yard. She waited for a sale and was able to purchase the velvet at $18 per yard. The pattern also called for two yards of reembroidered lace, which was $70 per yard. The empire-style dress had beaded lace at the waist, on the sleeves, and at the hem. The dress sounded exquisite, and the mother was very proud. What a lucky daughter!

WEARING YOUR MOTHER'S GOWN

Though, to some future brides, wearing your mother's gown may seem like a dreadful idea, if done right it can actually make a wedding picture perfect.

HOLLY'S STORY

Holly, one of our clients, shared some exciting news with us one day. We knew she was about to go gown shopping after combing bridal magazines for ideas. She was showing her mother several pictures when her mom asked her to come into her parent's bedroom. From the back of her closet, Holly's mother pulled out a large box. In it was the gown she had worn at her own wedding thirty-two years earlier. "Don't feel you must wear it if you don't like it, but it is somewhat like the pictures you have cut out," said her mother. She had been hesitant to bring it out, but her fears were put to rest when Holly tried it on and said, "I would love to wear it, Mom. It is beautiful." A few alterations were necessary, but an expert seamstress easily took care of them. It was professionally cleaned and pressed and looked brand new. Holly's mother had also saved her headpiece, but Holly felt the style looked too outdated. They chose a new head-piece with a shorter veil and no blusher, and it blended perfectly with the gown.

Some brides whose mothers have saved their gowns are not as fortunate. If a dress is stored away without being carefully cleaned, brown spots may appear. These stains are probably from the sugar in spilled champagne or white wine. Clear spills are not obvious on white fabric and most likely were not visible when the gown was stored. You can attempt to have the older gown cleaned, but more than likely the stains will remain. Depending on the age of the gown, you might have a chance. Some of the newer gowns are made of poly-ester and can be wet-cleaned even though the directions will say to dry-clean only. A gown of silk or acetate cannot be washed. This is not a job for your washing machine. Turn it over to a professional who has a lot of experience with wedding gowns.

Some companies specialize in renovating very old gowns, but this procedure is extremely expensive. Other suggestions for using an old gown are as follows:

1. If the bodice is in good shape, possibly a new skirt that would match could be made.
2. Perhaps lace used on the old gown could be transferred to another dress that has simple lines.
3. A headpiece that is a good style could be renovated using new tulle.

It would be wonderful if you could use part of an heirloom gown. We had a bride getting married on her parents' forty-ninth wedding anniversary. She was going to wear her mother's gown and looked like a dream in it. However, while trying on the dress, she could hear and feel the delicate lace on the shoulders breaking and tearing. It was just too fragile to wear. We found a seamstress who made a lining out of netting that was sewn in invisibly under the lace. The weight of the dress rested on this lining, taking the stress off the lace. The dress was perfect! After the ceremony, she changed into a very contemporary beaded cocktail dress for the rest of the evening. This was a wonderful solution so that a treasure could be worn.

Professionally Speaking

A *vintage dress with a stain problem can possibly be salvaged by making lace appliques and strategically placing them to cover the soiled areas.*

—Dee Kurtz, owner of Sunrise Cleaners, a store specializing in cleaning and restoring wedding gowns

---

The Right Veil and Headpiece

A VEIL should both frame the face and complement your dress. It is an important part of your bridal outfit, so do not rush into this decision. As with bridal gowns, most veils ordered are custom made, but they do not require as much lead time. We suggest having your veil made with a Velcro detachable option so that you may remove the

Styles for Veils and Headpieces

❧

A veil and headpiece can cost anywhere from $25 to $400. The best way to save money is to make your own. Of course, some brides today choose not to wear veils at all, which is an option for less formal weddings. The following sections define veil and headpiece terminology and give tips on veil making and purchasing.

VEILS

- **Blusher**   Veil worn forward over face or back over the headpiece.
- **Fly-Away**   Multiple layers that brush the shoulders.
- **Fingertip**   One or more layers of veiling extending to the fingertips.
- **Ballet or Tea Length**   Veiling to the ankles.
- **Chapel and Cathedral**   Veil cascading 2$^1/_3$ and 3$^1/_2$ yards, respectively, from the headpiece, usually worn with coordinating train.

HEADPIECES

- **Headband**   A decorative headband worn with or without a veil attached.
- **Mantilla**   A lace scarf draping over head.
- **Pillbox**   A small, round hat.
- **Tiara**   A crownlike headpiece.
- **Wreath**   A circle of flowers or other decorations.

tulle veiling from the headpiece after the ceremony and photos. This style makes dancing and hugging guests much easier because your veiling does not get caught. It also allows you to wear your headpiece throughout the day, which is important if it is an integral part of your hairdo.

Creating your own headpiece and veil or having a seamstress friend or relative make one for you is a surprisingly simple alternative.

This is definitely worth considering because the least expensive headpiece options we have seen in stores lately are $125. We suggest trying on headpieces and veils with your dress at the bridal store and choosing a style you think would complement your dress. Take a good look at the detail of the lace on your dress, if any, and look for similar lace in your favorite fabric store. With the broad range of laces available, we have found matching to be quite easy. Fabric stores carry "headpiece forms" of many shapes that can be decorated with details similar to the details on your dress. Tulle veiling can be purchased inexpensively and is easy to work with. We have used a couple of books that go through the process of making a headpiece step by step and will help you create a custom veil at a fraction of the price. Please refer to the appendix for the titles, or go to your local library's sewing section.

> **?**
>
> ### Do I have to wear a veil?
>
> *No. We suggest, though, that you keep in mind that this is the only day of your life in which it is appropriate to wear a veil, and you might want to consider such a special accessory. A nice compromise may be to take the entire headpiece off after the ceremony or pictures or to have the veiling attached to the headpiece with Velcro for ease in removing.*

The Right Train

As we have seen, there are several trains to choose from. One thing to keep in mind is that the longer trains need to be bustled. A bustle gathers up the train at the back of the dress for the reception. Many dresses are available with a bustling option, or a skilled seamstress can add one. We suggest buying a dress with a bustle or having one added because it is impractical to hold your train over your arm during the reception.

The Right Accessories

NEARLY as important as the wedding gown itself are the other, smaller items that complement your dress. You should give careful thought to your undergarments, shoes, and jewelry as they can beautifully enhance the entire outfit, making you feel all the more special. Accessories also can allow you, if you're so inclined, to indulge the superstition to wear "something old, something new; something borrowed, something blue."

UNDERGARMENTS

Remember the undergarments! Do not delay in choosing your undergarments to wear with your gown. These can play an important part in the fit and comfort of your dress and should be taken to every fitting. Some salons and seamstresses can sew in pads to certain styles of dresses so that a brassiere is not necessary. Inquire about your options and try on styles of brassieres at your bridal store. Some styles also require full slips and/or crinolines for the skirt to hang correctly and look full. Your consultant can offer you valuable advice in this area.

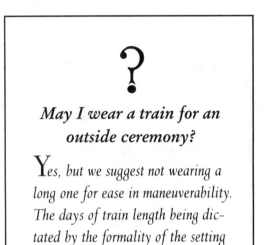

May I wear a train for an outside ceremony?

Yes, *but we suggest not wearing a long one for ease in maneuverability. The days of train length being dictated by the formality of the setting are in the past.*

Shopping for the proper undergarments is an activity where you should look around for the best price. Try your local department stores and compare prices.

SHOES

Choosing your wedding shoes is very important. Not only should your shoes be an appropriate height so that your hemline does not drag, but they also need to be comfortable. We have seen more than a dozen brides who have a hard time smiling only halfway through their wedding day because their shoes are hurting their feet. Although we make a point of telling all our brides to put function over fashion in the shoe department, some brides still choose beautiful shoes that are uncomfortable.

It is very popular now to wear dainty, satin shoes, but we suggest leather shoes. Satin shoes do not give or breathe and therefore can become uncomfortable after an hour or two of wear. Changing into ballet slipper–style shoes is also a comfortable option. Keep in mind, too, that with a floor-length gown, no one really sees your shoes.

STOCKINGS

Stockings that complement your gown in white or ivory are a must. Some brides choose to purchase nylons with an embellishment of a wedding bow or bell on the ankle. These are available in most bridal salons. A less expensive alternative would be to buy plain white or ivory stockings from your local department store. Again, like shoes, this isn't an article that is very noticeable. We suggest purchasing two pair of the stockings of your choice and taking them both to the site where you will be dressing. Wedding jitters definitely increase the chances of running your pantyhose while putting them on.

JEWELRY

Keeping jewelry to a minimum is a good idea, though a special piece or two can be appropriate. Finding earrings to complement your headpiece and dress may take some time. Many bridal salons offer selections, but you may also want to look at jewelry stores and department stores. Leaving your watch in the dressing room is a must; many photographers state that they are very obvious in pictures. Wearing

---

Timeless Traditions

Something old, something new; something borrowed, something blue—and a sixpence in your shoe. A bride having these items on her wedding day is thought to have good luck.

rings other than the wedding and engagement rings on the left hand can also detract from the wedding band during photos. Having all the bridesmaids wear matching earrings and/or necklaces is a nice way to complete their look. These items are popular gifts.

Bridesmaids' Dresses

THE gowns you choose for your bridesmaids will help set the scene for your wedding. Their dresses can be any color, and the style should complement that of your own gown. Their dresses may be a shorter length than the bridal gown but never longer. They may be a more simple design but never more formal.

We again suggest that only you and your honor attendant go looking for the dresses. Trying to find the dress that everyone thinks is perfect can be impossible. The two of you will want to keep in mind the following points:

1. The style of dress to complement your gown.
2. The style of dress that will look good on each of your attendants, considering their hairstyles, coloring, and different sizes.
3. The fabric and color choices that will go well with the season.
4. The budget and financial status of the members of your wedding party.

After choosing their gowns, the attendants will need to be measured before the order can be placed. Ask those who live locally to visit the store where you are purchasing the dresses. If you can organize a time when all the bridesmaids can go together, this would be a fun time for you all to go out to lunch or shopping afterward. For your attendants who are out of town, ask your bridal consultant what measurements are needed. They can go into a bridal or alteration store in their area and have these measurements taken. When ordering the gowns, in addition to the measurements, you may specify that you need extra length for a tall bridesmaid and petite sizing for a short one. Placing the order for all dresses together is important to ensure all dresses are made from the same dye lot. Dresses ordered individually may not match the others.

Once the gowns have arrived, your bridesmaids will need to be fitted. If your out-of-town attendants are unable to come to your area for fittings, have the gowns sent to them so they can have the fittings done in their locale.

We suggest the attendants wear leather shoes for comfort reasons. Sometimes our clients' bridesmaids have worn their own black shoes. If you decide to have shoes dyed to match their gowns, take all pairs to the store at the same time to guarantee a uniform color.

More and more of our brides are suggesting that their attendants wear a basic "little black" dress from their own wardrobe. The necklines usually differ, but the dresses have approximately the same look. The colors of the wedding can be carried off in the bridesmaids' bouquets.

LINDA'S STORY

One of our brides, Linda, chose a fabric for the bridesmaids' gowns and let her attendants pick the style dress they wanted to have made, with each choosing her own local seamstress. Because of a big difference in the sizes and ages of her attendants, Linda felt each would feel more comfortable with this arrangement. Her only stipulation was that the gowns be floor length and made of the fabric she chose. She had a fabric store hold a bolt of the desired material, and each attendant quickly picked a pattern they liked. Linda then bought the yardage needed for each gown, ordering extra for each attendant just to be on the safe side. Her attendants were very pleased with this arrangement, and each took responsibility for ensuring their dress was ready on time. On the day of the wedding, the attendants put on their gowns, and they all enjoyed seeing the same material done up in different styles. However, there was one problem. One of the dresses had been made with the dull side of the fabric on the outside rather than the shiny. Although the gowns were all the same purple, that one gown appeared to be a different shade. Beware of this possible problem if you choose to have dresses made. Both the bride and the attendant had a good sense of humor, so it was not a real catastrophe. During the picture taking, the photographer arranged the attendants in such a way that that dress was not noticeably different in color.

If you wish for your bridesmaids to wear a headpiece or a hat, consider each attendant's hairstyle. Most of our clients have the attendants decide what they want to do with their own hairstyle, and they wear nothing on their heads. One nice option we have seen at a casual outdoor wedding was the attendants wearing their hair in a French braid down the back with flowers in the braid. It was a lovely touch.

Flower Girls and Ring Bearers

OUTFITTING flower girls can be a lot of fun. The easiest solution is a ready-made dress in white or ivory to "match" the bridal gown. If choosing this dress quite a bit in advance, be sure to allow for growing room. If you would like the dress to have a sash, extra material of the same fabric of the bridesmaids' dresses should be ordered when their gowns are ordered. If a sash seems too heavy for the style of the dress, ribbon can be used to tie in the colors. Grosgrain ribbon stands a better chance of staying tied than a satin ribbon, although satin looks dressier.

Companies making bridesmaid gowns also make gowns for flower girls, but a very young child does not, for the most part, look good in a scaled-down version of a dress designed for an adult. If you want the child in a dress of the same fabric as the attendants' gowns, again order extra fabric. Make this decision when you order the gowns, as then all the fabric will be from the same dye lot.

Several years ago we coordinated a lovely winter wedding. The bridesmaids' dresses were black velvet, very simple and very exquisite. The mother of the flower girl found a lovely black velvet, young-looking dress for her daughter to wear. It had an empire waistline with a large satin collar. The little girl wore white patterned tights and patent-leather Mary Jane shoes. She looked darling.

Girls between the ages of ten and fifteen may be junior attendants. It is usually appropriate for their dresses to be the same as the brides-maids, depending on the style chosen.

Ring bearers often are dressed exactly like the groomsmen in a small version of the same tuxedo. They look very cute, but often it isn't much time until their shirttail is out and bow tie askew. We suggest that boys not be fitted more than two weeks before the wedding because they grow fast.

Several of our brides have dressed their ring bearers in suits. Eton-style suits—which include short pants (worn with knee socks), a jacket, a long-sleeved shirt, and a bow tie—look very sharp. One ring bearer's Eton suit was black velvet; another was in white linen. Another little guy wore a traditional charcoal suit and a bow tie. All looked very handsome.

Timeless Traditions

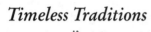

It has been a long tradition for bridesmaids and groomsmen to dress like the bridal couple. In the past, people believed that this was the best way to confuse evil spirits. How could the spirits jinx the couple's happiness if they could not tell the betrothed couple apart from the others?

Groom, Groomsmen, and Fathers

WITH all the fuss over the bride's and bridesmaids' dresses, the men sometimes seem to be forgotten. Such is not the case. To ensure the men are appropriately dressed, their clothing and accessories should also be chosen with the location, style of the wedding, and time of day in mind. Most men wear rented tuxedos. We suggest visiting a tuxedo rental store and spending some time looking at all your choices. Ask a staff member about the store's policies at this time. Some stores offer the groom's tux free when five or more tuxes are rented by the wedding party. Dividing this money among all the men can save everyone a bit.

Most coats come in single- or double-breasted styles, with notch, peak, or shawl lapels. The trousers are either pleated or double-inverted pleated and may have a matching fabric stripe on the legs. There is a myriad of choices of shirts, ties, cummerbunds, and vests, all available in many colors and patterns. If you're trying to match a color, it would be a good idea to take a bridesmaid's gown to the rental store. Look at them together in both outdoor and indoor lighting.

Included in the tuxedo rental price will be the tux, shirt, tie, cummerbund or vest, and studs (used in place of buttons). We do not recommend renting the shoes because they aren't very comfortable. Most men prefer to wear their own black dress shoes. We remind our grooms to be sure each pair is newly polished.

For your out-of-town groomsmen, they can take mail-in measurement forms to a tuxedo store in their area. Their measurements are recorded there, and this information is then sent to the store where the tuxes will be picked up. We suggest the tuxes be picked up early Friday afternoon for a Saturday wedding. This way, if there is a fitting problem, the store has time to correct it. We tell each groom to have every member of his party try on the entire outfit when picking up the tuxes. We can't stress enough how important this is to avoid confusion and frustration on the day of the wedding when the jacket sleeves are too short, a tie is missing, or the clasp on the cummerbund is broken.

Tuxedos are not necessary for all weddings. In some cases, the men wear their own suits. If you want a uniform look, we recommend you ask all the men involved to wear a dark suit. We recently were guests at a wedding where the groom was in a gray suit, the father of the bride wore a navy pinstripe suit, the father of the groom wore a casual brown suit, and the best man's suit was a gray tweed. They just didn't match!

We have had a groom and his groomsmen dressed in navy blazers with tan slacks and they really looked classy. The wedding and reception were held on a boat, so this attire was most appropriate.

Mother-of-the-Bride and Mother-of-the-Groom Dresses

AFTER the color and style of the bridesmaids' gowns are determined, the mother of the bride should start to look for her dress. It should complement both the bride's and the bridesmaids' dresses and may be of any length but not longer than the bride's.

After the bride's mother has chosen her dress, she should let the mother of the groom know her style and color. The groom's mother is then able to look for her dress in a coordinating color and similar style. In this way, no one feels that they are inappropriately attired, no matter the formality or informality of the day.

?

What should I say to the mother of the groom who does not want to wear anything that will clash with the mother of the bride?

Explain to her that the mother of the bride will select her outfit first (hopefully with plenty of time to spare), then she will describe it to the mother of the groom so she may choose a complementary one.

Remember to Organize

PLACE all attire information in your file folders labeled "Wedding Gown," "Bridesmaid Dresses/Women's Wear," and "Men's Wear." Enter the amount paid and the amount due on your payment schedule. Make a note of when the dresses are expected in, so that you may follow up with the stores around that time.

5

THE RECEPTION AND CATERING

CELEBRATING WITH FOOD AND DRINK

Your reception is the party celebrating your marriage. The guests look forward to this time to extend their best wishes to both of you and to socialize with other guests. You don't need to spend a fortune to make this a memorable occasion. No matter how many guests you invite or what type of reception you choose, it is important to carry off everything with as much class as possible. You want your guests to feel as comfortable and as pampered at the reception as you would like them to feel in your home.

In this chapter, we will review the appropriate foods to serve for each time of day, types of meals, menu suggestions, what to expect of an in-house caterer, your catering options, helpful hints on serving alcohol, the layout of the room and seating, and questions for caterers and rental companies.

Time of Day

The time of day you have your reception can have a big effect on your budget, since types of meals vary considerably in price. For example, a light brunch or an hors d'oeuvres buffet in the morning will cost far less than a full-course, sit-down dinner in the evening. The following sections describe some of the details that this particular consideration entails for your reception. Please refer to chapter 11, "Invitations," for suggested wording to clarify what kind of reception you are having.

MORNING OR NOON

A brunch is a possibility for this time of day. Normally served between 11:00 A.M. and 1:00 P.M., this meal features light fare such as fresh fruit, salads, quiche, egg dishes, breads, a cold meat selection, cheeses, pastries, fruit tarts, rolls, coffee, and juices. A champagne toast and a beautiful wedding cake would complete this meal nicely. A brunch like this is often a reasonably priced option to have professionally catered or prepared by volunteers.

Wedding Day Reflections

We wish we had ordered hors d'oeuvres for our guests to enjoy as soon as they arrived at the reception. The pictures at the church took longer than we had anticipated, and the guests dove in to the Jordan almond favors and were still hungry while waiting for our arrival from the church.

—Jill and Steve

EARLY AFTERNOON

This is a possible time to have a cake and champagne reception. Of course, other nonalcoholic beverages should be offered and may be served exclusively. Guests are not expecting a meal at this time of day, so it is your least expensive reception option.

To enhance the elegance of this event, we feel it is important to have the most stunning cake possible and make it the focal point of the room. Pay attention to other elegant details as well. A wonderful touch would be to have waiters circulating the room with champagne bottles wrapped with a white napkin. The champagne flutes should be made of glass, and the cake should be served on beautiful plates. Another option is to serve light hors d'oeuvres and have them passed on silver trays before cutting the cake.

A luncheon is also fitting for this time of day, if you wish to serve a meal, and may be served until approximately 4:00 P.M. It is a good idea to offer a choice of several salads—such as green, pasta, crab, potato, Caesar, and mixed vegetable—along with an entrée—such as chicken, a cold meat selection, or a warm carved meat selection.

LATE AFTERNOON

A late-afternoon ceremony may be followed by cake and champagne or light hors d'oeuvres if you're planning a short reception. A longer reception, however, calls for a larger meal.

EVENING

A 6:00 P.M. or later ceremony dictates a full meal will be served; therefore, this could be the most expensive time of day to have your reception. Whether buffet or sit-down, this meal is usually preceded by a cocktail hour when hors d'oeuvres are served. The menu may be similar to food served at a luncheon, but it should be heavier fare. An exception to the dinner rule for this time of day is a later, dessert-only reception.

SAM AND JANINE'S STORY

Sam and Janine wanted to have an inexpensive reception on a Friday evening. When they checked with their church, they learned a rehearsal was scheduled for 6:00 that evening for a wedding to be held Saturday. The couple could have a ceremony that evening, but it would have to be at 7:30 P.M. Decorating the church was not a problem because the florist could have access prior to the rehearsal. Because of the late hour, Sam and Janine decided to have a dessert-only reception, and to avoid any confusion for their guests, their invitations specified so. In addition to their wedding cake, they had a lovely selection of fruit and berry tarts, a variety of chocolate truffles, fruit that could be dipped in marshmallow sauces, chocolate mousse pastries, and petits fours, all of which were beautifully displayed. Also part of the festivities were an espresso bar, coffee and tea, and a champagne toast. This couple made the best of the late ceremony time, and the guests really enjoyed all the goodies.

Types of Meals and Menu Ideas

No matter the time of day or the type of reception, the presentation and the service is what makes fantastic party food different from ordinary food. The following sections offer detailed information on the different types of meals.

HORS D'OEUVRES

Hors d'oeuvres can comprise a light meal themselves or be used as a precursor to a heavier meal, perhaps a luncheon or dinner. They can be expensive because creating them is sometimes labor-intensive. Per-piece prices run from approximately $1.50 to $4.50. It is estimated that you should allow four pieces per person per hour when dinner is being served as well. If you are having a heavy hors d'oeuvre party at dinnertime and are not following it with a meal, it is recommended you plan twelve to fifteen hors d'oeuvres per person.

FOOD STATIONS

Food stations are becoming more popular for receptions and work well in a large room. The stations are actually individual buffets featuring different food categories set up at various locations around the room or rooms. Rather than everyone gathering in one line, guests are free to "graze" and move between the various stations at will.

Each station is a fairly large table with food displayed and accessibility from all angles. This arrangement is most appropriate when you want your guests to mingle. Smaller and fewer tables for the guests

Tasty Hors D'oeuvre Ideas

The following is a list of elegant and popular passed hors d'oeuvres that we have found to be reasonably priced by caterers or easily purchased or created by volunteers:

COLD

- Assorted canapés
- Cherry tomatoes stuffed with cheese
- Cucumber rounds with herb cream cheese
- Endive filled with Roquefort cheese
- Sliced prosciutto on honeydew melon slices

HOT

- English sausage in puff pastry
- Chicken wings
- Chicken teriyaki shish kabobs
- Bruschetta
- Pizzettes (mini pizzas)
- Shrimp-stuffed mushroom caps
- Cheese puffs

This selection can be supplemented with some of the following appetizers, which are best served on a table:

- Assorted cheese, crackers, and bread display
- Fresh fruit display
- Pâté and cracker display
- Fresh chopped vegetable display

are an option with this type of reception, but make sure that everyone at least has a chair since most of this food is eaten using utensils. Plates should be placed at each station; silverware and napkins may be at the stations or on the guest tables.

Food stations are a good option for catering by family and friends, because each volunteer can be responsible for one station. The following stations work well no matter who prepares the food:

+ Cheeses and breads
+ Pâté and crackers
+ Vegetables and dips
+ Fresh fruit and whipped cream
+ Various hors d'oeuvres
+ Variety of salads
+ Sushi
+ Crepes
+ Hot and cold pastas
+ Carving stations featuring one or more warm meats being sliced by an attendant
+ Cold meats offered unattended

BUFFET

With a buffet, all the food is displayed and the guests choose their own meals from among those dishes offered. A buffet works well for a brunch, luncheon, or dinner. The only things limiting your choices of what to offer here are your imagination and your budget.

Contrary to popular opinion, a buffet is not necessarily less expensive than a sit-down dinner, because more food needs to be prepared. If guests have an option to serve themselves, they are free to take as much as they like. A good way to have control over this is to have the buffet line manned, meaning that servers pass out each portion.

Listed here are our suggestions for the minimum of what should be offered for a buffet reception. Other selections, of course, may be substituted or chosen to supplement these suggestions.

- ◆ An assortment of vegetables
- ◆ Green salad
- ◆ Warm ravioli or other pasta or rice
- ◆ Chicken, fish, or beef selection

These selections are served with assorted breads and cheeses and perhaps hors d'oeuvres. Most professional caterers will vary the presentation heights of the main selections by using boxes or milk crates under the table linens. This setup adds interest and gives the illusion of more food being offered. Ivy wound between bowls or trays makes a nice garnish. A patterned fabric may also be draped along the table edges for interest.

One of the most unique buffets we have witnessed was a complete selection of Mexican entrées. Neither the bride nor the groom was of Latin American descent, but they enjoyed dining out on enchiladas, tamales, and Spanish rice and knew that their friends and families did also. All of the necessary components of a buffet dinner were present including meat and vegetarian selections, a vegetable accompaniment, and a salad. The buffet table was beautifully decorated with colorful woven Mexican blankets. All of this was complemented well with choices of Mexican beers and margaritas at the bar and appetizers of chips and salsa, which were a big hit with the guests. To arrange this, the couple simply contacted their favorite Mexican restaurant to handle the catering, and they were able to negotiate a reasonable per-person rate.

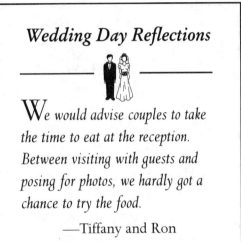

Wedding Day Reflections

We would advise couples to take the time to eat at the reception. Between visiting with guests and posing for photos, we hardly got a chance to try the food.

—Tiffany and Ron

SIT-DOWN MEAL

A served meal is the most elegant way to dine. The guests may come into the dining room to find salads already at their places, or this first course may be delivered after the guests are seated, followed by the entrée and appropriate accompaniments. Often wine is served at the table.

Sit-down meals can be the most expensive option, because of the heavier foods served and the need for a wait staff. Discuss expenses, though, with caterers before you decide that you cannot afford a sit-down meal. Caterers should be able to offer money-saving ideas and suggestions, and many also feel they can charge less for this option due to a limited amount of waste. Simply ask what they can offer you for under your per-person limit.

Tasty Sit-Down Meal Ideas

❧

The following are two sample menus of sit-down meals:

MENU 1
- Caesar salad
- Fettuccine with herb sauce
- Mixed warm vegetables
- Dijon chicken breasts
- A selection of rolls

MENU 2
- Mixed green salad with croutons
- Prime rib
- Grilled zucchini and red peppers
- Rice pilaf
- A selection of rolls

Types of Catering

THE sort of caterer you select—in-house, independent, culinary school, or family and friends—will depend on the sorts of foods you'd like served, the style of your reception, and your budget. Here we discuss all these options.

IN-HOUSE CATERING

If you have chosen a hotel or restaurant as the site for your reception, using its catering services will be mandatory. The staff there will have menu selections for everything from hors d'oeuvres to a sit-down meal. Some locations are open to you creating a custom menu and are happy to assist you with suggestions. They will probably require both a minimum number of guests and a minimum per-person cost. Be sure you know what is included in the quoted prices.

Beverages are charged on either a flat fee, per-person basis or on a consumption basis that is billed at the end of the event. If a consumption basis is used, ask what the per-person average is. Some facilities will let you bring in your own wine and/or champagne but will charge a corkage fee, in which case be sure to ask what that fee is per bottle. The average is $10 per bottle, but some corkage fees are higher, so it may not be worthwhile for you to shop for your own alcohol.

Facilities that offer catering will prepare a room layout showing where the bar, DJ or band, dance floor, buffet tables, guest tables, and other amenities will be placed. They also will suggest times for each event, such as hors d'oeuvres and cocktail hour, dinner, toasting, cake cutting, and dancing. See chapter 16, "The Day You've Been Waiting For," for schedule guidelines, if your location does not provide some.

Wedding cakes provided by the facility usually have no extra cake-cutting charge. Most facilities will let you bring in your wedding cake from an outside bakery but will then charge a cake-cutting fee of approximately $1.50 per person. If the facility's cake is reasonably priced, tastes good, and is decorated how you want it, then this might be your best option.

Some facilities provide items such as centerpieces, microphones, and dance floors at no extra charge. Remember to inquire about such details, because additional fees for these items can really add up fast.

Most facilities require a deposit to reserve the date. Please inquire so that you will have no surprises. It is usually not necessary to decide on your menu until about three months before your reception. At this time, the staff needs an approximation of the number of guests, and most require a 50% deposit based on that number. They will need a final head count ten days or a week before the event and will then calculate the final dollars due. Added to this price will be any applicable taxes and the location's gratuity fee, which is generally 18%. If more guests are actually served on the day of the event, you will be billed for those extra people. Some facilities expect payment immediately after the event while others will bill you within the following week. The bar tab will be billed at the same time as the reception tab.

INDEPENDENT CATERERS

Independent or off-premise caterers can be used at any location that does not have a mandatory in-house catering staff. These caterers can range from someone who prepares the food to be picked up, to a full-service caterer who orders all rental items (tables, chairs, glasses, plates, etc.), prepares the food, and provides a staff to serve and clean up.

The biggest advantage to working with an off-premise caterer is that you, assisted by the caterer's expertise, can design your own menu with no minimum requirements of a per-person rate. A good caterer is flexible, offering a variety of menus within your budget. Ask them what they can prepare within your per-person budget.

The full-service independent caterer will prepare a floor layout plan that should include all guest tables, the cake table, buffet or serving tables, bars, dance floor, and space for the DJ or band. This service will save you time and energy. If the caterer is ordering the rentals, the layout will be passed on to the rental company for the proper setup.

To locate a good caterer, ask staff at the facility you have reserved whether they have a list of recommended caterers who have worked at their site. Don't neglect word-of-mouth suggestions from friends, relatives, and coworkers who have recently married, too.

CULINARY OR RESTAURANT MANAGEMENT SCHOOLS

A culinary school can be a great source for good food at very reasonable prices. These schools prepare food at, or a little above, cost so their students have a chance to practice their skills. Contact a school in your area and ask about their policies and range of services.

CATERING BY FRIENDS AND FAMILY

If you are planning to serve food made by friends and family, allow plenty of time to try out recipes. We recently talked with a mother of the bride who was preparing all the food herself for an hors d'oeuvre reception for 100 guests. She spent countless hours determining what tasted best and what froze well—quite an ambitious project. She estimated her food costs would be about $700.

Your friends and family must take into account foods that complement each other well and decide on menus in advance. Normally each person volunteers to prepare a certain dish and you reimburse them for the cost of the food, but in some cases, they offer their contributions as their wedding gift.

If preparing all the food seems intimidating, consider supplementing your menu with already prepared foods from a store or an independent caterer. For example, one bride's family purchased a great selection of hors d'oeuvres from the frozen food section at a large discount warehouse. They also purchased big tubs of pasta salad, which was delicious.

A wedding we were recently involved with had a unique twist on the family catering idea. The parents of the bride bought ingredients for a variety of pasta, green, and fruit salads for a luncheon celebration. Different groups of family and friends were each assigned a salad to make. All of these were prepared in the family's kitchen the night before the wedding. The salads were kept chilled overnight in the neighbors' refrigerators. They were displayed in what appeared to be cut crystal bowls but were actually inexpensive molded plastic finds from a craft and party store. At the reception, these bowls were set on a rainbow of solid-color linens that belonged to a family member. These linens were strewn with buds of flowers snipped from the family yard. It was a very colorful sight, and the assorted salads won raves.

Questions to Ask All Caterers

❦

1. What menu choices do we have?
2. Will you provide a dish for special diet requirements?
3. Does your meal charge include nonalcoholic drinks such as punch, coffee, and tea?
4. Does your meal charge include the cost of the catering, serving, and cleanup staff?
5. What is the ratio of staff to guests?
6. What tableware is included, such as cloths, napkins, dishes, and silverware? May I see a sample?
7. Will you handle any necessary rentals such as tables and chairs?
8. Will your staff cut and serve the cake? What is the charge for this service?
9. How many hours before the event will you start setting up?
10. When will your staff start cleaning up? How long does someone stay at the reception?
11. What does your staff wear? Can they wear white shirts, black skirts or pants, and black bow ties?
12. What is your payment schedule?
13. When is the final count due?
14. May we see pictures of your work?
15. May we taste your work?
16. May we call several couples whose reception you have catered recently?

With this catering option, it is much easier if you choose foods that don't need to be served hot, don't need to be served at an exact time, and don't require a lot of work at the last minute. Foods that work well are salads, pâtés, herbed cheese spreads and crackers, and vegetable and fruit displays. Buffet or food stations are ideal arrangements for this type of production.

Wait Staff

EVEN if you opt to have your family and friends prepare the food in advance, we feel that to ensure a successful and fun reception, you need to hire a staff at least to help set up, serve, and clean up. This is a nice way to allow your friends and family to enjoy the reception after their hard preparation work. Staff can be hired to pass hors d'oeuvres, set up, restock and man a buffet, serve drinks, clear tables, and clean up after the reception. Money spent on wait staff is money well spent.

How do you find wait staff? Sometimes they find you! Recently we had lunch at a restaurant and our waiter looked very familiar. We told him we thought we had seen him somewhere, and when he learned our occupation, he said he had been a waiter at a recent wedding reception. He moonlights on weekends both for caterers and on his own as either a waiter or bartender, depending on what service is needed. He gave us his name and number and said he had five others he liked to work with and could put a crew together. How perfect!

We realize you might not have similar good luck in stumbling upon such an opportunity, but you can try locating qualified wait staff in various other ways. Call local culinary schools, for

> **?**
>
> *None of my friends have hired caterers lately. How can I find a good one?*
>
> Try calling your area's chamber of commerce to inquire which company won their most recent catering award. Another good source for referrals is wedding professionals. Wedding coordinators, photographers, and DJs are usually very willing to share their knowledge.

example. You might also ask a caterer for recommendations. Another good source for possible servers is the Hotel and Restaurant Employees Union; you'll find its number under "Labor Organizations" in the Yellow Pages.

Once you know your menu and have hired your wait staff, determine who will be your head server. Have a meeting with this person, and review what you expect from the waiters, describing your reception schedule, the menu being served, what service you would like, what equipment you have, and so forth. Ask your head server for input; he or she will likely have suggestions on what does and doesn't work and what equipment they need to do a good job for you.

Finally, as you do with your other vendors, remember to ask about fees and the specific services that will be provided. Try to get this information in writing, if possible. Typical hourly rates for good wait staff range between $10 and $15.

Alcoholic Beverages

DETERMINING whether to serve alcohol at your reception is a big decision. Take into account your personal feelings on the subject and whether you want to have alcohol served on your wedding day. Also, you must keep the location of your reception in mind. If your reception is being held at your church, check with your clergy or the church office to find out their guidelines for serving alcohol. Most denominations do not permit alcohol on the premises. Because alcohol definitely adds to the cost of the reception, your budget must also be taken into account.

We have worked with couples who have decided they did not want to serve any liquor at the reception because they do not drink and do not serve liquor to guests in their own home. In such a situation we suggest serving a sparkling cider for the toast, nonalcoholic punch (not sweet), soft drinks, and sparkling water. Another option is to hire an espresso bar and attendant to create all sorts of coffee drinks for your guests.

If you choose to serve alcohol, you can save money by serving only a selection of beer, wine, and nonalcoholic beverages and not including mixed drinks or hard liquor. Keep this in mind whether you are providing the drinks yourself or purchasing them through your reception location.

Drinks may be served at a reception in several ways. At a hosted bar, drinks are provided at no cost to the guests. A no-host bar is just the opposite: the guests pay for their own drinks. We do not consider a no-host bar to be an acceptable alternative. You would not offer a friend a glass of wine in your home and then ask for $3, please. We recommend not doing this at your reception if you want to have a classy event. If you can't afford to include drinks in your budget, don't serve them at all. If your reception is being held in a facility that has a completely separate bar, not provided in conjunction with your reception, it is acceptable for guests to adjourn to that area and buy drinks on their own. In that case you are not obligated.

ALCOHOL PROVIDED BY YOUR RECEPTION LOCATION

The liquor policy at your reception location will play a big part in determining this cost. Alcohol can be served on a flat, per-person rate or on a consumption basis. If you think you have "big drinkers" on your guest list, a flat rate may be advantageous. Some couples also like this method because they can budget in a known dollar amount. For a wine and beer bar, flat, per-person fees are usually $10 to $15. With the alternative, alcohol served on a consumption basis, the bartenders keep track of what they serve during the evening and then charge you for each drink.

PROVIDING THE ALCOHOL YOURSELF

If you are hiring a caterer for your food service, you may also need to hire a bar service. Some companies provide everything that is needed including the bar, alcohol, glasses, ice, and staff. This service is worth investigating as it certainly makes things easy for you.

If the bar service seems too expensive, consider purchasing the beer and wine yourself, using the guidelines presented here. We strongly urge you to hire a bartender to host your bar, however. The bartender will also be able to help with serving champagne just before the toasts. You should plan on one bartender for each fifty guests.

The following is an example of quantities you would need to provide for 100 guests for a three-hour reception:

- **Champagne** Decide whether you want to have champagne served only for the toast or available during your whole reception. Either way is appropriate. Always serve champagne well chilled. When it is served only for the toast, it is referred to as a champagne "skate."

    Each bottle serves six 4-ounce flutes.

    There are twelve bottles in one case.

    For a toast only: 1 1/2 cases.

    For continuous serving: three cases.

- **Wine** White and blush wines are served chilled; red wines at room temperature. Most guests prefer white over red.

    An average serving is four ounces of wine per glass.

    A 750-milliliter bottle is six servings.

    White wine: two cases.

    Red wine: one case.

- **Beer** Especially during the summer months, beer is very popular. If your guests include several younger males, be sure you have an adequate amount.

    Average beer consumption is four 12-ounce servings.

    One bottle is twelve ounces.

    One case is twenty-four bottles.

    Beer: four cases or one keg.

- **Alcohol-Free** Be sure to provide soft drinks and sparkling water for children, nondrinkers, and designated drivers.

    Half of the soft drinks should be diet.

    Assortment of soda and water: three cases.

These amounts are only general guidelines for 100 guests. Each reception is different and varies depending on the time of day or year, what kind of meal is being served, and your particular mix of guests.

BEVERAGE MISCELLANY

Your event will look infinitely classier if you serve your beverages in glasses. Figure two to three glasses per person. An all-purpose stem glass is the simplest. You also may buy large plastic beer glasses or rent glasses designed for beer.

Remember to provide cocktail napkins. You can purchase these in bulk from a party store at a minimal charge. White napkins are fine, unless you prefer to use your primary wedding color. You may also order napkins with your names and the date of your wedding printed on them. Please refer to chapter 11, "Invitations," for more information.

Finally, don't forget ice! Large tubs work well for keeping sodas, beer, white wine, and champagne chilled. You will also need to allow for extra ice to serve with the soft drinks.

Table Setups

WHETHER you are overseeing the reception catering yourself or hiring a caterer, the layout of the food stations or the buffet table is very important. We touched earlier on the various table arrangements depending on the sort of reception service you select, but now we go into greater detail on buffet setups, food stations, and guest tables.

BUFFET

If you've hired a caterer, ask to see pictures of buffets he or she has designed. If you and family or friends are doing the catering, we suggest you think a great deal about the presentation of your food. Either way, a lot of work has gone into this meal, and you will want your guests to view the food in its best light. Picture how the buffet table at a work potluck looks and use that as an example of what you *don't* want. A professionally done buffet will have dishes at graduated heights, swagged material (or tablecloths intertwined), and perhaps a flower arrangement or greens to set everything off.

To present a buffet yourself, start by deciding what food you are going to serve and then selecting the bowls and trays you'll use. Gather these service pieces together. Next, find a number of sturdy cardboard boxes of all sizes. Fill them with tightly packed newspapers or some other material to keep them from collapsing under the weight of the filled bowl or platter.

For illustrative purposes, let's prepare a buffet table for a luncheon. The plates should be at the beginning of the buffet, stacked at the front corner of the table and easy to reach. Start your food selection with salads. Place several boxes upside down, with the highest farther back on the table, the lower toward the front. Cover the boxes with cloths draped naturally, not smooth, so that they aren't readily recognizable as boxes but look more like raised platforms. Perhaps a bowl on the higher box could contain a pasta salad, while the lower box would support a large bowl with a Caesar salad. Next on the table would be a long basket with a fresh fruit display, placed perpendicular front to back so it doesn't take up excessive table space. We would then arrange several more boxes, again covered with draped cloths, to present a large bowl of roasted red potatoes and another of seasonal vegetables. Then at table level would be your entrée, perhaps chicken or turkey on large platters. If you want to serve these items hot, you would need to rent chafing trays. For extra touches, you could have a large flower arrangement on the table or greens and loose flowers around the boxes and the fruit basket. Set up a trial table in advance so you can see what looks

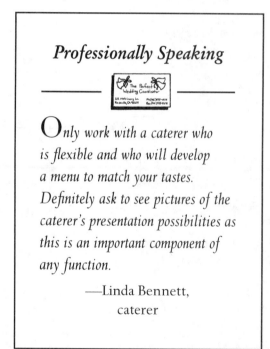

Professionally Speaking

O*nly work with a caterer who is flexible and who will develop a menu to match your tastes. Definitely ask to see pictures of the caterer's presentation possibilities as this is an important component of any function.*

—Linda Bennett, caterer

best where. By practicing, you have the opportunity to make changes while you have time and are not under the gun.

FOOD STATIONS

With food stations, as with buffets, it is important to have the food displayed both artistically and beautifully. Foods served at different heights and with draped cloths and ivy, flowers, or perhaps fruit and/or vegetables look more appetizing. Similar types of foods should be stationed together on the same table: raw crudités and dips at one station, salads at another, hot dishes at another, and so on. Small plates and napkins should be stacked at each food station for the guests' use, as well as any utensils they might need.

GUEST TABLES

If you are having a buffet, we feel it is a nice touch to have napkins, silverware, glassware, salt and pepper, and rolls and butter on each guest table. This saves your guests having to juggle a number of items while negotiating the buffet line. For a completely set table at a sit-down dinner, see Figure 5.1 below.

Figure 5.1

1. The dinner plate is in the center. If a salad is being served, the salad plate is placed in the center. After the salad course, wait staff will remove it and replace it with the dinner plate.
2. Forks are to the left of the dinner plate, with the salad fork to the outside.

3. A plate for bread and butter is on the left above the forks.

4. A butter knife (if available) is placed across the top of this small plate, with the tip of the blade to the inside.

5. The knife and spoon are to the right of the dinner plate.

6. If coffee is to be served with the meal, the cup and saucer will be on the table.

7. The water glass is directly above the knife.

8. The wineglass is to the right of the water glass, and the champagne flute (if on the table now instead of brought later for the champagne toast) is placed behind those two glasses.

9. A dessert fork may be placed above the dinner plate but is usually delivered with the pieces of cake later in the reception.

10. Napkins may be folded and placed on the dinner plate, to the left of the forks, or, as done quite frequently now, folded and placed in the water glass. This touch will be discussed more in chapter 9, "Decorations."

Layout of the Room

WHETHER your reception has in-house catering, you have hired a caterer, or your family and friends are preparing the food, a room layout is necessary to ensure that everything will fit nicely in your space. If you're using in-house or independent catering, the staff will prepare the layout. If you're handling your own reception, you will need to provide the rental delivery people with a layout if they have been hired to set up. If you plan on setting up tables and chairs with helpers the day before, allow about three hours for this project.

LAYOUT BASICS

Included in a typical floor layout should be the following pieces:

+ The head table
+ Guest tables

- Chairs
- The cake table
- A table to hold gifts brought to the reception
- A table for the guest book
- Tables for food service (buffet, hors d'oeuvres, and food stations)
- A table for punch and coffee
- A bar
- A dance floor
- Room for the DJ or band

To make sure everything will fit in your room, obtain the room's dimensions. Then create a rough "blueprint" of the room and the pieces you want in it on paper. Draw the room on a grid in proper proportions—say, with a half inch representing every foot—making note of doorways, windows, pillars, and any other unusual features. Depending on your number of guests, next determine the number of tables you will need. For guest tables, we feel round tables are more elegant and more conducive to visiting between guests. Figure on a table sixty inches in diameter seating eight guests and seventy-inch tables seating ten. Allow at least five feet between the tables so guests can easily pass and move chairs in and out. For the head table, tally the number of attendants when figuring the size you will need. Figure 5.2 illustrates an actual room layout for a dinner reception for seventy guests. The bride and groom each had four attendants, so the head table seated ten. The dinner was a served meal. When having food stations or a buffet, you must allow additional floor

?

Do we have to have a traditional long, straight head table?

No, *any table arrangement is possible. Many brides and grooms are opting for a few round head tables for themselves and attendants and inviting spouses and escorts of wedding attendants to join their partners. Another option is having a romantic table for two for the bride and groom.*

space for food tables. Be sure to allow ample space in front of a bar because people congregate there and don't move on quickly.

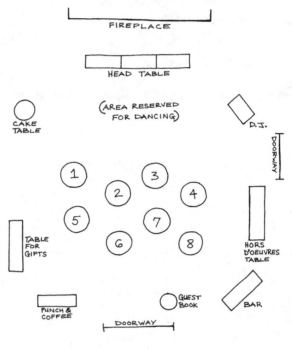

Figure 5.2

SEATING

The type of reception you are having will dictate the seating arrangements. Usually a head table is provided for the bride and groom and their attendants. This is generally a long table with the bridal couple in the middle, the bride on the groom's right, and either the attendants alternated (male, female) or all the men to the groom's left and the women on the bride's right. Our couples often choose rounds of eight or ten and include the attendants' spouses or dates at the same table. One couple recently opted to have their own table for just the two of them, with their attendants seated nearby at various rounds.

For buffet or sit-down meals, tables should be marked with a "Reserved" sign and set aside for the families and special guests, with perhaps the bride's side and the groom's side each having two reserved

The Rental List

🦢

Besides helping you make sure that everything you need for the reception will fit in a room, a layout also brings to your attention those items you'll need to rent. In our example the DJ brought his own equipment, as most do, but we needed to rent everything else. The rental list we composed for the above wedding is as follows:

- One portable bar
- Two 48-inch round tables (guest book and cake)
- Six 8-foot banquet tables (gifts, punch and coffee, hors d'oeuvres, and three for the head table)
- Eight 60-inch round tables
- Seventy-five white wooden chairs (five extra for the DJ, guest book attendant, etc.)
- Eight 120-inch round tablecloths (guest tables)
- Two 90-inch round tablecloths (cake and guest book tables)
- Six 60-inch × 120-inch tablecloths (two each for punch, gift, and hors d'oeuvres tables)
- Three 60-inch × 120-inch tablecloths (head table—this number gave us extra yardage to make swags in the skirting)
- Seventy-five linen dinner napkins

tables. We suggest place cards be made for the guests who have been invited to sit at these tables and that they all be told in advance that they will be at a reserved table. Guests often ask us, "Where are we to sit? We should be at the reserved table. We're relatives of the bride." Assigned place cards for reserved seating would eliminate this confusion.

At one wedding, the bride told us about the bad relations existing between her mother and her dad's mother owing to a less than friendly divorce. She said her grandmother would sit and give dirty looks to her mom all evening. We discussed our options and decided to place the two ladies at tables on opposite sides of the room. The grandmother would be seated at one facing the wall, and the mother at another facing a bank of windows. They would both have to stand up and turn around at the same time to see each other. The reception happily proceeded without incident.

Pondering where to set place cards at each table for every guest can get quite time-consuming for the bride. It is not easy trying to place guests with people they know or would be comfortable with. A recent *B.C.* cartoon defined "social science" as "Figuring out seating arrangements for a wedding reception." How true! A nice alternative is alphabetizing your place cards and placing them on a table near the entrance of the reception location so that guests can easily locate their own cards and place them themselves at the table where they would like to sit. Their spots are then "saved" for the remainder of the reception.

LINENS

When deciding what size linen you will need, measure the length and width of your table and add thirty-six to forty inches to each dimen-

---

Questions to Ask Rental Companies

❧

1. What are the rental prices for each item?
2. Does the price include delivery, setup, and pickup?
3. Can rentals be delivered the day before (if appropriate)?
4. When will you pick up, or when do we have to return, the pieces?
5. Do items (dishes, glasses) have to be returned clean?

sion. This size gives you an eighteen- to twenty-inch overhang on each side, which is knee length. If you wish the cloth to hang to the floor, standard table height is twenty-eight or twenty-nine inches, so add fifty-six inches to your table dimensions. The food and head table should have cloths to the floor. If the food table is against a wall, a seventy-two-inch cloth would work, with the cloth dropped to the floor and a slight overhang in the back.

Remember to Organize

DEPENDING on what type of catering you choose, you will need to create the appropriate files. These may be labeled with the hotel's or restaurant's name (e.g., "Chez Danielle"), the various caterers' names ("Linda's Catering"), or, if you and some volunteers are catering the reception and have selected menus, "Menus." If you are handling the renting of tables, chairs, and other items, compile a "Rental" file. Any contracts should be placed in the appropriate file. If you have no contracts, we suggest sending a confirmation letter to the vendor listing the date, time, service to be provided, and other specifics, and make a copy for your own files. Please refer to chapter 14, "Details, Details, Details," for a suggested format for this letter. Finally, remember to enter any deposits paid and the dollars due on your payment schedule.

Planning the reception is a lot of work. Don't get discouraged. Keep in mind that once the reception details are taken care of, you are really on your way to having planned your perfect wedding day.

6

PHOTOGRAPHY AND VIDEOGRAPHY

PRESERVING MEMORIES OF YOUR WEDDING ON FILM

WHEN YOUR WEDDING is over, you will want to savor every detail and have a record of everything that transpired for years to come. Such memories are, of course, best captured by photography or videography. On such an emotionally charged and busy day, it is easy for the couple to feel like "it flew by." Therefore, we remind all our clients, "When the wedding day is in the past, all you will have to remember it by is the photos."

Do not underestimate the importance of good-quality pictures. Photography is not an area where you should skimp. Neither is it necessary to spend a fortune. Photo and video professionals should be chosen early in your planning process because the popular ones who represent the best value are booked far in advance.

In this chapter, we will discuss all aspects of wedding photography and videography, as well as questions to ask the professionals.

Photography

As we already mentioned, it is important to choose your photographer early. Even if a friend or relative has offered to take photos as his

Wedding Day Reflections

Our photographer told us that there was no reason for him to take photos before the ceremony if we did not want to see each other. Not knowing any better, we agreed to this and as a result posed for far too many pictures between the ceremony and reception. Even having us pose for photos with our attendants before the ceremony would have saved precious minutes later.

—Jill and Steve

or her wedding gift, hire a professional for at least part of the day so you are assured of having beautiful pictures. For starters, ask friends, family, other wedding-related businesses, and church and reception staff for recommendations. Photographers rely a great deal on word-of-mouth advertising, so you're likely to come across a great photographer this way. Then, take the time to look at the work of various photographers by visiting a few studios, attending bridal fairs, and skimming through bridal magazines for ideas. Often discounts are offered to brides who choose a photographer at a bridal fair; however, don't get rushed into your decision because of a special offer. If you have misgivings of any nature, this photographer is not for you. Finally, if you are attending a wedding, even if it is out of town, observe the photographer in action. What did you like? What didn't you like? This will help you know what to look for while conducting your search.

WHAT DO YOU WANT IN A PHOTOGRAPHER?

In choosing a photographer, first and foremost you want someone who takes good pictures. How are the pictures put together? Are the backgrounds uncluttered? Are the subjects evenly spaced and looking at the camera? Is the bride's dress arranged nicely? Does everyone look neat, or are ties askew and men slouching? A good photographer takes the time to make sure everything looks perfect before snapping the picture.

The other important thing to notice in a photographer is his or her personality. You must feel comfortable with this professional, as you will be spending a great deal of time together on your wedding day. Is he or she calming to you or too hyper? Does he have a nice sense of humor, or is she too bossy? Our favorite photographers do a wonderful job of making everyone feel at ease as pictures are being taken, which makes it a fun experience rather than an ordeal.

One of our favorite photographers to work with is super at handling large bridal parties. He has a very outgoing personality and we have seen him command the attention of large bridal parties, which is no easy feat. At one wedding with eigtheen attendants, he wanted to pose all the attendants and the bride and groom on the front steps of the church. He knew the only time he could get this shot was immediately after the ceremony and before the guests had exited through the doors. He communicated his plan prior to the ceremony to the bridal party and they all dutifully arranged themselves, the large doors were closed behind them and a marvelous shot that would otherwise be lost was captured.

Efficiency should also be a priority. While interviewing prospective photographers, ask them how long it will take them to shoot the formals at the altar. If the answer is longer than thirty minutes, then go elsewhere. Your photographer should also be willing to take romantic shots of just the couple in a short period of time. Photographers more interested in posing brides and grooms than allowing them to enjoy their reception should not be in the wedding business. Beware of these! We have heard many complaints from bridal couples and guests about photographers who took up too much of the bride and groom's time.

Most photographers do their own work. However, some photography studios hire a number of photographers to take pictures at weddings for them. We don't feel comfortable with this arrangement because you don't have the opportunity to choose your own photographer and view that person's work. You are paying premium prices for an unknown entity.

When meeting with a photographer, ask to see the entire set of pictures from one wedding. This will let you see the quality of their complete work better than just seeing good shots from a number of weddings. It will also give you an idea of what your own album will be like.

COMPARING PACKAGES

Once you have found several photographers whose work you like, how do you decide which one to choose? We suggest comparing the different packages they offer. The following subsections will help you understand what each package contains.

TIME   Most packages have time constraints. We feel with careful scheduling, it is possible to have a photographer for a shorter time, which will cost you less money. Most packages average from two to eight hours of coverage. Overtime charges range from $85 to $250 per hour. Some photographers will only schedule one wedding on a Saturday and have no time limits.

NUMBER OF LOCATIONS   Some packages offer no location limit, while others specify one to four locations. The cost of the package increases with the number of locations. If you are dressing at the location where both your ceremony and reception are being held, the one-location package will be perfect for you. On the other hand, if you want pictures taken at your parent's home, then at the church, then at the reception location, you will need a three-location package. Keep in mind that some photographers charge a mileage fee if they travel more than fifty miles. Some of our photographers charge up to $1 per mile. Others charge a fee if they travel more than an hour to the location.

PRINTS   How many photos will be taken during the day and how many prints will you have to choose from? Different packages will offer varying numbers of prints. The more you can choose from, the better off you'll be. Photographers will take several shots of the same pose in case someone is not looking at the camera or not smiling. You will have all these different shots to choose from.

PREVIEW ALBUM   The preview album is usually available three to four weeks after your wedding. Along with the prints will be corresponding forms for you to complete stating how many copies of each print you would like. You may order photographs to go in your album or a parent's album, or as additional prints in enlarged sizes. This preview album makes the ordering process quite easy.

Most photographers have a limit of how many days you may keep the preview album. If you have relatives out of town who will want to order pictures, let the photographer know that you would like an extended time for returning the proofs.

WEDDING ALBUMS   Most packages include an album with a set number of prints. The albums are simulated or genuine leather, and the prints are 5×5, 5×7, or 8×10. We recently talked to a family friend whose album package contained only 8×10 pictures. It sounded nice until they realized they only got to choose twenty-four proofs for this album. Narrowing their choices down to twenty-four shots was difficult. For this reason, an assortment of sizes is usually the best.

Pages for albums usually range from twelve to forty-eight pages. Each page is matted and will hold one 8×10, two 5×7s, or four 5×5s. Ask whether there is flexibility in the layout of your album. You may want either more or fewer pages.

Some of the larger packages include a parent's album, usually containing twenty-four to forty pictures. Most parents choose pictures that are only pertinent to their own family, whereas the bridal album features pictures of both families. If not included in your package, a parent album may be ordered from the photographer and normally ranges from $150 to $300.

TYPES OF PICTURES

Many people don't realize the different photo options available.

TRADITIONAL   Traditional photography is formal photos with all pictures posed—for example, the pictures of the entire bridal party and the couple with both sides of the family inside the church. Some couples are opting to have these formal pictures taken before the ceremony. This may work for you if you don't mind seeing each other before the ceremony and if you want to immediately leave for the reception without the delay of picture taking. Posing before the ceremony does make taking these pictures easier. However, if you have looked forward to the emotion of seeing each other for the first time as you walk down the aisle, you have lost that precious moment.

To make picture taking after the ceremony go smoothly, we recommend talking to all the people who are to be included in those pictures ahead of time. After the recessional, these people need to return immediately to the altar area. Grandma doesn't get to stop and visit with Aunt Minnie, and the girls don't get to go find their friends. If all players are there, the skilled photographer can get through the traditional pictures very quickly.

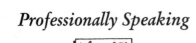

Professionally Speaking

We have found it to be best if brides avoid wearing frosted or glossy makeup. The flash tends to pick up and accentuate this shine. Matte finish makeup is more desirable for photographs.

—Debbie Jensen,
Bill and Debbie Jensen Photography

INFORMALS   Examples of informals are the bride getting ready with her attendants, the mother of the bride adjusting her daughter's veil, the dad and bride talking before getting into the limousine, the groom's mother pinning on her son's boutonniere, the groomsmen looking at their watches, and many other posed or semiposed shots of those involved in the day. These photos are fun and have a lighter note to them.

CANDIDS   Candid shots are pictures of people who may be unaware their pictures are being taken. These could be shots of guests arriving for the ceremony, signing the guest book, leaving for the reception, mingling over drinks, going through the buffet line, or dancing. Very often the best candid shots from your reception are those taken by your friends and family.

ROMANTICS Romantics are very special. These are photos of the couple during an intimate moment, perhaps outdoors making their way from the ceremony to the reception or sometime during the reception enjoying a little privacy, usually while guests are still eating. They include close-ups and are sometimes done with special lighting and muted lenses. They seem to capture the special feelings of your day and the moods you wish to remember.

PORTRAITURE This type of photography requires much equipment, screens, lighting, and assistants. Because portraiture entails quite a production and a great deal of time, we feel it is very obtrusive on the wedding day. The results might be good, but this much time should not be spent posing for pictures on your wedding day. If you want some formal portraits, we suggest you visit the photographer in his or her studio for special pictures taken either before or after your wedding.

PHOTOJOURNALISM We have had several brides request a photographer who will document the day without any posing. Your wedding album will thus be illustrated much like a magazine article, with shots of many activities. While this approach is refreshing, we feel some posed pictures are desirable.

BLACK-AND-WHITE Black-and-white photography is becoming quite popular, with more and more couples requesting it. This photography can also be reproduced on a range of papers that add texture and tone, for lovely results. It is now possible to have black-and-white prints made from color negatives. It is definitely a good idea to consider some black-and-white shots because they do not fade over time as color prints can.

Last fall we had a lovely wedding in which all the autumn hues were used in both the flowers and decorations. The couple chose to have all black-and-white photography and so had no colored pictures to showcase the beautiful colors they chose for their wedding. Now they wish they had taken a mix of black-and-white and color photos.

ITINERARY OF PHOTOS

A thorough photographer will meet with you several weeks before your wedding. At this meeting he or she will review with you the members in your bridal party, how many grandparents will be in attendance, whether your families are divorced, and other pertinent details. Be sure to describe any special shots you want the photographer to capture as well as any you specifically do *not* want taken. Large group pictures are definitely something that should be discussed with the photographer before the wedding day.

BETH'S STORY

At Beth's wedding, we had group pictures taken of both Beth's college track teammates and Jeff's cycling club friends. These pictures were taken on the front steps of the mansion. Group productions can go smoothly if the professional is forewarned. Pictures such as this are very popular for gifts. Years later, many of Beth's former teammates still have this picture hanging in their homes.

MONEY-SAVING TIPS

The least expensive way to have pictures taken would be to have Uncle Mike or some other amateur take your pictures. We do not suggest this option and in fact discourage it. Pictures of your wedding day are too important to take any chances.

Some professional photographers will take pictures and give the couple the undeveloped rolls of film. Because the photographer is not involved in the film processing, the fee may be less. Couples then may take the film to a professional lab and put together their own album.

Another option is using a photographer who gives you all the proofs so that you can create your own album. This is a good way to go if you are willing to do the album work. Keep in mind that you must buy your own album, all your pictures are the same size, and this deal doesn't include extras for family members. This option does not work well for everyone. We know one bride who was married seven years ago and still has not made her album. Because she now has small children who swallow her spare time, she estimates the album will be done by her twenty-fifth wedding anniversary! Other couples have stated they enjoyed making their albums because they had the flexibility to add pages and include their invitation, program, as well as pictures that guests had taken.

ENGAGEMENT PICTURES

When meeting with different photographers, discuss the cost of having engagement pictures also taken. Some photographers will reduce their normal fees if you are also hiring them for your wedding pictures.

Professionally Speaking

Be *on time. Be ready for pictures. When pictures start late, the rest of the day seems to go the same way. Sometimes I have areas planned for outside shots, and if the subjects are twenty minutes late, the sun has shifted, and the lighting is no longer perfect. Also, ask a potential photographer if you may see an entire set of proofs from a recent wedding. This way you can see shots more representative of the work you will receive, instead of twenty of the best shots the photographer has ever taken.*

—Mike Gomez,
The Photography Shoppe

For engagement photos, couples usually choose casual clothing and an outside location over more formal pictures. A casual engagement picture is fun to have on the guest book table because it lets guests see the "real" you. One of our couples posed for their casual engagement picture in jeans, white polo shirts, and bare feet, seated

Your Own Personal Photo Package

❦

The following is a list of possible photos that can be taken during the course of the day:

BEFORE THE CEREMONY

- Bride in dress
- Bride with mother
- Bride with father
- Bride with both parents
- Bride with siblings
- Bride with honor attendants
- Bride with all attendants
- Groom alone
- Groom with father
- Groom with mother
- Groom with both parents
- Groom with siblings
- Groom with best man
- Groom with all men

AT THE CEREMONY

- Guests outside the church
- Ushers escorting guests
- Guest book attendant
- Harpist or special musicians
- Bride and father getting out of the car
- Grandparents being seated

- Groom's parents being seated
- Mother of the bride being seated
- Groom and groomsmen at the altar
- Attendants' processional
- Ring bearer and flower girl
- Bride and father processional
- Bride and groom exchanging vows*
- Bride and groom exchanging rings
- Bride and groom kissing
- Unity candle lighting
- Bride and groom coming up aisle

FORMAL PICTURES TAKEN IMMEDIATELY AFTER CEREMONY

- Bride alone
- Bride and groom together
- Bride and groom with bride's parents—add in siblings, then grandparents**

- Bride and groom with groom's parents—add in siblings, then grandparents**
- Bride and groom with honor attendants**
- Bride and groom with all attendants**

AT THE RECEPTION

- Bride and groom getting out of the car
- Bride and groom entering
- Receiving line
- Buffet table
- Parents' table
- Bride and groom at the head table

- Wedding party at the head table
- Romantic shots***
- Toast by best man
- Bride and groom cutting the cake
- Bride's and groom's hands showing rings
- Bride and groom's first dance
- Bride dancing with her father
- Groom dancing with his mother
- Bride tossing her bouquet
- Groom removing and tossing the garter
- Bride and groom with persons who caught the bouquet and garter
- Bride and groom leaving the reception

* During this portion of Beth's younger sister Kim's wedding, our photographer took a picture of the sanctuary using a star filter. The shot was taken from the balcony of the church, and the altar and pew candles all glistened beautifully. Ask your photographer if you can see an example of this shot. It is truly the most beautiful picture we have seen taken during a ceremony.

** To avoid a big delay after the ceremony and before the reception, it is very important that you let all the people who are to be involved in having their pictures taken know that they must not stray. These pictures will be taken quickly, and everyone must be present. It is not fair to expect the photographer to be finished in a short time if the photo subjects are all not there.

*** Between the meal and the toast is a great time for romantics. The bride and groom are usually relaxed. For example, during this time, Beth and Jeff, along with their photographer, went outside to the area where their ceremony was held. The photographer took a wonderful shot with a muted filter with them sitting between the two altar arrangements. Beth's dress looks like it is floating, and they both have a most contented look on their faces. This is our favorite picture from their entire wedding.

on a boat dock with their feet dangling in the water. It's their favorite shot of themselves.

A WRAP-UP OF OUR SUGGESTIONS

When someone asks us about the best approach for photography, we suggest the couple order the minimum package of a professional photographer. Schedule this photographer to take the pictures immediately before, during, and after the ceremony. Most packages include extra items such as an 11 × 14 wall portrait. If you don't think you would want such a large picture, ask whether you can substitute a second location or another hour of time. The photographers who are worth working with are willing to change their packages to make each couple happy. Photographers are especially flexible for weddings in the off months, such as January, when they aren't busy and really want your business.

The minimum packages include a limited number of hours of photo coverage, usually three to four hours. It is difficult to take all of the ceremony pictures and all of the reception pictures within this time limit. Avoid this problem by having the photographer stage some of your reception pictures—for example, the cutting of the cake or the first dance. We had one couple pose for their "first dance" a whole hour before the actual music started! This worked well: it was not obvious to the guests what was being done, the couple had the picture they wanted, and the photographer was able to leave within the budgeted time frame.

Another suggestion is to have disposable cameras on each table with a note asking the guests to take pictures during the reception. Guests really seem to enjoy taking pictures, and some of the results

---

?

Should I buy disposable cameras for each table?

We have heard the following quote many times from clients: "The candid photos that the guests captured with the disposable cameras were priceless!" By all means, purchase these cameras for the reception; they're an inexpensive yet fun touch.

are good. Kodak has a disposable wedding camera with flash (important), fifteen exposures, and instructions printed on the camera. The guests can return the cameras in a basket on the guest book table when they are finished, or someone can be assigned to gather them at the end of the reception.

Finally, by all means avoid "the wait." We hear all too often a tale from a disgruntled wedding guest that goes something like this: "We sat there for more than an hour waiting for anything to happen. There was no sign of the bride and groom, nothing available to eat, and an absurdly long line at the bar." The moral of the story? Don't allow the guests to wait too long between the ceremony and reception. Since this "downtime" is one of our pet peeves, we definitely discourage couples from hiring photographers who take up too much of their time between the ceremony and reception. We also encourage

Questions to Ask Your Photographer

1. Will *you* be taking our pictures?
2. What sorts of packages do you have, and how much do they cost?
3. May we substitute an extra hour if we prefer not to have any of the extras included in your package?
4. Do you have another wedding scheduled for that day?
5. When will you arrive? How long will you stay?
6. How long does it usually take you to complete the photos after the ceremony?
7. Do you carry backup film and cameras?
8. When will you have the preview album ready?
9. How long do you keep negatives?
10. Is it possible for us to create our own album?
11. What should we know about your work?

our clients to provide hors d'oeuvres, music, and plenty of bartenders at the reception site so guests feel that the celebration has started, even if the wedding couple has not yet arrived.

Videography

MORE and more couples today want their wedding day captured on videotape as well as still photography. Videography is another way to preserve the ambiance of this unique day, with the advantages over regular photography of recording sound, too, if you like and capturing live-action moments a photograph cannot.

The trick to finding a good videographer is to ask around. Start by asking recently married couples whether they hired a videographer and were pleased with the results. Who would they recommend? Another great source for a videographer is your photographer. The videographer and photographer must work well together, and the photographer will certainly have knowledge of who is good and who isn't.

Like photographers, videographers offer different packages, and you need to compare carefully. The choices can range from simply taping the ceremony with one camera to a package including a collage of childhood pictures, an aerial shot of the location, three cameras at the ceremony, two cameras at the reception, and a conclusion with interviews of your guests—all set to the music of your choice. These packages range from $300 to over $2,000, with most packages averaging about $1,000.

Guest Appeal

We attended a wedding reception where we thought we were watching the filming of a movie. The videographer had an assistant with a spotlight, and they followed the bride and groom everywhere. We could not even talk to them. They taped an endless amount of dances with the bride and groom and relatives, etcetera. Dinner was not served until 10:00 P.M., when the videographer left. I have seen many videographers at weddings, but none that so completely took over.

—Matt Jones, wedding guest

When budget is a constraint, we suggest having a videographer for the ceremony only. The vows are the most important part of the day and a part that the photographer cannot capture word for word. If you plan on only having one camera, we suggest the camera be discreetly placed on the altar (with the church's approval) pointing toward the faces of the bride and groom. Most officiants are very happy to cooperate by wearing a clip-on microphone for recording the ceremony. Usually their only concern is that the video camera does not distract from the ceremony. You may consider two cameras, one at the altar and another in the back of the church. The camera in the back would record the ceremony from that angle. Although not as important as the camera in the front, it would be nice to have that view also.

Wedding Day Reflections

Our wedding day was such a blur. We wish we had hired a professional videographer so that we could see some of the highlights of the ceremony and reception again.

—Nicqueline and Skip

SCOTT AND KIM'S STORY

A couple we recently coordinated for, Scott and Kim, shared with us that Kim's grandparents were unable to travel to the couple's wedding due to poor health. We suggested that it would be a nice idea for the couple to hire a videographer to tape their ceremony. They did so and the tape was ready when they returned from their honeymoon. They immediately mailed it off to Kim's grandparents. The grandparents were so thrilled to be able to see the ceremony and are reportedly reviewing it daily— what a great thing for grandparents to have. (Scott and Kim are enjoying their copy also!)

MONEY-SAVING TIPS

A great way to keep the costs of videography down is to ask a relative or friend to take footage at the reception. This amateur can be anyone who owns a video camera or at least is familiar with using one. You may also rent a video camera from some camera stores. If you do rent one, have whoever is willing to take the pictures practice beforehand so he or she becomes familiar with the machine and learns what settings for light and sound work best.

Beware of the following possible problem: A recent wedding couple had trouble with the uncle who had volunteered to take videos during the reception. He was in the restroom during the cake cutting and out on the deck having a smoke when the toasts were being given. These were the only two parts of the reception that the couple had really wanted captured. To avoid this problem, be specific and give your volunteer videographer a schedule and a list of "must have" scenes.

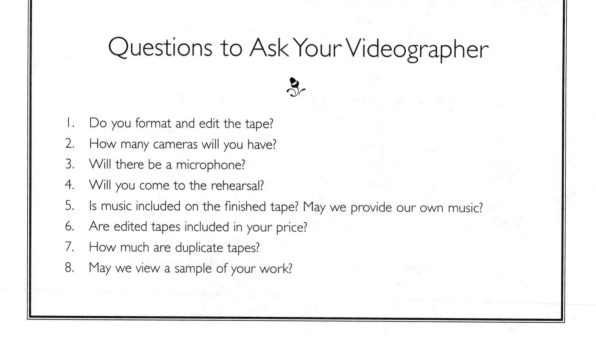

Questions to Ask Your Videographer

1. Do you format and edit the tape?
2. How many cameras will you have?
3. Will there be a microphone?
4. Will you come to the rehearsal?
5. Is music included on the finished tape? May we provide our own music?
6. Are edited tapes included in your price?
7. How much are duplicate tapes?
8. May we view a sample of your work?

Remember to Organize

INSERT any notes, contracts, and confirmation letters you've sent your photographer and/or videographer in your "Photographer & Videographer" file. Be sure you've discussed times of arrival at the ceremony, when certain photos will be taken both there and at the reception, and the types of poses you especially would like (and would not like). Record any deposits made on your payment schedule and note the due dates of payments and the final balance.

7

MUSIC

CREATING AND ADDING PERFECT HARMONY

Music PLAYS A major role throughout your wedding day. Whether you choose a harp or an organ for your ceremony, a DJ or a ten-piece band for your reception, you should select your music carefully to evoke the desired mood. Your choices are many and should reflect the style of your wedding as well as your personal tastes. In this chapter we offer dozens of ideas for using music and musicians to make your wedding uniquely yours.

Music for the Ceremony

CEREMONY music can range from soft and romantic to majestic and uplifting. The style and location of your ceremony will greatly affect your choices. If your ceremony is in a church, during your first meeting, we suggest you ask your officiant whether there are restrictions as to musicians and/or music. Some churches will limit your ceremony music to what their organ and organist plays. Others will allow outside musicians to play for your ceremony but require you first to clear any songs you select with their musical director. Some churches are much more lenient, allowing any music as long as it is in good taste.

For religious ceremonies, most couples will opt to use the church or synagogue organist for their music. A well-played organ has such wonderful sound capabilities and can fill the church with great emotion. This is an inexpensive choice for music because the organist's fees are usually quite nominal.

Usually soloists are also available, and the organist will suggest times during the ceremony when a solo would be appropriate. Also, using a soloist who has sung with your organist helps guarantee a better performance than if you hire one who is not familiar with either the building's acoustics or the organist. Rehearsals will be required, and that extra time could be billed to you. It is a good idea to hear any soloists sing before you choose them. Ask when they will be singing at another wedding and whether you may attend to listen. We suggest you choose only one or two songs so that your ceremony doesn't seem like a voice recital.

If your church or synagogue is in agreement, there is no need to limit yourself to the traditional organist and soloist. Most churches allow piano and harp music. If your ceremony is held outside a house of worship, your possibilities are endless. Some popular choices include a harp, a harp and flute duo, or a string quartet. Remember, too, that the song lists we provide in the following sections are more traditional suggestions; some appear in several categories. Each couple can choose the music they like and where they think it will fit well. For a very untraditional twist, at one wedding we coordinated, the couple chose "Send in the Clowns" by Stephen Sondheim, from the Broadway musical *A Little Night Music,* as their processional. They were a bunch of jokesters and the title definitely fit!

At a family member's wedding, we chose to have the church's

organist play all the music for the ceremony. We also hired a trumpeter to join the organist in playing the bride's processional. He stood at the very front of the altar and accompanied the organ, and the combination was wonderful! We had several guests tell us they got goose bumps because it was unexpected and so beautiful.

At a recent large cathedral wedding, we had a magnificent-sounding, five-piece brass ensemble comprised of two trumpets, a trombone, a tuba, and a French horn. The bride's processional was "The Prince of Denmarks's March" by Clarke. We have also had a woodwind quartet in the same cathedral, and they sounded equally fine. That groom was quite a talented oboe player and wanted woodwind instrumentals for his ceremony. This choice meant something to the couple, and their selection of musicians reflected their interests.

At several of our weddings a piano has been played for the prelude and the seating of grandparents and mothers, and then the church organ for the processionals and recessional. Going from piano to organ is a nice change that signals the start of the ceremony.

> ## Professionally Speaking
>
> Most brides choose 'Bridal Chorus' from the Lohengrin opera by Wagner or 'Wedding March' from A Midsummer Night's Dream by Mendelssohn for their processional. I try to acquaint them with other music. There is beautiful English and German baroque music. Two excellent compact discs to help couples with their wedding music selections are Classical Weddings and Joyous Weddings by Hope Publishing. They feature organ and trumpet selections.
>
> —Philip Jonathan Angove, trumpeter

Strings, including everything from a harp to a string quartet, add much to the romantic feeling of the day. These instruments seem to work well in any setting. We have even had a guitar be the only music for a ceremony. Especially in a casual, outdoor setting, this works perfectly. At another ceremony, a harp and flute duo were placed in a gazebo and looked just beautiful. Because a harp must be in the shade at all times, placing these musicians in the gazebo worked well. We recently had this same duo play for a small ceremony at a country club. After the ceremony, they moved to the room where the reception was being held and played during the dinner. It was a very elegant affair, and their music added the perfect touch.

At several outdoor weddings, at which no piano or organ was available, we have had a keyboard played with great results. Electricity must be available for amplification, and extension cords work wonders!

We have also had disc jockeys play music for the ceremony and then play for the reception. The couples usually choose beautiful prelude music and traditional music for the processional and recessional. The DJ is discreetly out of sight and uses small hidden speakers. This approach is fairly inexpensive and works well at a ceremony location different from a church setting.

To help you with your music selections, we suggest you listen to tapes or CDs of wedding music and decide what you both like. We have a tape entitled *The Wedding Album,* by Anthony Newman, organist (Sony Music), that we loan our couples. They find it very helpful when they start discussing music they would like to include in their ceremony.

Prelude Music

❧

Several songs make for traditional prelude music. Listed here are some of the selections our couples have made:

Andante/Harps in D, J. S. Bach
"Arioso," J. S. Bach
Prelude in C Major, J. S. Bach
"Jesu, Joy of Man's Desiring,"
    J. S. Bach
"Ode to Joy," Beethoven
"Panis Angelicus," Franck
"Air" from *Water Music Suite,*
    Handel
"Pastoral Symphony" from *Messiah,*
    Handel
"Where'er You Walk," Handel
Canon in D, Pachelbel
Four Seasons, Vivaldi
"Spring," Vivaldi

PRELUDE MUSIC

Prelude music is played before the start of the ceremony while your guests are being seated. It is usually upbeat. Often churches are more lax with music choices at this time, so couples may pick what they like. We have heard everything from Broadway hits played on a harp to *Fiddler on the Roof* music played on an organ, and Enya music played by a string quartet—and they all sounded great.

It is important that your musicians be ready to play the prelude music a half an hour before the ceremony is scheduled to start. Some guests, especially the older ones, will arrive at the ceremony location early so they can get a good seat. They might not be ready to be seated immediately as they will want to visit with friends, but the music will let them know they are anticipated and welcome—another nice touch!

After the prelude music is played, special songs can be chosen for the seating of grandparents and mothers. It is often nice to have these relatives choose their favorite piece of music. They love to be asked and feel they are very honored, as they should be. If there is just one grandparent or mother to be seated, a shortened version can be played. Musicians should be told how many grandparents there are and whether there are also stepmothers to be seated in order for them to plan the duration of each tune played.

Music for Seating Parents and Grandparents

🌹

A signal from the church hostess or your "coordinator" to the musician or musicians will let them know the grandparents and mothers are ready to be seated. The following are possible songs for their seating:

Air on the G String, J. S. Bach
"Jesu, Joy of Man's Desiring,"
    J. S. Bach
Water Music Suite, Handel
"Con Moto Maestoso" from Organ
    Sonata III, Mendelssohn
Canon in D, Pachelbel
"Ave Maria," J. S. Bach/Gounod

Processional Music for the Attendants

❧

The following traditional music is often chosen for the attendants' processional:

"Jesu, Joy of Man's Desiring,"
    J. S. Bach (most popular)
"Trumpet Voluntary," Clarke
"Lèvres," Gustafson
"Air" from *Water Music Suite,*
    Handel
Canon in D, Pachelbel
Four Seasons, Vivaldi

A pause in the music after the seating of the mothers lets the guests know that the ceremony is about to begin. One couple had quite a dramatic pause before the ceremony started. They asked their church choir to sing at their wedding. The first time the guests heard the choir was immediately after the mothers were seated. From the back of the church, out of sight in the choir loft, came the choir's voices singing "Ave Maria." Immediately after the couple was pronounced man and wife and before the lighting of the unity candle, the choir also sang "The Lord's Prayer." It was very impressive.

BRIDAL PARTY PROCESSIONAL

During the processional, your bridal party elegantly enters and walks toward the altar. Be sure your musicians know how many attendants you have and whether you also have a ring bearer and/or a flower girl. Because they are so small, it is easy for musicians not to be able to see the children. For the correct order of your attendants' processional, refer to the rehearsal section in chapter 15, "The Finishing Touches."

BRIDE'S PROCESSIONAL

After the entire bridal party has reached the altar, including the flower girl and ring bearer, the music changes with great flair to the bride's processional. As the first notes play, the mother of the bride should rise and turn toward the back. This signals the guests also to stand and turn to witness the bride and her father entering. Many a mom has cried while watching her husband proudly escorting her daughter down the aisle.

LIGHTING OF THE UNITY CANDLE

During the unity candle portion of the ceremony, it is nice to have music. This prevents people from getting restless or distracted, and it can also set a more meaningful and romantic scene.

HOW TO CHOOSE MUSICIANS

If your ceremony is being held in a house of worship, start there. Talk with the organist or the musical director to learn what guidelines you need to follow and to get recommendations for a soloist, if desired. If you think you would like a harp, strings, or other instruments, ask whether that arrangement is possible.

If your ceremony is not in a house of worship and you have an idea of what you would like, ask your location for suggestions. They may have the name of a good musical group or a particularly talented soloist.

The music department of our local college has been a wonderful source of musicians for us. Talking to one or two of the professors has put us in touch with many talented people. A local symphony orchestra is another wonderful source of talent. Music stores also have knowledge of talented musicians. Another possibility is calling the American Federation of Musicians union in your area for referrals.

Processional Music for the Bride

❦

The following sections are appropriate for the bride's processional:

"The Prince of Denmark's March,"
    Clarke (most popular by far)
"Wedding March" from
    A Midsummer Night's Dream,
    Mendelssohn
Canon in D, Pachelbel
"Trumpet Tune," Purcell (second
    most popular)
"Bridal Chorus" from *Lohengrin,*
    Wagner

When choosing musicians, ask whether you can attend one of their performances. By seeing and hearing them in person you will be able to get a good idea of what music they are most comfortable with and determine whether it will work for you. We went to a downtown coffee shop one Sunday with a couple to listen to a trio they were considering for their ceremony. Over mochas and croissants, we had our own personal concert. The couple hired them on the spot!

Music for the Reception

PICTURE a gathering of seventy guests sipping champagne and tasting hors d'oeuvres while a selection of George Winston tunes plays in the background. Now picture that same scene with no accompaniment of any sort. The gathering would become less than a celebration and more like a business gathering. Music at your reception is very important. It can range from your own CDs playing with a predetermined mix of tunes to a five-piece band playing old-time favorites.

For a quiet gathering where no dancing is desired, a piano, a harp, a harp and flute, a strolling violin, or a flute and guitar all work well for background music. One of our bride's dads wanted Gershwin music played during his daughter's reception. A small combo made up of piano, bass, and drums was perfect for this type of background music. We had a groom and his family from New Orleans request that a jazz band perform during their brunch reception. They played Dixieland music so that guests felt like they were in the French Quarter.

Communion Music

❧

If communion is being served, the following music has often been played:

"Panis Angelicus," Franck
"One Bread, One Body," Foley
"The Lord's Prayer," Malotte
"How Beautiful," Paris

If dancing is on your agenda, decide on the type of music you want played. Many couples choose a disc jockey to provide their music. If you are looking for a band, a four-piece band composed of keyboard, bass, guitar, and drums works well; a saxophone or trumpet might be added if your budget allows.

HOW TO CHOOSE A DISC JOCKEY

Disc jockeys (DJs) are very popular because they can play anything under the sun and usually have a large repertoire. Many people prefer this option to a live band, and it is definitely a less expensive alternative. DJs come in all shapes, sizes, and energy levels, all with varying styles. We have had DJs ranging from absolutely great to most obnoxious. Some feel *they* are the evening's entertainment and will bring strobe lights, costumes, props, and games—quite inappropriate at a wedding reception.

Our ideal DJ is someone who is neat, dresses appropriately, and has high-quality equipment with no loose cords or wires exposed. He or she also has a large selection of songs, welcomes input from the bride and groom, has a nice speaking voice but doesn't use it unless there is a good reason, and uses a cordless microphone. A great DJ makes a good party even better. He or she will play mood music for the meal portion of the evening. The DJ may also act as an emcee, if you wish, and announce your arrival at the reception, announce when the food is being served, call

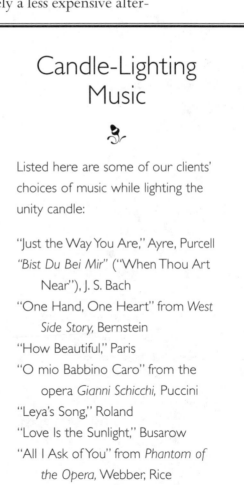

Candle-Lighting
Music

❧

Listed here are some of our clients' choices of music while lighting the unity candle:

"Just the Way You Are," Ayre, Purcell
Bist Du Bei Mir ("When Thou Art Near"), J. S. Bach
"One Hand, One Heart" from *West Side Story*, Bernstein
"How Beautiful," Paris
"O mio Babbino Caro" from the opera *Gianni Schicchi*, Puccini
"Leya's Song," Roland
"Love Is the Sunlight," Busarow
"All I Ask of You" from *Phantom of the Opera*, Webber, Rice

Recessional Music

🎵

The recessional music should be a joyful, rousing announcement that you are married. Some of our couples' choices have been as follows:

"Sleepers Awake," J. S. Bach

"Rigaudon," Campra

"Allego Mustro," Handel

"Awake, the Trumpet's Lofty Sound," Handel

Finale from *Water Music Suite*, Handel

Hornpipe Allegro in D from *Water Music Suite*, Handel

"La Rejouissance" from *Music for the Royal Fireworks*, Handel

"Wedding March" from *A Midsummer Night's Dream*, Mendelssohn (most popular)

Trumpet Fanfare from *Rondeau*, Mouret

Sonata in D Major, Purcell

"Trumpet Tune," Purcell (second-most popular)

individual tables to the buffet line, and announce the toast, cake cutting, first dance, and bouquet and garter toss. A good DJ "reads" a crowd and can get everyone on the dance floor.

Arrange to meet with the DJ to describe how you would like the reception handled. Also discuss your choice for your couple's first dance, whether there will be a father/daughter dance, and whether the parents and wedding attendants will be joining in and when. Most important, let your DJ know your music preferences. If you don't want to write out a specific song list, at least let him or her know whether you prefer a particular type of music. The broad types of music are often broken down into the following categories:

- Big Band/Swing Era
- '50s/'60s Rock
- Classic Rock
- Funk/Disco
- Motown
- Country
- Alternative Rock
- R&B/Hip Hop
- Top Hits
- Ethnic
- Group/Line Dances

When choosing a DJ, ask whether you can peek in at a reception where he or she will be working. Find out approximately when the first dance will be, and show up just a little after that time. If the reception allows, discreetly peek in and listen for a minute or two. The guests will first be starting to dance then, and you should get a good idea of how the DJ works.

HOW TO CHOOSE A BAND

Many of the principles for hiring musicians also apply here. For hiring bands, we again suggest the music department of a college, music stores, and your reception location as potential sources. Call and get prices and ask to hear a tape of theirs, or, better yet, go listen to them play. Interview the leader and prepare a list of the music you would like played. Inquire about the cost, playing time, and what the members will wear. Bands often take breaks. Ask whether they could time their breaks during the toasts and cake cutting.

Professionally Speaking

When you talk to a disc jockey you like on the phone, go watch his [or her] work. Find one you feel comfortable with and whose style you like.

—Bill Vanderveer,
SJ's Disc Jockey Service

Before signing a contract, make sure everything you have discussed is included. Know what equipment the band will bring and what you have to provide. Take the time to read all the fine print and cover every detail.

KRIS AND DAVID'S STORY

One of our biggest wedding-coordinating nightmares involved reading the fine print on a band contract. One of our lovely couples, Kris and David, hired a band from southern California that they and a group of friends had seen perform many times. This band imitated a well-known rock group, with everything from the music to the moves. The couple was very excited and was keeping the band's appearance a secret from their guests; they assured us that everything was taken care of for the band. The week of the wedding, one of us awoke in a fright worrying about the fine print in the band's contract. Indeed, as we found out later, there was a reason to be worried! Under Article VII (in mighty small print) were the words: "soundboard to be provided along with sound technician." We frantically called the reception location, which put us in touch with a theatrical lighting company, which gave us the names of several soundmen. Only one was available, and after learning his cost, we had to break the news to the bride's parents. We all knew we had no choice at this point, so the soundman, who saved the day, along with his soundboard, was hired. The band that had seemed affordable was suddenly more expensive. Nonetheless, the band sounded great, and the friends of the happy couple were wonderfully surprised and danced the night away.

No matter which musician, band, or DJ you choose, you are not on their books until they have your deposit and a signed contract. We received a call recently from a groom who was desperate to find a DJ for his wedding two weeks later. He and his fiancée thought they had a DJ reserved because six months before, they had talked to one they really liked. He knew the date of their wedding, and the couple thought that was all they had to do to reserve him. When they called, he had another wedding booked for their date. The DJ had not received a deposit check from the couple and thought they decided to hire someone else. Don't let this happen to you—follow up! Make sure everything is in order.

Remember to Organize

AFTER you have made the decisions on your music, create two files, "Music for Ceremony" and "Music for Reception." Enter your contacts' names and phone numbers on the inside of each folder. Record any deposits made on your payment schedule and note when the balance is due for both of them.

8

FLOWERS

ADDING JUST THE RIGHT TOUCH TO YOUR DAY

NOTHING SYMBOLIZES A wedding more than a beautiful bouquet of flowers. Whether you picture a small nosegay of rosebuds or a flowing cascade of stephanotis and ivy, romance always comes to mind when you see a bouquet. Flowers are a wonderful way to bring nature's beauty to your celebration and to express your individuality. The flowers you choose should have special meaning to you.

Take the time to look through magazines and floral books to gather ideas. It is easy to find many varieties of bouquet ideas in these publications. We have listed a few of our favorite floral books in the appendix. These should assist you in visualizing your perfect bouquet. We would like all of the brides who read this book to be able to say that they had the bouquet of their dreams. This goal is achievable if you know how to choose a florist, have tips on creating floral pieces with help, and take our suggestions on saving money on your floral bill. We will discuss these items in this chapter, as well as share ideas that our clients have successfully used.

Selecting the Flowers

WE have helped brides with no idea of what floral accents they wanted and those who had very definite opinions of what they wanted and why.

MICHELLE'S STORY

Michelle, a bride-to-be who knew exactly what she wanted, had decided on her flowers a year before her wedding. She chose to have a bouquet of gardenias and tuberose for their fragrances and added roses for their romance. She chose to complete her bouquet with ferns for contrast, eucalyptus for its dramatic look, and small evergreen sprigs for her groom, who had grown up among pine trees. Michelle enjoyed carrying this meaningful bouquet and planned the rest of her bridal flowers around it.

Choosing your wedding-day blossoms may seem like a huge project, but if you break it down into categories, it is not too overwhelming. Decisions need to be made on the bouquets and corsages and boutonnieres, or personal flowers. You may make the bouquets and personal flowers all the same, or you may make each one unique. Other floral accents are altar sprays for the ceremony location, unity candle arrangements, reception table centerpieces, and any other floral accents you choose.

Checklist for Flowers

WE have prepared a checklist for flowers. Go over this list before you visit with a florist so you have a better idea of your floral wants and needs in terms of quantities.

Bridal Party

Quantity

___ Bride's bouquet.   ___

___ Maid/matron of honor's bouquet.   ___

___ Bridesmaids' bouquets.   ___

___ Flower girl—what type of accent?   ___

___ Groom's boutonniere.   ___

___ Best man's boutonniere.   ___

___ Groomsmen's boutonnieres.   ___

___ Ushers' boutonnieres.   ___

___ Ring bearer's boutonniere.   ___

Personal Flowers

Quantity

___ Bride's mother's corsage.   ___

___ Groom's mother's corsage.   ___

___ Grandmothers' corsages.   ___

___ Godmother's corsage.   ___

___ Other corsages (for anyone you wish to honor,
such as guest book attendant, candle lighters,
readers, sisters, aunts, wedding "coordinators").   ___

___ Bride's father's boutonniere.   ___

___ Groom's father's boutonniere.   ___

___ Grandfathers' boutonnieres.   ___

___ Godfather's boutonniere.   ___

___ Other boutonnieres (for anyone you wish to honor
such as uncles, brothers, readers, candle lighters).   ___

Decorations at Church

Quantity

___ Pew bows.   ___

___ Unity candle arrangement.   ___

___ Altar sprays.   ___

___ Candelabra.   ___

Decorations for Reception	Quantity
___ Cake.	___
___ Cake table.	___
___ Decorations on cake knives and toasting goblets.	___
___ Head table.	___
___ Guest tables.	___
___ Guest book table.	___
___ Throwaway bouquet.	___
___ Anything else?	___

This list includes everything you could possibly want to order or discuss with a florist. Later in this chapter, and in chapter 9, "Decorations" and chapter 10, "The Cake," we describe some alternatives to ordering everything from the florist.

Bouquets

THE bride's and attendants' flowers should complement the bride's gown and the entire wedding's style. Your attendants' bouquets should complement their gowns and reflect the colors you have chosen as the predominant colors of your wedding day. Usually the maid of honor's bouquet differs slightly from the other attendants'.

Floral Options for Mothers and Grandmothers

SEVERAL lovely floral items for mothers and grandmothers may serve as alternatives to the traditional choice of a rose corsage. Many are choosing to have orchids for their simplicity and gardenias or tuberoses for their fragrance. Rather than having corsages, we have had mothers choose to have flowers on their purses or worn as a wristlet. Two mothers of our clients opted to carry small bouquets on the wedding day. Be sure to ask mothers what type of personal floral accent they would prefer.

Beautiful Bouquets

&

The following is a list of the most common bouquet styles:

- **Cascade**   Flowing flowers up and out of the center and down the front, for the appearance of a cascade of flowers .
- **Presentation**   The shape of bouquets that beauty pageant winners are handed. This bouquet would rest on the bride's left arm as her right arm holds onto her father's, as they walk down the aisle.
- **Loose-Tied Bouquet**   Reminiscent of the just-picked-from-the-garden look. Bouquets of greens and various flowers are tied with any type of ribbon.
- **Round Cluster**   A small, tightly arranged bouquet with a minimum of greens or none at all.
- **Nosegay**   A small grouping of flowers with short stems, secured with flower wire and ribbon.

Flower Girl

BASKETS filled with flowers or floral petals look very charming. Petals may be strewn along the aisle by the young participant. Old-fashioned wire hoops decorated with flowers are also returning in popularity, adding a touch of Victorian splendor. For a whimsical look, the bride may consider floral wreaths for the young girl's hair.

Perhaps you would like to have two young attendants. They may carry a swag or ribbon held at each end, decorated with flowers or not. This is a classic option that also keeps the girls together. Another idea that one of our clients created for her two flower girls was for them to carry pomanders. These are round balls decorated with flowers and greenery and held by a ribbon. The bride stated that these were quite simple to create because she just stuck stems of flowers into Styrofoam balls purchased at a yardage shop and secured the ribbon well with a pin.

Boutonnieres

BOUTONNIERES are small floral accents with a bit of greenery pinned on a man's lapel. They are worn by any men with an honored role on the wedding day. Traditionally, the groom's boutonniere complements the bride's bouquet. All the other men's boutonnieres should be slightly different from the groom's, whether in flower or color.

Choosing a Florist

WE suggest hiring a florist that specializes in weddings. Although your neighborhood florist may create lovely arrangements, it is a different skill to assemble bouquets and corsages that are unique and look fresh all day. A talented wedding floral designer will listen carefully to everything that you describe and also give you ideas to supplement your thoughts. It is worth interviewing a few florists because they all have different styles and personalities, and you want to work with one who clicks with you. Choosing wedding flowers can be a lot of fun, and working with someone you enjoy can make it even more so.

One way of narrowing the list of floral shops in your area is to ask friends and relatives for recommendations, especially those whose wedding flowers you may have admired. Another possibility is attending a bridal fair. Florists bring samples of their work to these fairs, and this is a good way to weed out businesses whose designs look too sloppy or whose styles you don't find attractive.

Once you have developed a list of potential florists, call to make an appointment with their main wedding designer. This will assure that the professional will have time to discuss your needs fully with you. It is a good idea to fill out our floral item checklist before your appointment so that you know what exactly you'd like and how many people you would like to honor with a corsage before being put on the spot by the florist. Take the following items with you:

1. A picture of your dress or a similar dress
2. Swatches of fabric from the bridesmaids' dresses or similar fabric
3. Pictures of floral designs you like
4. A list of floral items you need (from the checklist)

During the meeting, let the designer know what your wedding budget will accommodate for floral expenses. The designer will ask for the date, location, and time of your wedding and your floral likes and dislikes. He or she should listen intently to your opinions and show you pictures of recent work. The designer will record everything that you wish to order (e.g., three bridesmaids' bouquets, two mothers' corsages, etc.) and which flowers you wish to feature. After you have discussed all your floral needs, the florist will mail you an estimate. You may also want to ask the florist to bid on areas that you were considering creating yourself. This will give you an idea of whether the time and money you were planning to spend on that project are worthwhile.

It is important to meet with several florists before deciding on one. All flower shops are different. Besides better prices, you may find one with a friendlier staff or more intriguing bouquet ideas and better creativity.

Professionally Speaking

The bride on a budget can still have flowers that make an impact. Instead of a big bunch of inexpensive flowers, choose something elegant to carry such as one Casa Blanca lily or one Ecuadorian rose. Have the stem wrapped with a beautiful, good-quality wired ribbon. Make it look like your intention was to carry one singularly fantastic bloom.

—Cathy Brooks
Visual Impact Florist

TASHA'S STORY

Many years ago we went with Tasha, another one of our brides-to-be, to find a florist in her small town. She really wanted to use local vendors to support the community and to save her from driving twenty-five miles into the city for each meeting. We understood and hoped that one of the two florists in town could serve our needs. The first florist met us at the door and escorted us to a seating area with a few books on the coffee table. She asked us to look through them and tell her what we liked. Her books were three years' worth of FTD arrangements; each had approximately two pages on "wedding flowers." The arrangements and bouquets were nice, but there was absolutely nothing unique about them. We asked whether we could see pictures of weddings the florist had recently completed. She said, "No, I don't have any pictures, but I can copy anything that you liked from the books." We left there discouraged and worried that the other florist would be similar. Much to our delight, the cross-town rival had no intention of creating "cookie cutter" bouquets. She quizzed Tasha, went into the cooler, and came out with a lovely bouquet she had just created. "Is this the country garden look you are trying to achieve?" she asked. "Yes!" Tasha exclaimed, "with satin ribbon braided down the stems." "Fantastic!" the florist replied, and spurred on by her creative energy, we planned the rest of the flowers around that bouquet. We left there very pleased because we had all feared that we would be "stuck" with boring flowers.

After you have reviewed bids and decided on a florist, send the florist you choose a deposit check and a confirmation letter. Keep a copy of the check and the letter for your records. Ensure that your letter states the date of your function, the times and addresses of deliveries, and the agreed-on services. If there are items in the bid you do not wish to order, cross them out and send an amended copy of the bid with your deposit. If you feel some part of the bid is higher

Questions to Ask the Florist

❧

1. I am able to spend this amount. Are you willing to work within this budget with me?
2. Are there delivery/setup fees?
3. Do you have columns, urns, or centerpieces I could rent?
4. Do you have plants for rent?
5. How many weddings do you do in a day?
6. Are you familiar with my locations?
7. Is a throwaway bouquet complimentary?
8. Will you stay to pin on boutonnieres and corsages?
9. Will you tag each floral piece with the individual's name and role?

than you want to spend, discuss it with your florist. Ask whether other flowers could be substituted to reduce the cost. Often a slight variation in design or a comparable flower that is more readily available, and thus more affordable, can make a big difference in the overall cost.

In Season Or . . .

THE "have to have daffodils" bride will be disappointed if she is being wed in September. Daffodils are not considered in season in the summer or fall. We encourage every bride to talk with her florist about what is considered in season in their area. To get the most blooms for your buck, let your florist know that you do not wish to consider out-of-season choices. Don't worry—this approach will not completely

What *Not* to Say to a Florist

❦

If you want to stay within your budget, keep away from the following statements and questions:

- ◆ "I do not care how much they cost—I think they are beautiful."
- ◆ "Can you get a tulip in September?" (The answer would be yes, but the cost would be big!)
- ◆ "I want roses, roses everywhere!"

limit your choices. Many popular flowers such as carnations, roses, freesias, and gardenias are available all year. Out-of-season flowers may still be available, but only through special growers or from overseas, at a premium price.

Creating Floral Decorations with Your Friends and Family

We really do not think it is practical to ask friends and family to create all of your floral arrangements, and you certainly will not have time to do it the day before or the day of your wedding. We can imagine taking on creating the centerpieces or the altar arrangements, but brides and their families have plenty to worry about without tackling all the rest of the flowers. The biggest drawback of creating floral decorations is that to remain fresh, they must be completed within thirty-six hours of the wedding! This really limits how much time brides and family members can commit to such a project. If you do decide to create floral bouquets and arrangements, please refer to the books listed in the Appendix. They showcase many designs and have detailed "how-to" descriptions.

We offer a myriad of nonfloral decorating ideas in the next chapter, "Decorations." These decorations are easy to create weeks in advance and can enhance your floral arrangements. Another great way to help your floral dollars go further is by supplementing what you have contracted the floral designer to do in various ways. Many of our clients have created their own imaginative additions. If you have clever and creative people willing to help you and you are extremely organized, you may want to consider some of the ideas described here:

> ### Wedding Day Reflections
>
> We *saved money by not ordering floral decorations for our head table or our cake table. We simply set the four bridesmaids' bouquets along the edge of the head table and placed my bouquet on the cake table, and they both looked "decorated."*
>
> —Denise and Mike

 • Some wholesale flower marts are open to the public and will let you and your "floral designer" friends buy flowers. Remember only to commit to making the number of arrangements that you can keep refrigerated between your shopping trip and your wedding day.

 • Cutting greenery, especially ivy or ever-greens, is a viable option. These pieces of greens are easy to wash and work well as decorations or arrangements and as great fillers for decorating arches. Pine boughs lend a lovely scent to a room and can enhance the mood of a winter wedding. Ivy may also be formed into swags for tables or staircases with the help of green floral tape and wire.

Marvelous Ideas Worth Duplicating

HERE are some creative yet economical ideas illustrating floral touches you can prepare yourself or ask your professional florist to arrange for you.

A lovely outdoor country wedding showcased beautiful bouquets. They were loosely tied, the bride's was mostly white roses, and the three bridesmaids' were a colorful mixture of wildflowers and roses. These colors were echoed on the tall white cake, where the florist placed many blooms between layers. The bride splurged on a lily of the valley corsage for her mom but saved money on the floral center-pieces for the reception. The bride's mother and her neighbors began growing sweet peas in the winter, and they harvested all of them at their peak in June, just in time for the wedding. On the morning of the wedding, they made the centerpieces by placing the sweet peas in two semicircular terra-cotta pots that encircled the pole of the umbrellaed reception tables. This colorful centerpiece was easy to assemble and only cost $5 per table.

An outdoor ceremony lends itself well to saving money on floral arrangements. With a naturally beautiful setting, altar arrangements are not necessary. One of our clients was able to keep floral costs to a minimum because of the naturally beautiful surroundings of a win-ery. This feat was especially remarkable because the bride had seven bridesmaids and seven groomsmen. The bride's entire order from the florist was one large vase of white flowers for the table at the altar, ten white rose boutonnieres, two white rose corsages for the mothers, and twelve long-stemmed and eighteen short-stemmed roses. She asked friends to tie white organza ribbons on seven of the long-stemmed roses, and they were carried by the bridesmaids. The roses made quite an elegant statement against the bridesmaids' navy gowns. The remaining long-stemmed roses were tied for the bride's bouquet. The short-stemmed roses were formed into a crown and circled the top of the cake. The beautiful setting and the elegant flowers lent very nicely to having very simple centerpieces of five white votive candles.

Another client was concerned about keeping her floral costs low because she had twenty small tables in a mansion to decorate for her reception. She and her fiancé originally were afraid they could not have any floral centerpieces for less than $20 each. This amount alone would have already put their floral costs at a formidable $400, without any personal flowers! Then the couple had the idea to inquire with mansion management about any vases that might be available for use. Indeed, beautiful narrow crystal vases were available at no charge. The florist was then requested to place a single rose with a fern accompaniment in each vase. This was a lovely look on the small tables, and the cost was only $5 apiece, for a total of $100 for reception decorations.

Twenty-inch, narrow glass vases for centerpieces have become popular in our area. Most of the florists we work with use these frequently. With just a few blossoms, a touch of greenery, and a decorative twig or two, they liven up a room and a table. Because the number of blooms used is small, we have seen these available for a low cost of between $10 and $15 each. These vases achieve a very finished look and are ideal for a room with high ceilings.

Money-Saving Tips

THERE are so many points to consider, and creative ideas to choose from, when you start cutting costs. Because it's easy to get excited over the big day and overlook details, we've provided a list of things you may not think of—and that will help you keep your budget right where you want it.

♦ Do not choose a wedding date near Valentine's Day or Mother's Day. Not only will you have a hard time finding a florist willing to commit to your event, you will also be charged top dollar because demand for flowers is high at these times of year.

♦ Choose flowers that are in season. Tulips, for example, are abundant in the winter and are therefore affordable in January and February. In the summer, tulips would have to be shipped from overseas, if they are available at all, and they will cost a pretty penny.

♦ Move the altar arrangements from the ceremony location to the reception. We have volunteered to do this job at several friends' weddings. The job is best handled by two people—one to drive and one to sit in the back seat to keep the vases upright. Normally we place the flowers near the cake table at the reception. They form a nice backdrop for the photos taken in that area.

♦ Consider hiring a floral school in your area to do your flowers. Most often they will only charge you for the cost of the materials.

♦ Agree to a "market buy." The wholesale markets where florists purchase their flowers often have weekly specials. If you are open to not knowing what your flowers are until the week of your wedding, discuss this option with your florist.

♦ For altar sprays, request only larger, less expensive flowers whose colors and shapes will complement your wedding colors. Smaller flowers tend to be lost in large arrangements, and it does not make sense to pay top dollar for a gardenia here when a less expensive zinnia packs the same amount of punch in these large arrangements. Other examples of less expensive, larger flowers are statice, stock, chrysanthemums, and gladiolus.

♦ Instead of purchasing an arrangement to grace the guest book table, place your throwaway bouquet there. Some florists provide a complimentary throwaway bouquet for their brides. If your florist does so but you are not going to throw a bouquet, ask whether you could substitute a small arrangement on the guest book table, still at no cost.

Wedding Day Reflections

We chose to hire the local floral decorating school. We were very pleased with the flowers and are glad that we were able to make our money for flowers go further.

—Mike and Joanne

♦ Ask your church or ceremony location for the name and phone number of the couple that may be getting married a few hours before or a few hours after you. Call them to see whether you could perhaps coordinate and share the costs of decorating the pews and altar area.

♦ Remember, it is not necessary to order corsages or boutonnieres for anyone whom you have hired for the day, such as soloists or musicians.

♦ Consider flowers besides roses for corsages and boutonnieres. Bachelor buttons and zinnias are less expensive yet still pretty alternatives. Ask your florist for ideas.

♦ Silk flowers are an option for altar decorations. If found on sale, these flowers can be used quite inexpensively. We recommend limiting silk flowers for altar sprays and other accents that are not near guests. The scent of natural flowers is definitely part of their appeal and something that members of your wedding party and family should be treated to.

Remember to Organize

CREATE a "Florist" file. Keep in it pictures of flowers and bouquets you like. When you have decided on your florist, enter the name and telephone number on the inside of the folder. Insert copies of your final contract and letter of confirmation. Record any deposits made on the payment schedule and note when the final dollars are due (usually ten days or a week before the wedding).

9

DECORATIONS

PICKING THE PERFECT ACCENTS

Decorations set the scene for your special day. Decorative touches can transform a blank-canvas setting into one that boldly announces that a wonderful celebration will be held here today. Use your imagination to add your unique, personal touch to convey the color scheme and style of your wedding day. Let the decorations reflect your personalities and tastes. In this chapter we will discuss decorations for churches and other ceremony locations and dispense ideas for livening up and personalizing reception sites.

Decorating for the Ceremony

Because of the architectural detail of many places of worship, such as high ceilings, stained glass windows, wooden pews, and lovely altars, only a minimal amount of decorating is necessary in some settings. Before planning any decorations for your church, consult your officiant or the church office. Some churches prefer no flowers or candles at all, while others permit the use of all types of decorations.

Professionally Speaking

Altar arrangements usually need to be very large to be impressive at the front of the church and can get very expensive just by the sheer numbers of flowers required to fill them. Eliminate these arrangements. All eyes will be focused on the bride and groom and their attendants in their beautiful dress attire and their hand-held arrangements. If you must have altar arrangements, use large fern plants that can be purchased at your discount nursery for under $15 each. Set them on a pedestal and add baby's breath, trailing ivy, and brightly colored status flowers to match your colors, if desired.

—Mary Kuyper
Garden Wishes florist

ALTAR DECORATIONS

When planning your altar decorations, remember that your bridal party will serve as decoration themselves and you, the bride and groom, will be the center of attention. Having more than two large altar sprays and two candelabras, therefore, is not necessary on most church altars. Take into account what your guests will be able to see when the bridal party is in place. Raise the large altar sprays by putting them in a tall brass or wicker standard. Some churches provide standards, or they can be rented from a rental company or your florist. When considering altar arrangements, ask your florist what they could create inexpensively that would not appear sparse.

If you decide to make these arrangements yourself, a large block of florist's foam placed in a pot and secured with chicken wire will serve as a good base for the flowers. Choose inexpensive flowers that blend with your bouquets. Good choices would include statice, stock, and gladiolus. If the church is dark, the flowers should be in light shades so that they are easily visible.

Instead of having flower arrangements, several of our brides have rented wicker baskets and then purchased large ferns as their altar arrangements. The ferns added an airy touch of nature and were quite inexpensive. White artificial marble columns are also possible. These are available in heights of six and eight feet and are very lightweight and easy to move. Arrangements of flowers or plants look beautiful placed on them, especially with ivy or ribbons trailing.

A money-saving idea is to have the altar arrangements transferred from the church to the reception location as decorations. Some florists include this transferring service in their fee. If your florist does not or if you are making the arrangements, request the assistance of a couple people to move them. Still another time- and money-saving idea is not to have any large arrangements at all. If your decorating budget is tight and you don't feel they are necessary, this is a good item to eliminate altogether. Also, ask your church whether another ceremony is scheduled before or after yours; perhaps you could share all or some of the decorations with another couple.

CANDELABRA

Most churches have tall floor candelabras of brass or copper available at no charge. These add a nice finishing touch to the altar and can serve as an alternative or addition to altar sprays. Candelabras usually hold a minimum of five candles, and most churches require that you use dripless candles. Ask whether you need to provide the candles. The candelabras look very nice when simply decorated with bows and/or greenery.

UNITY CANDLES

If you choose to have a unity candle included in your ceremony, keep in mind that you don't need to spend $25 or more to buy an "official" candle as sold in wedding-oriented stores. A ribbon tied around an ordinary candle makes a beautiful unity candle. Simple greenery around the base also is very pretty. Several of our couples have chosen greenery with baby's breath or other small flowers placed in the greenery. Your photographer may reenact the lighting of your candle for your album, and these touches add interest and contrast for these photos.

ALTAR RAILINGS

We have had clients spend a great deal of money on swags for altar railings only for them not to be visible because their wedding party stands between the railing and the guests. Ropes or swags of greenery are labor-intensive and thus quite expensive. We suggest eliminating this decoration unless a friend or family member offers to do them for free. One of our bride's grandmothers had beds of small English ivy in her yard, and she made two ivy ropes for the railings on either side of the altar. After the ceremony, while pictures were being taken and guests were lingering in front of the church, two of the bride's cousins quickly removed the ivy ropes. They immediately took them to the reception site where one rope was draped on the cake table and the other on the front of the head table. Detailed instructions and the necessary equipment were given to the cousins in advance so they were confident with their assignment.

PEW BOWS

Unlike decorated altar railings, pew bows are very visible to your guests. If you wish to include them, by all means do so. Couples and their families can easily and inexpensively make these decorations in advance. Our clients have coordinated their pew bows so that they pull together the style and decorations also used at the reception, using a variety of fabrics:

- **Tulle** A light, airy feeling, perfect for spring and summer.

- **Polished Cotton** A very finished look, available in a variety of colors to match or coordinate with bridesmaids' dresses, flowers, and time of year.

- **Plaid, Floral, or Check Pattern** A more casual look. We have had a red plaid for a Christmas wedding, and floral and check patterns used at outdoor receptions.

- **Brocade** A more formal look. One couple used this fabric at their cake table, as the head table runner, and on the ring pillow (for their canine ring bearer—we'll tell you about that story later).

In making pew bows ourselves, we have found three yards of fabric makes the prettiest bow. It is not, however, necessary for the bow to be the full width of the material. Standard fabric widths are thirty-

six, forty-five, or fifty-two inches, which can be cut in half, thirds, or
even quarters. Experiment and decide what you think looks best.
Craft stores have a spray-on stiffener that can be used to help keep
bows from drooping.

Bows can be used alone or with floral and/or greenery adorn-
ments. Small arrangements have included daisies, daffodils, and roses.
One bride had a large herb garden and created nosegays of fragrant
herbs to hang upside down from the bows. Our couples have used a
variety of floral arrangements with bows.

TOM AND AMY'S STORY

Tom and Amy chose to have a very lovely, understated
wedding with moss green and ivory as their colors. The bride,
who had gorgeous red hair, chose an ivory dress with a tulle
skirt. Her bridesmaids wore very simple moss green dresses.
Their bouquets were predominately English ivy with a few roses.
The bride's bouquet was mostly roses with a little English ivy.
A beautiful sight! Several months before the wedding, Amy and
her mother made bows of ivory tulle they purchased at a fabric
store for $1.19 a yard, for a fifty-two-inch width. They figured for
each bow, they would use three yards of tulle, cut in half; their
cost then was just $1.78 per bow (three yards at $1.19 = $3.57,
divided by 2). They made twelve pew bows, two bows for the
church candelabra, four for the cake table, and four for the
head table, all for less than $40. English ivy from their garden
was added to each bow the day before the wedding. The
simplicity of the two understated colors was breathtaking.
A little later in this chapter we will tell you about their table
centerpieces.

Ask your church what they require to attach the decorations. You
may have to buy plastic clip-ons that will be attached to the back of
your bows. These will not scratch the pews, but we suggest you try

them on the pews first, because some pews are too thick for the clips. Some churches require rubber bands or ribbons. Churches will not allow the use of wire or tape to attach bows.

PEW CANDLES

The warm glow of candles can add much to a church aisle. Pew candles are particularly fitting for an evening or winter wedding. It is possible to rent these candle stands, which stand about five feet tall, rest on the floor, and are attached to the end of a pew with a clamp or vice. These are often brass or wrought iron candleholders with glass hurricane globes that typically encase eight- or ten-inch candles, which you will need to provide. Pew bows or flowers can then be attached to the candleholder or base of the standard itself. A large church where we have had several weddings has beautiful wooden pew candleholders for their couples to use if they wish. These were lovingly made and donated to the church by an elderly parishioner.

For pew decorations of any variety, we suggest you place them at the first few rows where family will sit and then at every other row or every third row. You don't need to decorate every pew. Remember to double your count when making decorations, as you have two sides of the aisle to adorn.

AISLE RUNNERS

An aisle runner is optional. We've heard that even weddings at the White House no longer use them, because it was felt that a wedding gown does not show off well when photographed on runners. Nonetheless, some brides opt to use them for another elegant touch during the ceremony. Linen aisle runners and gold holders can be rented from rental companies for approximately $50. A disposable fabric-like paper runner with an attractive white-on-white pattern can be purchased at rental or craft stores for approximately $25. Usually the florist lays the runner before the guests arrive. However, one couple chose to have it laid ceremoniously, after the mothers were seated.

RYAN AND KIMBERLY'S STORY

In Ryan and Kimberly's wedding, two groomsmen came down the aisle pulling a decorative gold roller that held the runner between them. As the men walked, the runner unrolled behind them and covered the aisle. At this point, we quickly pinned the runner at the back of the church to avoid having one of the bridesmaids or the bride and her father trip over it. We of course practiced this at the rehearsal and carefully marked where the men should begin so the material would end just before the altar steps. When the men reached the front of the church, they smoothed the runner on the floor and inserted a long pin on each side of the runner, attaching it to the carpet. They then joined the other groomsmen at the altar. The aisle runner being laid this way added a special touch. If this is something you choose to do at your wedding, be sure you inform your musicians so they are prepared to play during this time.

DECORATING FOR A CEREMONY IN A SETTING OTHER THAN A CHURCH

When having your ceremony at a location other than a place of worship, try to draw attention to the area where you are going to exchange your vows. Some settings have an obvious "perfect" spot; at others, one must be created.

For outdoor ceremonies, a large tree, a gazebo, or a beautiful view can serve as a backdrop. Remember to be aware where the sun will be at the time of your ceremony—you don't want your bridal party or guests squinting into the sun. If there is no "perfect" spot, a rented arch or potted plants work well for creating a focal point. We have even had a ceremony spot set off with stacked bales of hay. There was no question where the ceremony was being held! Whatever you choose, take into account a strong breeze could be a possibility and your "altar" should be fairly sturdy.

For indoor ceremonies, you have more choices for your altar. A table covered with a full-length cloth can spotlight an area and lends itself to including a unity candle in your ceremony. Marble-looking columns or brass or wicker standards with flowers or greenery work well. Again, a wooden or wicker arch is beautiful, and decorated with flowers or greenery it can create a garden-like feeling to an indoor location. A wooden arch decorated with poufed tulle and tulle bows lends a heavenly look to a ceremony spot. Huppas (or chupas), the canopies used in Jewish ceremonies, may be free-standing or held by four people, and may be decorated with flowers or greenery. These, too, set off a ceremony location perfectly.

CEREMONY SETUP NOTES

For either indoor or outdoor ceremonies, chairs are set up with an aisle and, again, pew bows or other decorations are a nice touch. Practice attaching your pew bows to the chairs you'll be using in the ceremony; a light-gauge wire used in floral arrangements might work best. An aisle runner will further delineate the ceremony location. A paper runner works well indoors and outdoors. Most rental companies will not rent a linen runner for outside use because grass stains are very hard to remove.

OTHER FUN TOUCHES

Several of our brides have put wreaths on the big double doors at the entrance of their ceremony location for a festive, inviting welcome to their guests. Another couple had the wrought iron railing on the steps leading into their building decorated with ivy and ribbon. Yet another unique idea involved two stone lions flanking the steps of a bed-and-breakfast ceremony location. The bride softened their look by placing around their necks grapevine wreaths wound with the ribbon she used as accents indoors.

Decorating for the Reception

AND now it is off to the celebration! Most guests (and brides and grooms) can barely wait to get to the party following the ceremony. Let the decorations you choose for your reception location reflect your personal tastes and the feeling you want to convey to your guests. Every couple would like to create an occasion unlike any other, and the reception is the perfect arena to let your individuality be seen.

TOM AND AMY'S STORY

Tom and Amy were the soon-to-be newlyweds who chose moss green and ivory as their colors. Well, they repeated their understated elegance at their reception. Their cake table had a simple overskirt of moss green polished cotton, gathered up with four ivory tulle bows. The cake was made of three stacked squares with smooth icing in a polka dot design. English ivy was laid around the cake's base. Amy's bouquet was placed on the cake table to serve as a decoration. The toasting goblets and cake knives had small moss green ribbons tied to them and were the only other decoration on that table. The mother of the bride made swags of English ivy the week before the wedding and stored them in her refrigerator. The head table was adorned with these swags, which were held in place with ivory tulle bows. The bridesmaids' bouquets were placed along the front edge of the head table to double as decoration. Much to her delight, Amy's mother had accidentally stumbled on a sale of ivy topiaries at the nursery department of a building supply store. They were regularly $20.00 but on sale then for $12.95. She purchased eight of these for table centerpieces. Each topiary was adorned with a piece of tulle and a strand of moss green wired ribbon. This same ribbon was tied around the napkins on the plate at each place setting. The ribbon was $1.44 per yard and each bow used one yard, as did each topiary, so the total ribbon cost for the eighty guests was $115.20 before tax. The guests noticed the special touches, and none would have ever believed that the family had spent less than $275 for decorations at both the church and the reception.

THE ENTRANCE

The entrance is the first impression that your guests will have of your celebration and thus deserves special attention. An arbor festooned with greenery or a billowing arc of balloons can make the guests feel that they have entered a special festivity. Other simple yet powerful statements here could be potted trees or bushes lining the entrance walkway. Bows and lights can transform a borrowed or rented plant into a dazzling addition to an entrance.

Wedding Day Reflections

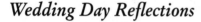

We rented ivy topiary centerpieces and tucked a string of battery-powered small white lights between leaves. This little touch made the whole room glow. We enjoyed walking in to the reception because it had such a warm feeling.

—Kim and Matt

GIFT TABLE

Set a table aside for gifts your guests will invariably bring to the reception. Although this table does not *require* decorations other than a tablecloth, it can be decorated very simply to tie in with your other reception decorations. We suggest you place a basket on this table for guests who bring cards. It is easy for cards to be misplaced or mistakenly put with the wrong gift. You can also decorate the basket in your wedding theme. Placing an empty envelope with your names on it in the basket lets the first guests know what the basket is intended for.

CAKE TABLE

Because so many pictures are taken here, your cake table should be decorated attractively. Anything other than a plain wall behind the table will add interest to the photos. If you have the space, it is nice to bring the cake away from the wall and place a rented tree or altar sprays behind it. Another good backdrop is a lattice screen that can be decorated to tie it in with the rest of your theme. Greenery works especially well as it is a good contrast to light-colored icing on the cake. For actual decorations on the cake table, please refer to chapter 10, "The Cake."

CENTERPIECES

Anything you could possibly imagine adorning a table can serve as a centerpiece. In chapter 8, "Flowers," we discussed floral arrangements for table focal points, but of course there are many other options. Following are some examples.

COLLECTIONS If you or someone in your family collects teapots, baskets, antique bottles, or almost anything else, this is a great place to showcase them. Most collectors love to show off their items, and a garnish of fresh or dried flowers makes them a lovely decoration and conversation piece.

SEASONAL TOUCHES By all means take advantage of nature's bounty of seasonal decorations. Spring and summer weddings may feature whatever is in great abundance in your circle of friends' gardens. Wild flowers and even fruit are possibilities. Fresh-smelling lemons stacked in a bowl with a ribbon bow on top is a marvelous example. In the fall, baskets of small gourds and pumpkins would make a colorful centerpiece and pull together a harvest theme.

Professionally Speaking

Beautiful flowering plants can be purchased at your discount nursery and make wonderful centerpieces when placed in the right container to match your wedding colors or theme; later you can plant them in your garden. Or on a larger scale, use one-gallon flowering plants such as marguerite daisies, mums, or any perennial in bloom wrapped in lace cello with tulle bows. These can be placed down the aisle of the church at every other pew. Then you are well on your way to landscaping your new home!

—Mary Kuyper,
Garden Wishes florist

These rich colors can be echoed in the floral arrangements. Holiday weddings have many options including poinsettias, which may be purchased fairly inexpensively, and evergreen boughs, which can be arranged with holly, pine cones, and a red ornament or two for contrast.

ALISON'S STORY

What could one possibly do with a paper lunch sack, a gold cord, walnuts, a candle, and two pomegranates? That is what we wondered when Alison, one of our clever brides-to-be, showed us what she was using to make her centerpieces for her holiday season wedding. We were going to guess she was making lunch for a squirrel! Instead, she spray-painted everything gold except the candle, folded down the paper bag, and filled it with the nuts and pomegranates. She placed the candle in the middle and tied a cord bow around the bag. These were spectacularly unique centerpieces just perfect for her tables of four. They added a festive touch without being overly "Christmassy." Another great thing about these decorations is that the bride was able to start making them a month in advance.

OTHER CENTERPIECE IDEAS Plants look great as centerpieces. Plant rental companies are a good place to discover a variety of choices. Purchasing flowers at a nursery and placing them in baskets is another super idea. The potting soil may be covered up with moss and a ribbon added and voilà—a lovely centerpiece!

The possibilities for centerpieces are endless. Use your imagination and ask friends for ideas also. It is the unique little touches that guests remember the most when the wedding is over.

Candles

❧

A flickering candle adds a lot of ambiance to a table, and numerous candles add a lovely glow to a whole room. Candles can make a large impact for a small amount of money. It is not hard to find votive candles for less than $0.50 each or tapers for less than $1.00 each. We have seen candles used in many imaginative ways. The following is a sampling:

- A hurricane-globed candleholder encased a large ivory candle and had ivy and the occasional bachelor button flower wrapped around the base. The holders were purchased at a craft store for $3.50 each including candles, and the florist charged $5.00 to decorate each one.

- Floating candles of blue and maroon were the perfect centerpiece for an outdoor evening reception. The scented candles were found on sale for $4 for three, and they floated in clear fishbowl-shaped vases. The reflection of the flame on the water cast a nice light on the dinner tables. Floating candles are also a possible compromise at a location that does not otherwise allow candles for safety reasons.

- Candles in any holder reflect nicely off a mirror square placed in the center of the table. This is a very modern, minimalist look that can be achieved quite inexpensively. Glass stores are able to custom-cut larger mirrors to your size specifications.

- Polished silver candelabras are available complimentarily at two of our favorite reception locations; the couple just needs to supply the candles. These have such a classic, elegant look that no other decorating touch is necessary on the tables. Ask your reception location whether they offer something similar. Some caterers also provide them.

- Votive candles are a nice way to add interest and ambiance. One wedding we attended featured votives in small clay pots that had been hand decorated by the bride with white and gold paint. There was one at every seat, and each guest was encouraged to take the unique decoration home as a favor.

Table Linens

Do not underestimate the power of color! Linens in colors other than white can really liven up your reception. Most rental companies now charge the same amount for a rainbow of colored linens as they do for white. Of course, all white or ivory linens can make a bold statement also, but if your location is fairly drab, a splash of color on napkins or table linens may be just the answer. Adding a colored square over a white or ivory floor-length linen can add a nice contrast. These colored squares are available for less than $10 each at rental supply stores. A less expensive way to have a contrasting color square would be to buy fabric. We recently found a cotton-blend material on sale for $0.99

Tips for Finding the Perfect Centerpiece

❧

1. Do not forget to ask your location whether they offer complimentary options.
2. Ask your reception location for the name and phone number of the other people who are using the facility that day. Perhaps you can share centerpieces or other decorations.
3. Centerpieces should not block the view of guests across the table. To avoid this, restrict shorter arrangements to no more than fifteen inches high and keep taller ones very thin and between fifteen and twenty-one inches high. A topiary makes an excellent centerpiece, as it is narrow in the middle and won't obstruct views.
4. Several candles near each other burn faster than a single candle.
5. Put someone in charge of keeping an eye on all candles. Some tables may have candles that burn faster than others, and these may need extinguishing while the guests are dancing. Be very careful because a candle might easily ignite a ribbon or decorative twig.

for a 45 × 36" piece of fabric. Two yards could be sewn together for a square on a sixty-inch round and 2½ yards for a seventy-inch round.

RUNNERS

Runners, like colored squares, are a perfect way to add interest to straight or round tabletops. Sewing the edges of the fabric of your choice creates a finished look. A floral-patterned runner is a great option for a bride who would like a floral look but has opted for a few candles rather than flower arrangements on tables.

NAPKINS

Simply adding a bow to napkins is a nice touch at each guest's table setting. One bride's mother recently cut out tin purchased at a craft store into the shape of hearts, making them look like pewter hearts. She then fastened a tag to each heart that said "Thank You for Sharing Our Special Day." She attached these hearts to the ribbons tied around the napkins. The guests were impressed with their thoughtfulness. Many locations have various-colored napkins from which you can choose. Napkins can also be folded in special ways and displayed in the water glasses for visual interest at each table.

> ### Wedding Day Reflections
>
> We're glad we saved money on the centerpieces. We were originally considering centerpieces that were quite expensive, but then opted to use the facility's three-tiered hurricane candleholders free of charge. We only had to purchase the candles. These were a nice complement to the patio's outdoor surroundings.
>
> —Suzanne and Russell

Decorative Favors

FAVORS can serve as another nice decorative touch at each place setting. Not having favors is a great way to save money, but if you do choose to offer some, the sky is the limit. Hershey's chocolate kisses or Jordan almonds in tulle netting tied with ribbons are popular favors. Several of our couples have presented a luscious truffle in a small gift

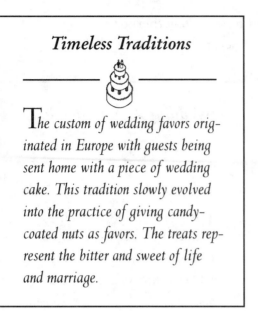

Timeless Traditions

The custom of wedding favors originated in Europe with guests being sent home with a piece of wedding cake. This tradition slowly evolved into the practice of giving candy-coated nuts as favors. The treats represent the bitter and sweet of life and marriage.

box for each guest. Another couple created a scroll with a romantic poem on one side and a thank-you note to their guests on the other side. The scrolls were rolled up, tied with a ribbon, and set at each place setting. One bride and groom gave their guests a "guardian angel" pin attached to a card with the couple's wedding date on it.

Our favorite favors were tree seedlings presented at a reception. The groom worked for the Department of Forestry and was able to get these seedlings through his job. The couple attached a printed tab that read, "As this tree grows, so will our love for each other. Thank you for being with us on our special day." Here was a favor that you felt wouldn't be thrown away after the reception but rather taken home and planted to serve as a lovely memento over the years.

Questions to Ask Both the Ceremony and Reception Locations

1. When may we have access to decorate?
2. What are your rules as to what we can and cannot do?
3. Do we need to remove the decorations? If so, by when?
4. What is available complimentarily for our use?
5. May we use thumbtacks? Tape?

Illuminating Ideas

OH, the magic of lights! Evening functions, whether inside or out, can be brightened up with lights. Drape little white lights (or "twinks") in trees or around a railing to add a touch of romance. Also try hanging them around the walls of a room or suspending them in plants. This decoration will allow you to turn down the bright lights and enjoy a softer glow. Strands of white lights are available at after-Christmas sales for about $1 each, and ten of these sets can work wonders. Be sure to allow yourself and your volunteers plenty of time for this sort of decorating, and determine ahead of time the number of extension cords your plans require.

A LAST WORD ON THE "BLANK CANVAS"

We like to think of a reception room as a blank canvas—some need a little more "paint" than others. Keep in mind, though, that even the blandest room can take on a festive mood when it's full of party-goers. The two most important areas for you to concentrate on decorating, as we mentioned before, are the entrance and the area around the cake table. For very blank canvases, if space and your budget will allow, rental trees or bushes add a lot. Look up plant rentals in your local Yellow Pages and ask to see their selection. Four trees on four different walls can "pull together" a room and make a cavernous room appear more intimate.

> **?**
>
> *Our reception hall is rather dark because of the paneling. What can we do?*
>
> We *suggest small white lights, or "twinks," everywhere. Keep your decorations light and airy, such as tulle bows. Add twinks in tulle swags on the head table and cake table. You will have a very different feeling in the room for a very low price.*

Remember to Organize

CREATE two folders entitled "Ceremony Decorations" and "Reception Decorations." Keep all of your notes, pictures of ideas you like, and work estimates in these folders.

10

THE CAKE

SELECTING A MAGNIFICENT EDIBLE SHOWPIECE

IT'S NOT A party without a cake! A major focus of any wedding reception, no matter the style, time of day, or number of guests, is the cake. It is beautifully displayed at the reception, rating its own table in a conspicuous location. It is always included in the pictures with quite a ritual made of the cutting as all eyes are focused on the bride and groom. Guests often ask us what time the cake is being cut. They undeniably look forward to eating the cake!

The History of Wedding Cakes

QUITE a bit of history is behind the tradition of the wedding cake. Greek couples are reported to have shared a sesame cake as a symbol of fertility. The Romans started their ceremonies with an offer of wheat cake that was then crumbled over the bride and groom's heads. The crumbs were gathered by guests and thought to be good luck. In medieval England, guests brought small cakes to weddings and put them in a pile, one on top of the other. The bride and groom then kissed over this stack. A French chef attending one of these receptions decided to spread icing over a pile of cakes, which is how the tiered wedding cake was created—or so the story goes.

A Myriad of Taste and Design Possibilities

YOUR choices for wedding cakes are unlimited. Some couples feel the design of the cake is paramount and spend a lot of time pouring over pictures, looking for the perfect style. Other couples are much more

What a Lovely Cake . . . and So Delicious

🌤

No longer are you limited to the plain white cake with white frosting. A sampling of the flavors our couples have chosen are as follows:

- Carrot
- Mocha
- Chocolate mousse
- Spice

- Lemon chiffon
- Raspberry truffle
- Chocolate and vanilla sponge cake

Each tier of cake is usually four inches high and composed of three or four layers of cake and two or three layers of filling. You also have many choices for fillings, such as these:

- Pineapple
- Amaretto custard
- Amaretto mousse
- Lemon cream
- Lemon mousse
- Chocolate mousse
- Raspberry

- Mocha
- Chocolate Bavarian
- Cream cheese
- Hazelnut
- Strawberry cream
- Chocolate orange cream

interested in how the cake will taste, and they cut a taste-testing swath through town.

Cakes with fresh fruit fillings are quite popular in the summer months.

SHERRI AND MIKE 'S STORY

A cake filled with fresh strawberries and whipped cream was a big hit at Sherri and Mike's wedding last summer. The couple had a casual picnic-like reception. The guests sat at tables covered with red-and-white checked tablecloths. A restaurant catered a rib dinner and actually barbecued during the reception over large grills. The very generous portions of ribs were served with potato salad, baked beans, and rolls. After the heavy meal, the light cake was perfect. It was decorated with smooth icing and had large red strawberries and kiwi slices as its only garnish. Strawberries were cut in half and stuck in the frosting on the sides of each layer. The top layer was completely covered with whole strawberries. It looked absolutely delectable, and the berries' red color matched the color scheme of the reception.

If you have pictures of cakes you really like, take them along when you visit bakeries. Ask to see pictures of cakes the bakery has made for previous weddings for more ideas. Cakes come in shapes other than the round design that first comes to mind; imagine an oblong, square, oval, hexagonal, or even heart-shaped one.

Wedding cakes are traditionally layered creations, with possible variations. Those with each tier resting directly on the lower tier are called stacked. Others have risers or columns of varying heights between each

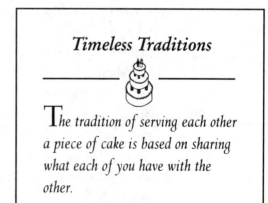

Timeless Traditions

The tradition of serving each other a piece of cake is based on sharing what each of you have with the other.

tier. Many of our couples have chosen a third look, in which each tier is placed on a separate stand, and all stands are of varying heights. The largest-diameter tier is on the lowest stand, whereas the smallest is on the highest stand. When the stands are clear acrylic, each tier appears to be floating (see Figure 10.1). This cake is beautiful when surrounded by flowers and greenery.

Figure 10.1

Icing on the Cake

"THAT was the icing on the cake!" How often have we heard that expression? For an actual wedding cake, icing can indeed make a powerful statement, in terms of both taste and decoration. Gone is the very sweet, nothing-but-sugar icing. Today, most brides choose a butter creme frosting that is not overly rich. This type also lends itself to just about any style of decorating.

Many of our brides have been tempted to choose the expensive fondant icing. Fondant icing looks smooth and neat, but because it is hard, it is very difficult to cut. It also doesn't taste good. Fondant's history dates back several hundred years, before finely ground flour and baking powder were introduced, so the cakes were dark cakes filled with fruit and nuts. This "fruitcake" was prepared several weeks before the reception, covered by an apricot glaze, and then preserved by using a heavy, hard, impenetrable topping, which was fondant. The baker then could take his time with the decorating with no fear of the cake spoiling. The smooth look of fondant can now be duplicated in butter creme frosting—a very popular look with our brides.

Designs created using butter creme or sugar frosting include basket weave, lace, lattice, rope, and various garland patterns. While most cakes are decorated with white frosting with a little color used in the design, some of our couples have chosen a slightly tinted frosting. One couple had peach-tinted frosting for their autumn wedding, and each tier was covered with flowers in fall colors. Another couple had a dark chocolate icing with a beaded border in ecru, or beige, tinted frosting. Both cakes were beautiful.

Cakes can also be decorated with icing made to look like ribbon, which is very lovely. Several of our couples have had bows made of real ribbon in their wedding colors placed in the frosting. One of our brides chose to have the cake decorated with beautiful flowers made from frosting on the sides of each layer, with gold paper leaves placed on either side of each flower. The table centerpieces had gold accents, so the cake tied into the overall scheme very nicely. When planning your cake, take into account your style of wedding, the colors of your wedding, and the type of reception you are having. The cake helps to pull everything together.

Cake Tops

No longer are couples limited to the plastic bride and groom models for the top of their cake. Our couples have been most innovative in their selections. One bride used a pair of kissing cherubs that she had played with at her grandparents' home as a child. Even though her groom pointed out that one cherub had been broken and poorly glued back together, she insisted that it would look fine. The florist placed the pair amid flowers on the cake top, strategically arranging several flowers so they covered the cracked wings.

One of our couples visited Disneyland prior to their wedding and had a blown glass Minnie and Mickey made for their cake top. Their first date had been at Disneyland when they were in college, and they felt Minnie and Mickey played a big role in their romance. Because of the delicacy of the blown glass, the "mice" looked quite beautiful. Yes, they stopped at Disneyland on their honeymoon!

Another couple who were avid skiers had a pair of ceramic skiers on their cake top. They had kidded about even making the entire cake look like a giant ski slope, and we were all relieved when they chose a more traditional cake.

Another bride and groom who are both very active politically, and of different parties, good-naturedly teased each other whether the donkey or the elephant on their cake top would be larger. At the last minute they decided to have neither and chose to have flowers instead.

One couple chose not to have a cake top as such but chose a Lladro figurine of a bridal couple as a table decoration instead. The statue was very heavy, so it needed to be placed directly on the table and not on the cake. The table looked very beautiful, and the Lladro definitely had a place of honor.

Cakes adorned with flowers on each tier and on top are by far our couples' favorite choices. Flowers on the cake tie in all the decorations together, from the bride's and attendants' bouquets to the table centerpieces.

LIZ AND ZACK'S STORY

We have only had one real cake disaster, or almost disaster, out of all the weddings we've coordinated. The bride, Liz, said her cake was the most important part of her wedding, so she contracted with a very popular, European-style bakery for a very expensive cake. Several months before the wedding, the owner of the bakery retired and sold the business. It was purchased by a man who had no experience in running a bakery, let alone a bakery with many cakes going out on a busy Saturday in June. Our bride's cake was to be delivered at 4:00 P.M. to the reception location, which was about an hour's drive from the bakery. The florist was done with all the other decorating and was standing by to decorate the cake. At 5:00 the reception started, and the cake still had not been delivered. The florist was still standing by! The only thing that saved the day was that the reception was outside on the lawns of a large bed-and-breakfast inn. The cake was going to be in a gazebo on the other side of the inn and was out of sight of the guests. The bride, groom, and the guests were not aware the cake had not arrived and did not see the hand wringing of the rest of us. A panicked call to the bakery at 5:00 let us know the cake was just leaving the bakery. We estimated it would arrive at 6:00—two hours late! Sure enough, just a little before six, two ladies arrived with the cake. All three tiers had large cracks in them from being jostled on their fast drive. The caterer, the florist, the photographer's assistant, and the two of us grabbed the three tiers, hastily stacked them, attempted to smooth the icing, and then "decorated" the cake. We completely covered each tier with flowers until the large fissures were not visible. The cake looked absolutely gorgeous, although more like a floral arrangement than a cake! We finished just in time to call the guests over for the cake-cutting ceremony, and no one was aware of the drama or delay that had taken place. We shared the story with the bride and groom at the end of the reception, and they were most grateful for everyone's part in saving the cake. (The bakery is no longer in business. Evidently this wasn't the only cake that hadn't been delivered on time!)

Groom's Cake

SOME weddings also have groom's cakes. This is a fun southern tradition that is spreading its way across the country. The groom's cake is a small cake, and the bride usually plans it to reflect her groom's interests, such as sports. In one case, the bride had the bakery design a cake to resemble the groom's dog. His dog was jealous of the time the groom spent with the bride, and the bride thought this might put her in better standing with the pooch. (We hear the three are now doing well together.)

Most grooms' cakes are chocolate with chocolate frosting, but, again, your choices are limitless. If you decide to have one, we suggest serving it along with the "bride's" cake so that you can order a smaller wedding cake and thus save some money.

How to Choose a Bakery

Professionally Speaking

I encourage couples that are comparing bakeries to taste their work as well as look at photos from past creations. It is also a good idea to ask to see thank-you letters from past clients. Any good bakery will have them!

—Tom Wall, Cakemasters bakery

BY now you have chosen a florist and a photographer, and both are wonderful sources of referrals for bakeries, as they have seen many cakes at weddings. They may not have tasted them or know each bakery's prices, but they certainly know who decorates beautifully. Call the bakeries they suggest and make an appointment to go in and taste. Another great source is a bridal fair where you can both see and taste cakes. Don't limit yourself to just the bridal fair bakeries, however, as many established bakeries do not exhibit at fairs.

Sizes and Prices of Cakes

WHEN selecting a cake, have an idea of your number of guests, since the size of the cake and number of layers needed are normally determined by your guest count. For a small group—say, forty to fifty guests—a six-inch and a ten-inch tier would work well. With a group of 100 or more, three or even four tiers might be necessary. Ask each

Questions to Ask the Bakery

❧

1. May we set an appointment to taste your cakes?
2. What is your most popular design?
3. What are your most popular flavors?
4. May we see pictures of cakes you have made?
5. What size of cake do we need? What is the per-piece cost?
6. When will the cake be made? When will it be decorated?
7. Is there a delivery and setup charge?
8. Do you pick up the cake board and pillars after the reception, or must we return them?

baker what size and how many tiers they suggest for your group. Cakes run an average of $1.65 to $4.00 per serving.

Following are a few ideas to help you trim cake costs. Consider purchasing two cakes: a smaller-tiered, decorated cake at $3 per person to serve about fifty people, and an equally delicious sheet cake at about $1.65 per person to be cut in the back room and served to the rest of the guests.

Another suggestion is to serve the entire cake and not save the top tier. Brides often say they want a piece or a top tier of their cake to eat on their first anniversary and then wind up not doing so a year later. Cakes as a rule don't freeze well for any length of time, but if you really want to save the top tier or just a piece of your cake, we understand that spice and carrot cakes freeze the best.

The Cake Table

THE cake table commands a great deal of attention and should be nicely decorated. Usually it is round and covered with a white or ivory floor-length cloth. Our brides usually have a second cloth, sometimes a square of a contrasting color or another round cloth gathered up in three or four places around the diameter and held in place by bows as shown in Figure 10.2.

Figure 10.2

If you are having a small cake, we suggest the cake be placed on an overturned crate atop the table. A plastic one that holds rental glasses is perfect. Whatever you use, it must be sturdy. Drape a cloth over the crate to create a great raised platform for your cake display. A gold or silver lamé cloth is perfect because it drapes so nicely. One bride used a piece of velvet, which also looked beautiful.

The cake usually has flowers and/or greenery around its base. These same flowers may or may not be used to decorate the cake. Also on the cake table will be your cake-cutting knife or knives. Ribbons around the handle are a nice touch but not necessary. Several of our brides have taken their knives to the florist for both ribbons and flowers to be added. If you will have the toast at the cake table, your toasting goblets could also be on the table. Some couples use their goblets all evening, so they are placed on the head table at the start of the reception. We also suggest a small plate for a damp napkin or other cloth on the table for use after the cutting—your fingers may get sticky from the frosting.

Some photographers put the bride's and bridesmaids' bouquets on the cake table just before the cake cutting. This gives the illusion of flowers everywhere for the pictures.

When cutting the cake, again for pictures, the groom's right hand is placed over the bride's right hand, and the first cut is made. We recently worked with a photographer who had the couple use their left hands so their wedding rings were in the picture. They quickly switched to their right hands for the actual cutting. The first slice (cut from the bottom tier) is placed on a plate. The couple feed each other a piece. Gone are the days of the wedding cake food fight (thank goodness). Several of our couples, after sharing the first piece of cake with each other, have cut more pieces and each presented their new parents-in-law with the first pieces—a very nice touch. The cake is then cut by the catering staff or family friends. On a stacked cake, the bottom tier is cut first and cut in as deep as the next tier, as shown in Figure 10.3. After the bottom layer is completely cut, the next layer up is cut until it is all gone. Then the servers finish cutting the bottom layer. If the tiers on the cake are on risers or pedestals, the top layers are individually removed before the cutting begins.

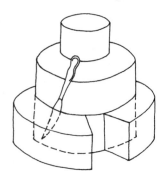

Figure 10.3

Remember to Organize

Create a "Cake" file to hold photos of decorating ideas you like. After you've placed your order, enter your bakery's information on the inside cover of the file, and insert notes about any other agreed-to details, such as delivery time. Record the deposit you gave the bakery on your payment schedule, and note when the final payment is due.

11

INVITATIONS

Asking Friends and Family to Share in Your Special Day

Your invitations will be the first impression your guests receive of your wedding day. Whether you purchase invitations or create your own, they should reflect the style of your wedding. We will take you through the process of determining how many invitations you will need as well as describe various design ideas, the correct wording for all pieces, and inserts to enclose such as maps and accommodation listings.

Guest List

It is time to make your actual guest list. Until now, you might have had an arbitrary number of guests in mind for general planning purposes. Now you need to begin compiling names to determine a more precise number. A general rule of thumb is to allocate 25% of the guest list to the bride, 25% to the groom, and 25% to each of the families. Of course, such neat prioritizing will not work in all instances. For example, if the groom's family lives far from the location of the ceremony, the people from their list might be few. Take your unique situation into account when working this out.

185

We suggest each person involved in determining the guest list create their own list of who they would like to have attend, independent of the others. To facilitate putting this all together, we suggest a card system that several of our clients and we have used successfully. Some computer-savvy couples prefer to compile the guest list on their computer, but our low-tech approach is tried and true, not to mention very portable.

Purchase 3 x 5 cards in four or more differing colors. You will also need a set of 3 x 5 manila dividers and a plastic recipe file box. Give each inviter (i.e., the bride, groom, family of the bride, and family of the groom) cards of a different color to complete, along with a rough idea of how many guests they may invite. If there are remarriages among the parents, perhaps you will also use a fifth or sixth color. Each card will have the names of those invited written at the top. If children are invited, put their names under their parents' names. For engaged couples or couples living together, both must be invited. Add up the total number of guests on each card, and write that number at the top right-hand corner. The card should look something like this:

```
                                                      4

JOHNSON, Mr. and Mrs. Thomas R.
Sarah and Tommy

```

Addresses are not required at this point. After everyone has compiled their own list, put all the cards together in alphabetical order and eliminate any duplications. Count the number in the top right-hand corner for a total of the guests you would all like to include. Is this a manageable amount? If not, it is back to the drawing board. After you have reached a satisfactory number of invitees, each card needs to be completed by adding the full address; a telephone number is also useful but not necessary. Allow plenty of time for this task, as it is sometimes difficult to get current addresses. After the addresses are added, the cards are ready to be filed in alphabetical order in the file box. Create a divider entitled "Invitations." All of the cards should be behind this divider for now. The other dividers should be labeled as follows:

+ Acceptances
+ Regrets
+ Thank you notes to do
+ Thank you notes done

Put these dividers in the back of the box for now. We will discuss them later in the chapter.

Now go through your box and count each 3 × 5 card as one invitation. Don't count the number of guests—count each card. This total will be the number of invitations you will actually send. We suggest you order twenty-five additional invitations. You and the families will want to have extras as mementos, envelopes will invariably be ruined in addressing, and more times than not, someone will be remembered at the last minute. Be sure to send an invitation to the officiant at your ceremony and his or her spouse. Also, any children over the age of eighteen, even if living at home, should receive their own invitation.

Wedding Day Reflections

We had a disposable camera on each reception table and had the snapshots developed. We enclosed some of these shots from the reception in each thank-you note. This was a nice way to share some of the memories of the day.

—Joanne and Mike

CHILDREN AT THE CEREMONY AND RECEPTION

It is important to decide early in your planning whether you will invite children to your wedding and reception. Many brides and grooms struggle with this decision. In some families with a small number of children, there is no question—these children are almost always included. For very large extended families, inviting children could instantly double the guest list; understandably, then, children are often not included in these cases. Some couples don't want children

?

***How do we nicely inform
people that we do not wish
for children to attend
our wedding?***

I*f children are not included on the
inner envelope, guests should realize
that children are not invited. If you
do receive responses of four people
attending when you have invited
only two, it is acceptable to call the
guests and explain to them that you
are unable to include children
because of a limited guest list.*

at the ceremony for fear they will cry or fuss but would like them to attend the reception. In this case, let the parents know that baby-sitting is provided in the church nursery or that a crying room is available. For evening dinners followed by dancing, it probably would not be appropriate to have children attend, as such an event will make for a late evening for them.

As we mention later in this chapter when we present some samples of wording, if the children's names do not appear on the inner envelope, they are not invited. If an invited couple notes on their response card that they are bringing their uninvited children, it is perfectly acceptable to call them and say, "Due to our limited guest list, we are unable to have children attend. I hope you'll be able to make alternate arrangements for them so you can still be with us."

Every Style Imaginable

INVITATIONS come in all shapes, sizes, colors, and designs. The classic card is white or ecru, folded, and printed on the front side. It might be plain or have single, double, or triple panels as borders. If you are using white in your wedding, such as your gown and tablecloths, set the scene with white invitations. If your gown is ivory, you might want to choose a matching shade for your invitations.

In addition to traditional styles, many decorative options are available. Some have embossed flowers or a design framing the wording; others depict a Cinderella-looking castle or a teddy bear bride and groom. The cutesy ones certainly don't suggest an elegant affair and

Making Your Own Invitations

Creating your own invitations truly indulges a boundless imagination. Our clients have come up with the following ideas:

- A very artistic groom painted entwined flowers on a small canvas, then had the canvas color-photocopied on the front of nice card stock. He also handwrote the wording, which was professionally copied on the inside of the invitation.

- One couple hired a calligrapher to write their wording. They then took this text to a printer, who reduced the writing and printed it on paper with a soft floral design in the background. Their colored envelopes picked up a light green in the design.

- The most creative invitation we have seen was very big; in fact, it was so big, we referred to it as the "book": "How is the book coming along?" "Is the book done yet?" Their invitation had a card-stock cover and four inner pages. The first page had the traditional invitation wording, which they created on their computer with a unique font. The second page told about the reception, the third page gave directions to both sites, and the fourth had hotel accommodations. A raffia bow held it all together. Very well done!

are rarely chosen. A fairly new design is invitations with an opaque vellum panel, which are gorgeous but also quite expensive. Another popular style has ribbons attached to the front. One of our couples chose an invitation they really liked, but they didn't like the ribbon as shown. We placed the order without the ribbons and received a 20% discount as a result. The couple then purchased ribbon more to their liking and customized their invitations.

Putting Your Invitations into Words

THE wording of your invitations usually follows some well-established guidelines that respect the nature of your specific family. The following is traditional wording with the parents of the bride extending the invitation:

Mr. and Mrs. Robert Edward Taylor
request the honor of your presence
at the marriage of their daughter
Kimberly Sue
to
Mr. Michael Thomas Ford
on Saturday, the fifth of June
nineteen hundred and ninety-nine
at three o'clock in the afternoon
St. John's Methodist Church
1721 L Street
Davis, California

If the wedding is being held at a home, instead of listing the church say:

at the residence of
Mr. and Mrs. Mark Edward Taylor
324 Meadow Drive
Davis, California

If the wedding is taking place at a location outside a church, instead of the church name simply substitute:

Twelve Oak Park
Main Street
Miami, Florida

When the couple wishes to extend the invitation themselves, follow this format:

Miss Kimberly Sue Taylor
and
Mr. Michael Thomas Ford
request the honor of your presence
at their marriage

A popular alternative to this wording is as follows:

Together with their parents
Kimberly Sue Taylor
and
Michael Thomas Ford
request the honor of your presence
at their marriage

When both the bride's and groom's parents are issuing the invitation, another variation is used:

Mr. and Mrs. Robert Edward Taylor
and
Mr. and Mrs. Thomas James Ford
request the honor of your presence
at the marriage of their children
Kimberly Sue
and
Michael Thomas

Divorced parents issuing the invitation will likely use this wording:

Mrs. Carol Smith Taylor
and
Mr. Robert Edward Taylor
request the honor of your presence
at the marriage of their daughter

The bride's mother and stepfather issuing the invitation calls for this wording:

Mr. and Mrs. James Lawrence Wood
request the honor of your presence
at the marriage of her daughter
Kimberly Sue Taylor

When the bride's father is deceased, follow this guideline:

Mrs. Robert Edward Taylor
requests the honor of your presence
at the marriage of her daughter

For other examples, the front section of almost every large invitation catalog has a number of variations on the accepted wordings for invitations.

Thermography versus Engraving

UNTIL about twenty years ago, your only option for invitations was engraving. Now there is a printing process called thermography that mimics engraved printing at a much-reduced cost. It is also possible to choose from different-colored inks with thermography. Very few of our couples have opted for engraving, given its high cost. Both options have raised print, and only a discerning fingertip can feel the difference on the back of the engraved invitation—it is indented and thermography is not.

Thermographed invitations from the printer arrive with a packet of tissue paper. These were necessary years ago to help keep the invitations from getting smudged when engraving was widely used. They are not necessary with thermographed invitations but are used with them anyway for decoration.

Inking and Lettering Styles

WHEN ordering invitations from a large album, you will see a page in the front with your ink color selection. There is no additional charge for black ink, but there is an additional charge for the other colors (about $6 per batch of invitations, plus $6 for each batch of response cards, etc.). Many companies also offer foil-stamped ink. We do not suggest ordering this ink because it is quite a bit more expensive (approximately $40 additional for 100 invitations) and because it is harder to read due to its shininess.

The invitation catalog will also include several pages with examples of the available lettering styles, or fonts. You may choose anything from a very plain type to a very fancy script. Some of the fonts look very bold when done in black ink. In that case, a good alternative is to choose the gray ink; remember, however, it will be at an additional charge. We suggest you go through the album looking at the lettering styles rather than just looking at the individual letters on the sample page.

Envelope Styles

MOST invitations come with both an inner and an outer envelope. You may choose to have the inner envelope lined with a coordinating color or pattern. These linings run about $20 per 100. We suggest you have your return address imprinted on the back of the outer envelope, even though the additional charge is about $30 per 100. This extra will save you a lot of writing and time.

Reception Cards

IF your ceremony and reception are at the same location, you do not need this card. A simple "Reception immediately following ceremony" on the bottom left of the invitation is sufficient. However, if you are having the reception at a different site, you will need a reception card. We suggest you mention the type of reception you are having, such as "Brunch Reception" or "Dinner and Dance Reception"; your guests will appreciate knowing what to expect. An example is as follows:

Brunch Reception
immediately following ceremony
Grand Island Mansion
2123 Briar Lane
Salt Lake City, UT

Response Cards and Envelopes

IN the past when guests received an invitation to an event, they would send a handwritten response to their hostess with their acceptance or regret. Today, instead of expecting a reply on the guest's initiative, we provide them with small response cards, along with a preaddressed and already stamped envelope, and keep our fingers crossed that they remember to send them back!

The date you specify on the response card coincides with the date you need to know your final count for the food service. Have your "respond by" date be at least a weekend before this final count due date. We can almost guarantee you will need to contact some people who haven't yet responded. Hopefully you will be able to reach them over that weekend and still have an accurate head count in on time. We have had brides say they were so frustrated with not getting their response cards returned, but they also had to admit they themselves had not been careful about returning them in the past.

For a wedding on September 15, the response could read:

Please respond on or before
September 5, 1999

M _____

_____ *accept with pleasure*

_____ *decline with regret*

OR

Kindly respond on or before
September 5, 1999

M _____

_____ *will attend*

_____ *not able to attend*

OR

The favour of a reply is requested
before September 5, 1999

M _____

_____ *accepts* _____ *regrets*

As your response cards are returned, take the 3 × 5 card for that person out of the file box and place it behind the appropriate divider, either "Acceptances" or "Regrets." It is fun to see these sections start to fill.

Informals

INFORMALS are small cards with the couple's names or monogram on the front; they are perfect for thank-you notes for wedding gifts. (Cards with the couple's names or monogram should not be used for thank-you's before the wedding.) They are also handy cards to use during your married life to invite someone for dinner, to thank someone when they have had you as a guest in their home or for a gift, or to just send a thinking-of-you note. Very classy!

Some samples of informals are as follows:

Mr. and Mrs. Michael Thomas Ford

OR

Kim and Mike Ford

OR

K F M

OR

Kimberly F Michael

When you open your wedding gifts after the ceremony, take out the 3 x 5 card of the giver and write on the bottom of the card what gift they gave you. This card can then be put behind the divider that reads "Thank you notes to do." All the information you need such as proper spellings and addresses is right there and easily transportable. You can write several thank-you notes on your lunch hour, for example, and soon the big task of thank-you's doesn't seem so daunting. After the thank-you is sent, put that 3 x 5 card back in the box behind "Thank you notes done." You really feel like you have accomplished something as that category starts filling up.

Announcements

ALTHOUGH not commonly used, announcements are sent to people who are not invited to the wedding but whom you want to inform that you are married. These are mailed the same day as the wedding or within several days afterward; never before the wedding takes place. Sending announcements is quite expensive, because the cost is the same as ordering invitations.

Following are examples of two announcement styles:

Mr. and Mrs. Robert Edward Taylor
announce the marriage
of their daughter
Kimberly Sue
to Mr. Michael Thomas Ford
Saturday, the fifth of June
nineteen hundred and ninety-nine
Denver, Colorado

OR

Mr. and Mrs. Robert Edward Taylor
have the honor of announcing
the marriage of their daughter

Please note that the specific ceremony location is not mentioned on the announcement, just the city and state.

Placing Your Order

PLEASE allow yourself an ample amount of time for both the ordering and the addressing process. To not waste time and money with errors, we suggest you order your invitations from someone who specializes

Wedding Day Reflections

Make your deadline very clear to the printer. The independent printer we originally went to saw from the date on the invitation that our wedding was three months off and moved our order to the low-priority pile. We had purposely ordered early to give ourselves plenty of time to address the envelopes, and they were waiting at his store to have the return address engraved! The two weeks that he sat on our order forced us to have only two weeks to address everything, and we felt rushed.

—Jody and Matthew

in wedding invitations. The young person working part-time at the local specialty card or party supply store probably does not have the knowledge necessary to order invitations properly. A local wedding coordinator might be an excellent source of referrals, and most carry a large range of choices from inexpensive to expensive. Some coordinators let you take the sample books home to browse at your leisure. Look in your Yellow Pages under the "Invitations" heading. Your florist or photographer also might have recommendations. We do not suggest ordering invitations through a mail-order company. The quality of paper is not good from some companies, and we have had to pick up the pieces on several botched orders that a mail-order company would not correct.

Before ordering your invitations, ask whether a discount is available and whether you will be charged a shipping fee. When ordering, have the complete wording correctly typed out (proofread!), including all names, dates, and addresses, to eliminate any problems caused by less than perfect handwriting. Ask for an invoice with the total amount due. Expect to pay half, or perhaps all, of the amount at the time you place your order.

Addressing Envelopes

ENVELOPES should be addressed using no abbreviations except for *Mr., Mrs., Ms.,* or *Dr.* Religious (e.g., *Reverend, Sister, Father*) and military (e.g., *General, Colonel*) titles should be written in full. Between names, write out *and,* as in Dr. *and* Mrs. Do not use *Mr. and Mrs. . . . and family.* Children's names only appear on the inner envelope (if they're invited). An example of an inner envelope when children have not been invited is as follows:

Mr. and Mrs. Jones

An inner envelope when children are included would read:

Mr. and Mrs. Jones
Sarah and Thomas

Only the outer envelope includes the street address after the names. Spell out *Street, Avenue, Boulevard,* and other such terms; all numbers except house numbers; and the name of the state. An example of an addressed outer envelope is as follows:

Mr. and Mrs. Matthew Robert Jones
2123 First Avenue
Spreckels, Ohio 43210

Do not use stickers with your return address. If you didn't order your address printed on the back of the outer envelope, you should write it out by hand. A carefully placed "love" or beautiful floral stamp completes your package. Before buying postage, take a completely assembled set including all enclosures to the post office and have it weighed. You don't want your guests receiving your invitation with postage due. Some odd-shaped envelopes cost more than the standard amount even if they don't weigh more. Don't forget that you also need stamps for your enclosed response envelopes.

?

We would like to invite children to our celebration. How do we address the envelopes?

Only the parents' names appear on the outer envelope. Children's names should then be written on the inner envelope, under the parents' names.

Professionally Speaking

If you are using a professional cal-ligrapher (or a volunteer with nice handwriting), give them one com-plete list of names and addresses that has been typewritten or compu-ter generated. Phoning in changes and updates at a later time definitely slows down the process.

—Sandra Torguson,
calligrapher

Invitations should be mailed six weeks in advance to all guests, or six to eight weeks to out-of-town guests and no less than four weeks to nearby guests. If your wedding is on a holiday weekend or near Thanksgiving, Christmas, or Hanukkah, a call or note to guests well in advance letting them know the date will be appreciated. We suggest mailing your invitation on a Thursday, with your guests hopefully receiving the invita-tion on Saturday. They will have more time to read it on the weekend and will possibly return the response card quickly.

CALLIGRAPHY

Envelopes addressed using calligraphy are beautiful works of art all by themselves. Your guests will be impressed the second they pull the invitation out of their mailbox. Calligraphy is certainly not necessary—just using a calligraphy pen can help make even ordinary writing look pretty. The most important thing is that the writing is neat and legible.

You can hire a calligrapher to address your invitations at a cost of $2 to $3 for both the inner and outer envelopes. Several of our brides, however, have learned this art themselves. Stationery or office-supply stores carry calligraphy pens, and classes are commonly offered through adult education or parks and recreation departments. Libraries and bookstores also carry books on this subject for self-instruction. Consider calligraphy as another simple touch lending elegance to your wedding.

Other Invitation Inserts

Maps are a big help to people unfamiliar with the locations of your ceremony and reception. The least expensive way to prepare these is to make them yourself on a computer. Another option is to take a sketch of what you want included to a print shop that has a map-making computer program. Also bring one of your invitations to match the color of the paper stock you choose; please don't include a plain white map with a beautiful invitation in ecru. A nice touch for out-of-town guests is to have names of convenient hotels both shown on the map and listed on the reverse side with addresses and telephone numbers (preferably a toll-free number) for ease in making reservations. In chapter 14, "Details, Details, Details," we will discuss reserving a block of rooms for your guests.

SHARON AND JERRY'S STORY

Instead of a map, Sharon and Jerry wrote out very detailed directions to a very hard-to-find location. The directions told guests to follow a road for 2.3 miles and take a hard right, then go 1.4 miles to a drawbridge, then left at the first driveway, and so forth. On the reverse side of the directions, they described the mansion where the festivities would take place: it was built in 1917 by so-and-so, it was 20,000 square feet with fifty-eight rooms, and more. They mentioned what events had transpired there over the years and even listed notables who had visited in recent years. After reading this enticing description, the invitees were looking forward to being guests there, too.

One thing that should *not* be included as an insert in your invitation is a list of stores where you are registered. Let family and close friends know personally where you have registered, and they can pass this information on to guests who might inquire.

Programs and Napkins

ALTHOUGH you can order other wedding-related printed material from the same sample catalogs as your invitations, we suggest you use other more economical options. For example, you can prepare your own programs and have them printed at a local print shop, which allows you to customize them and costs less, too. Again, choose a paper stock that will match your invitations and maps. We discuss programs in detail and offer several samples in chapter 13, "A Personalized Ceremony."

Unless you really want your names and the date on your beverage and luncheon napkins, we suggest you simply buy plain napkins at a party supply store. Take a sample of the colors you are using in your wedding to match or coordinate. For drinks or hors d'oeuvres, plan on at least three napkins per guest.

Regret Notices

OCCASIONALLY it is necessary to postpone or cancel a wedding. Last-minute cancellations require telephone calls. If there is time, you can have notifications printed.

If the wedding is postponed, it is customary to give an explanation—for example:

Mr. and Mrs. Robert Edward Taylor
regret that owing to the illness of their daughter
Kimberly Sue
they are obliged to recall invitations to her wedding
to Mr. Michael Thomas Ford

OR

Mr. and Mrs. Robert Edward Taylor
regret that they are obliged to recall the

invitation to the marriage of their daughter
Kimberly Sue

to

Mr. Michael Thomas Ford
owing to the recent death of Mr. Ford's father
Mr. Thomas James Ford

If the engagement is broken, a very brief statement can be made:

Mr. and Mrs. Robert Edward Taylor

announce that the marriage of their daughter
Kimberly Sue

to

Mr. Michael Thomas Ford

will not take place

A friend recently received a variation of this notice that read:

Dear Family and Friends,
This is to inform you, that by mutual consent,
the marriage of _____ and _____
will not take place.
We regret any inconvenience this may cause you.
Sincerely,
[signed by both sets of parents]

Remember to Organize

CREATE a file called "Invitations." Record the dollars paid and still due on your payment schedule. Keep copies of the information you have given when ordering the invitations to check for errors.

12

TRANSPORTATION

ARRIVING IN STYLE AND ON TIME

Get me to the church on time! That old song sums it up. When planning your means of transportation, you want everyone to be where they are supposed to be at the correct time. Arranging transportation is a very important part of your planning. Once again, organization is key. The final details can be worked out after you have prepared a schedule for your wedding day, but before that, determine how many people need transportation, where they need to be picked up, and where they need to go.

The least expensive transportation is to have a friend or family member who is not in the wedding party act as a chauffeur. This way those involved in the wedding do not have to worry about the traffic and parking. One of our grooms had two cousins and two friends drive the wedding party around in family cars. On the day before the wedding, the four guys washed the cars and vacuumed the interiors. They wore black pants and white shirts on Saturday, looking quite professional and acting the part. They took the wedding party to the church and then from the church to the reception. All four of them joined the friends and family at the reception.

This example illustrates an inexpensive way to provide rides for the wedding party. We discuss other options in this chapter as well.

Limousines

IF it will fit into your budget, hiring a limousine adds an elegant element to your day. Stretch limousines can carry up to ten people. Before looking at cars, determine the maximum number of people who will need transportation at one time. If there isn't much of a distance between point A and point B, it is very feasible to have a limousine make multiple trips.

When you know the size of the car you need, make some calls and get an idea of the costs and required minimum rental time. Ask friends and wedding professionals who they feel is a good, reliable limousine company. Don't let price be your only required standard—choose a company with an impeccable reputation. We have found hourly rates to average $50 to $75, but they vary depending on the size, year, and make of the limousines. Most companies require a two- to three-hour minimum.

If the quote seems within your budget, make arrangements to visit and see the actual vehicle you are renting. While there, ask to see their TCP license and certificate of insurance. If they can't or won't produce these, do not use that company. More than likely, they do not have the proper authorization to transport people. The company you choose will prepare a contract and

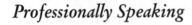

Professionally Speaking

In finding a reputable limousine company, look past the Yellow Page ads. Go to the company and look at their cars. Some companies boast of cars they actually don't have, and some have one or two newer cars and the rest are considerably older. Look at the license plate. In California it should have "Livery" printed across the bottom in red. Also, a good idea is to call the Public Utilities Commission, which oversees the limousine industry. The PUC can verify the validity of their operating permit (TCP number). Limousine companies do get revoked for violations, such as nonpayment of insurance.

—Rick English,
director of operations,
Carey Limousines

require a deposit or credit card number to reserve the date. Inquire what form of payment they will accept. Most transportation companies we have worked with won't accept personal checks close to the date of your wedding. When making the reservation, also approximate the start time and duration of rental for the limo. As soon as you know your actual schedule, send the company a letter with the specifics and then follow up with a phone call approximately ten days before your wedding day. Finally, limousine drivers receive a gratuity of 15% to 20%, so figure that into your total cost. When making your final payment, usually by credit card on the day of the wedding, you can include the tip at that time so no one will need to worry about cash.

Other Transportation Options

TRANSPORTATION choices are not limited to limousines. By far the most popular for our couples has been a horse and carriage; it lends an aura of romantic times gone by as it pulls away with the horse's slow clip-clopping. A carriage taking the bride and groom from the church to the reception is also a wonderful opportunity for the couple to have some time all to themselves and be able to talk and savor their day. Our clients have made "Just Married" signs to be attached to the carriages and of course have adorned the horse's leather tack with flowers and bows. Several brides have even provided carrots for their steeds, which have been happily devoured.

The next favorite mode of transportation has been antique cars. While we feel it is best to go with a professional company, one of our grooms located an antique car

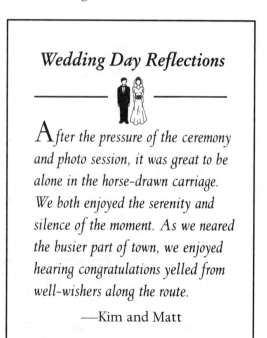

Wedding Day Reflections

After the pressure of the ceremony and photo session, it was great to be alone in the horse-drawn carriage. We both enjoyed the serenity and silence of the moment. As we neared the busier part of town, we enjoyed hearing congratulations yelled from well-wishers along the route.

—Kim and Matt

Making a Transportation Schedule

❧

We recently worked out a schedule for a limousine that was hired for six hours. The limo picked up the bridesmaids at the bride's home prior to their hair appointment, transported everyone to the wedding, and finished up by taking the bride and groom from the church to the reception. Everyone had previously left cars at the reception location for their own transportation at the end of the festivities. This schedule is presented here as an example for you:

9:30 A.M.	Pick up four bridesmaids and bride at bride's home 231 Hidden Lane
10:00 A.M.	Drop off at hair appointments Wendelyn's Hair Boutique, 2242 South Avenue
12:00 P.M.	Take bridesmaids and bride to church to dress St. John's, 1721 L Street
12:30 P.M.	Pick up bride's parents at their home and take to church 231 Hidden Lane to 1721 L Street
1:00 P.M.	Pick up groom's parents at hotel and take to church Hyatt at 630 L Street to 1721 L Street
2:00 P.M.	Ceremony
3:00 P.M.	After family pictures at altar, take both sets of parents to reception Clubhouse at McKinley Park, 2340 McKinley Boulevard
3:15 P.M.	Return to church—after pictures of couple with attendants, take bride and groom to reception. (The bridesmaids rode with groomsmen to reception.)
3:30 P.M.	Finished with limo.

club by calling an auto parts store that only sells parts for older model Fords. The store gave him the names of several of their customers whom he contacted. These car owners were pleased to do it, as they love taking their cars out—and enjoyed making some extra money.

PAM AND COLIN'S STORY

A dear friend of Pam's family, who just happened to be the proud restorer of a 1933 Bentley, asked if he could drive for Pam and Colin on their wedding day as his gift. He had known Pam since she was four years old and felt like her pseudo-grandfather. He took Pam and her father to the ceremony, and then the bride and groom to the reception. He was all dressed up in a 1930s-style suit complete with a chauffeur's hat, and enjoyed playing the part.

Several couples have rented vintage Rolls-Royce sedans from the late 1950s. We found these cars by calling the concierge's desk at a local hotel. Concierges often procure transportation for hotel guests and are happy to share the names and numbers of people they work with. Following are some amusing yet romantic examples of couples' different means of transportation.

The big red fire engine cruised through the intersection and then, with siren blasting, circled around the park reception site. The just married bride and groom had hopped on the back running board to depart the reception. The engine turned back to let the guests get one more glimpse of the couple as they held onto the back bar with one hand and waved happily to their guests with the other. The groom organized this great getaway plan through the local fire department where he worked. The department agreed to allow their extra engine to be used that afternoon. As you can imagine, the pictures were priceless.

We have coordinated several weddings for cycling enthusiasts, too.

One groom fixed up a rickshaw-type bike. One of his teammates dressed in a tuxedo jacket and wore cycling shorts. He pedaled the bike while the couple rode in the rickshaw from the ceremony to the reception. Rain had threatened the entire day, but the sun actually peeked through for their trip.

Another couple decided to leave their reception on a bicycle built for two. The bike was hidden behind a building, so their means of exiting was a real surprise. At the end of the reception, the couple stood at the front of the dance floor and did a quick change. The bride slipped off the skirt of her dress, which had been specially made with hooks for detachment, and modeled her white cycling shorts on underneath. At the same time, the groom took off his tuxedo pants to reveal his black cycling shorts. The best man wheeled the tandem bike around front, and the couple rode off with her short veil blowing in the wind. There were many whoops and hollers from the guests. The couple was delighted they had pulled off a really great surprise.

Beth and Jeff left their reception on a boat. A friend of our family had a ski boat and was asked to help out. The boat was decorated with bows in the wedding colors and moored at the mansion's river dock but was out of sight of guests. Jeff had told Beth early in their planning stages that he wanted to leave the reception in a unique way and in a casual outfit. One day while we were shopping, we happened upon the perfect going-away outfit for Beth: a sailor suit. The outfit was navy, complete with a middy collar and skorts. In keeping with the nautical theme, we found Jeff a navy and white horizontal striped cotton knit shirt, and we let him wear his khaki shorts. Their outfits were darling, and they looked like they were ready to swab a deck! They surprised all the guests by leaving on the boat. The guests stood, waving from the levee, and a few of them promptly broke into the theme from *Gilligan's Island*.

Parking Options

ADEQUATE parking for your guests at both the ceremony and reception is a must. If a parking garage or other location is available, a note on the map enclosed with the invitation is a good place to mention this.

We have had couples who have thoughtfully prepaid their guests' parking fees in a garage. Toward the reception's end, parking vouchers were handed out to the guests, and the guests in turn presented them to the attendant when exiting the garage.

If parking is awkward, offering valet parking is most helpful to guests. Companies offer this service and will work at your location. We have also had one reception in which young men who were family friends of driving age served as valet parkers. They waited for a car to pull up, offered to park the car, asked the car's driver to wait a moment, and then returned the keys to the driver immediately. This method of service alleviated any chance of keys getting mixed up since we were dealing with nonprofessional valets. The guests then retrieved their own cars from the parking area after the reception. The parkers knew several Jaguars and Porches were coming, and each hoped he would be the one to park those cars. This was a fun touch for the guests and even more fun for the young volunteers!

?

Do we need to provide transportation for our attendants?

You *do not need to rent a limousine; however, if you have out-of-town attendants, arrange a way for them to get from their lodging to the festivities and back again.*

Providing Maps

As we briefly mentioned, providing maps for your guests is very helpful (see also chapter 11, "Invitations," under the heading Other Invitation Inserts). Drive the route several times yourself from all

?

There are only two miles between the church and the reception site. Is it okay to reserve a smaller limousine and ask the driver to make a few trips?

Y*es. There is often a significant price difference between smaller and larger vehicles. It is better to utilize the limousine instead of paying for it to be parked somewhere. Let the company know your plans ahead of time. For example, if you are having photos taken of the families and bridal party immediately after the ceremony and you wish to have family members and the bridal party shuttled to the reception (an especially good idea if parking at the reception location is at a premium), simply let everyone involved know that this shuttle service is available to them. They should proceed directly to the limousine after their pictures are taken.*

directions, and determine the easiest way to have your guests travel. Pay close attention to exactly what the road signs say. Don't necessarily have guests go the fastest way or your own usual way but rather the easiest route for people unfamiliar with the area. Show freeway off ramps and one-way streets, if applicable.

Noting parking locations on the map is important. A simple "Parking Available at Back of Church" can save a frustrated guest from driving around the block ten times looking for a parking spot to appear. It also is helpful to note driving times if your locations are somewhat remote. A note saying "Allow an Hour and a Half Driving Time from City" on the map can save you from having very tardy and embarrassed guests.

Remember to Organize

AFTER you have decided on your transportation needs, start a "Transportation" file with any contracts and notes you have taken. Record any deposits made and dollars due on your payment schedule. Include a copy of your wedding-day schedule for the limousine driver, or, if you have a volunteer chauffeur, write a letter outlining the date, times, and locations. This will lessen the chance of any misunderstandings. Follow up closer to your date with any changes and to reconfirm all details.

13

A PERSONALIZED CEREMONY

INDIVIDUALIZING THE WEDDING RITUAL

Although all marriage ceremonies share many similarities, each has its own unique qualities that reflect your personal tastes, values, and beliefs. Take the time to ensure your ceremony reflects *you*. The vows you take reflect the seriousness of the commitment you are making to each other and should not be taken lightly.

Religious Ceremony

If you are being married in a religious ceremony, you will meet with the priest, pastor, or rabbi during your course of planning. You may have some requirements to fulfill such as premarital classes, counseling sessions, or Engagement Encounter weekends. At a meeting with your clergy or perhaps at a class, the various parts of the ceremony will be discussed. The specific elements of the ceremony will vary with each religion and even with each clergyperson. Your wedding may include the words "dearly beloved" found at the beginning of a Protestant ceremony, or the "giving of gifts" included in a Nuptial Mass in a Catholic church, or the ritual of crushing the wineglass at the end of a Jewish ceremony. Whatever is included will serve to make your ceremony very special to you.

Interfaith Ceremony

IF you and your fiancé are of different religions, you may be able to combine the rituals inherent to each and have clergy representing both faiths involved in your ceremony. Such a ceremony takes more time to arrange, but many clergy are willing to take part in this type of service. Your efforts can make for a unique ceremony that will have a lot of meaning for both you and your groom.

JENNY AND TRENT'S STORY

Several years ago we coordinated an interfaith ceremony performed by a Protestant minister and a Jewish rabbi. Very few rabbis will do this, by the way, but this rabbi was associated with the Reform Jewish Outreach at the Union of American Hebrew Congregations. (For referrals to rabbis who participate in interfaith ceremonies, see the Appendix.) The rabbi asked both the bride and the groom to write a letter to him and the minister that included humorous or moving moments throughout their relationship; traits and values each admired in the other; and special tributes to family members and friends who have been especially supportive in their relationship. They were asked to indicate whether there were portions of the letter they did not want read aloud and shared with their guests during the ceremony. Otherwise, the officiants would use their own discretion. The two men alternated reading parts of the letters, and it was wonderful. Their guests and we enjoyed hearing about their courtship and their dreams for their life together. These letters became a touching feature of the ceremony.

Civil Ceremony

A CIVIL ceremony is defined as a ceremony officiated by someone who is not representing a formal religious faith. Most often a judge fills this role. When choosing a civil ceremony, you have great leeway in styles. You may opt to be married by a civil servant at the same location where you get your marriage license, but you also can have a civil ceremony in many beautiful locations.

Some of the most touching weddings we have been involved with are civil ceremonies. The following is a sample ceremony that a judge, whom we frequently hire, gives to his couples as a possibility for their vows. We both feel it is simply lovely.

Family and Friends
We are gathered together in the presence of these witnesses to join _____ and _____ in matrimony. Marriage is an honorable estate and therefore is not to be entered into lightly or unadvisedly, but discreetly, soberly, and with love.

Your wedding is a beautiful beginning to a lifetime of love. It is two radiant people so deeply in love beginning a future they are both dreaming of. It is family and friends gathering to share in the glad celebration of two hearts that care. It is the making of vows, the rings and the kiss; it's a beautiful service; and yet, more than this, it is a promise fulfilled, a dream that's come true, and the first happy step in a life shared by two. It is a time to be treasured the rest of your life; it's that wonderful moment you become husband and wife.

A good marriage must be created. In the art of marriage, the little things are the big things.

It is never being too old to hold hands.

It is remembering to say, "I love you" at least once each day.

It is never going to sleep angry.

It is having a mutual sense of values and common objectives; it is standing together facing the world.

It is forming a circle of love that gathers in the whole family.

It is speaking words of appreciation and demonstrating gratitude in thoughtful ways.

It is having the capacity to forgive and forget.

It is giving each other an atmosphere in which each can grow.

It is finding room for the things of the spirit.

It is a common search for the good and the beautiful.

It is not only marrying the right partner, it is being the right partner.

Remember that love and loyalty are the foundation on which a happy home is built. If the solemn vows that you are about to accept are kept, and if you steadfastly endeavor to lead honorable and worthwhile lives, the home that you establish will abide in peace and the marriage will be lasting.

No other human ties are more tender, or vows more sacred, than those that you are now about to assume.

Please join hands and face one another.

Will you _____ have _____ to be your wife, to love, honor, and cherish her so long as you both shall live?

Will you _____ have _____ to be your husband, to love, honor, and cherish him so long as you both shall live?

Place the ring on her/his finger and repeat these words after me:

With this ring as a token of my faith and as a symbol of my love, I take you as my wife/husband.

The ring is a symbol of your marriage, symbolic of the fact that you have this day pledged yourselves in marriage, and as the ring is a perfect circle without end, it is the wish and hope of all that your marriage will be perfect and will be without end.

And now, inasmuch as _____ and _____ have consented together in wedlock and have witnessed the same before these witnesses, and thereto have pledged their troth, each to the other, and have declared the same by joining hands, and in the giving of rings, by virtue of the authority invested in me, I now pronounce you husband and wife. You may kiss the bride.

Ladies and gentlemen, I proudly present to you Mr. and Mrs. _____.

Writing Your Own Vows

WRITING your own vows makes a ceremony uniquely your own. We recently helped with a wedding where the couple wrote their own individual vows and did not share what each had written in advance. While the groom was reciting his part, he mentioned why the bride was so special to him and she broke down crying. The ceremony came to a halt while she collected herself, and then everything continued. We aren't suggesting you make each other cry, but this example shows how very personal and touching composing your own vows can be.

If you are writing your vows to each other, allow time to research, write, rewrite, and memorize. In the appendix we list some books that our couples have referred to when writing their vows or incorporating customs from varying religions. Again, reciting vows is a very important part of your ceremony, and you should take the time to give this much thought. Don't wait until the week before!

> **?**
>
> ### *Can we personalize our ceremony?*
>
> *This decision is between you and your officiant. You may choose to write your own vows, select readings, incorporate a unity candle, or make a presentation of flowers to the mothers. The appendix lists books to help you with these choices.*

Specific Details

ALL ceremonies necessitate decisions about items you wish to be included or not. Many points arise, but the most controversial point from several years back was "Do I have to say 'obey' in the ceremony?" The word *obey* seems now to have been stricken from ceremonies and is no longer an issue. Today the biggest question is "I have lived away from home for eight years. Does my father still have to 'give me away'?" Some churches are omitting the question "Who gives this woman to be married to this man?" and are instead posing a question to the families of the couple. At a recent wedding, for example, the minister asked, "Will you give your blessing to _____ and _____ in their new relationship? Will you support them with the love and freedom they need? Will you share your experience and wisdom with them as they seek it, as you learn from them as well?" The parents responded, "We will."

Readings

A POPULAR part of many ceremonies is the reading. Readings can be delivered by the officiant, but are more commonly read by friends or relatives. For religious ceremonies our couples often choose 1 Corinthians 13: 1–13: "Love is patient and kind; love is not jealous or boastful; it is not arrogant or rude. Love does not insist on its own way; it is not irritable or resentful; it does not rejoice at wrong, but rejoices in the right. Love bears all things, believes all things, hopes all things, endures all things. Love never ends." For couples who do not want to have any religious references in their ceremony, they have instead selected beautiful love poems or, in several cases, words to a song they both liked.

Wedding Day Reflections

We wanted the congregation to have a feeling of community and being involved in the ceremony, so various guests read readings from their seats in the pews.

—Suzanne and Russell

Choosing Music

As we suggested in chapter 7, "Music," listen to several albums to help you with your music choices. After you have some idea of what you both like, make an appointment with your church organist or musicians to decide on your ceremony music. They may suggest some additional music that they feel worked well at other ceremonies.

Meeting with musicians and soloists early allows you the opportunity to see and hear them perform before booking them.

Wedding Traditions

DIFFERENT religions, nationalities, and ethnic groups have special rituals that are part of their wedding ceremonies. A Protestant wedding often includes the recitation of the Lord's Prayer. Another example is instead of a bouquet, occasionally a bride will carry a family Bible that her mother or a grandmother had carried.

A Catholic wedding often entails many rituals. A presentation of gifts (wine and the host) precedes communion. If the couple wishes, they may place the bride's bouquet (or a specially prepared one) at the statue of Mary while prayers are being said. We have had several Catholic weddings with families of Hispanic ancestry in which *arras* were given. *Arras* are gold coins, and the groom gives thirteen of them to his bride as a symbol of his love and commitment to ensure that their household never goes without necessities. These same weddings included a *lasso,* which is a cord that represents the unification of two into one in the sight of God. The *lasso* was placed over the couple's heads by their mothers as an outward display of their blessing on the marriages.

In both Protestant and Catholic ceremonies, quite a few of our couples choose to have a unity candle during their service. The unity candle ceremony involves the bride and groom lighting one large candle together with two smaller ones to signify their new life as one. Often the two tapers are lit along with other candles before the service starts. Occasionally, the mothers of the bride and groom will each light a taper just before the processional begins. See chapter 9, "Decorations," for tips about purchasing and decorating the unity candle.

We recently suggested a beautiful alternative to a unity candle at an outdoor ceremony. Both mothers were escorted down the aisle at the beginning of the ceremony carrying a single rose. At a given time in the ceremony, both sets of parents went forward with the rose. The bride's parents gave their rose to the groom, and the groom's parents gave theirs to the bride. Much hugging and a few tears signified that each was welcomed into the other's family. The parents returned to their seats, and the couple turned, placing the two roses into one vase. The unity theme was the same, and the roses made a good alternative to trying to keep candles lit outside.

Jewish ceremonies include a variation of the unity candle. At the beginning of the ceremony two candles are lit either by the bride and groom, by their mothers, or by other family members or friends. After the candles are lit, a blessing in Hebrew is given: "We give thanks to the Source of Life, in Whose Presence we kindle these Lights of Joy." Later in the ceremony, after the vow and ring exchange, these candles are used to light the Candle of Union, a braided candle called a Havdalah Candle. A blessing is again given: "We give thanks to the Source of Life in Whose Presence we kindle this Light of Union." Also part of a Jewish ceremony is the couple sharing wine (or grape juice) from one glass. This same glass is then placed in a bag (to contain the broken glass) and is stepped on by the groom at the end of the ceremony.

Wedding Day Reflections

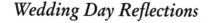

We are so glad we had a unity candle. Each year on our anniversary we have a quiet dinner and light our candle. It is romantic and a nice remembrance of our special day.

—Shannah and John

Several of our couples, at the conclusion of their ceremonies, have stopped where their parents were seated. They have taken two flowers from the bride's bouquet and presented one to the bride's mother and then one to the groom's mother before proceeding down the aisle. This special touch was unexpected by the mothers and was a very nice symbol of thanks.

At the end of several outdoor weddings, our couples have chosen to release two doves (which were actually white homing pigeons)—a very pretty sight. Another couple and their attendants released butterflies at the end of their reception. Again, this was a colorful and unexpected touch. Lovely!

After your ceremony is planned, make a list of any special items you will need to get together. Review these items with your officiant so that nothing is accidentally omitted.

Programs for Ceremonies

A NUMBER of our couples choose to offer their guests programs that describe the order of the service, the music, and any readings they have chosen. If your guests will be asked to participate in prayers, it would be helpful to have these passages appear. Some couples include the names of their attendants and, in some cases, their relationship to them and a little about each person. If you plan on having readers or guest book attendants, it is nice to mention their names also. Some couples add the history of the church or ceremony location, and invariably the couple thanks their parents and those who have helped put the day together, such as their "coordinators" or any other volunteers. Also included could be a message to the guests, such as "To our guests: thank you for sharing this happy day with us." Although programs are certainly not necessary, they are a very nice token showing all the thought that has gone into the ceremony. Guests enjoy reading them after they are seated and waiting for the ceremony to start. They also make great fans if the day is warm!

> **?**
>
> *We want to have a program for the ceremony. What do we put in it?*
>
> The main part of your program should be the order of your ceremony. It is nice to include your musical selections for the processional and recessional as well as readings. The names of your attendants are a popular addition, too.

Once you know what you want included, we suggest you do the layout yourself on a computer to save a printer's hefty "typeset" charge. Take your layout to a print shop along with your invitation so you can match up shades of paper. These businesses also have books of clip art you can choose to decorate your cover. Several of our couples have used a rendering of their church (perhaps what is used on the Sunday bulletin). Many couples have their invitation reprinted on the cover of their program.

Rather than having your programs printed, compare the cost to have your text photocopied. Print shops usually have large, high-quality copy machines, and you really can't tell the difference between copying and printing. Several of our couples have used their own personal printer. If you choose card stock (heavy paper), it will need to be scored before it can be folded, which makes it more expensive than lighter paper (approximately 12 weight). With the lighter paper, especially if you use a bold font, it is possible for your print to show through from the other side. Ask the printer to see a sample before you approve an order.

Because we are asked repeatedly for suggestions for programs, we are providing samples of actual programs our clients have created.

This ceremony was held at a Catholic church:

THE CEREMONY

Presider—The Right Reverend _____

Prelude	Preceremony Medley
Seating of the Family	Canon in D, by Pachelbel
Processional	"Jesu, Joy of Man's Desiring," by J. S. Bach
Bride's Processional	"The Prince of Denmark's March," by Clarke
Opening Prayer	
First Reading	Tobit 8: 4–9
Responsorial Psalm	Psalm 145: 8–9, 10, 15, 17-18 "The Lord Is Compassionate"
Second Reading	Romans 12: 1–2, 9–18
Gospel	John 15: 12–16
Homily	

Prayer of the Faithful
Exchange of Vows
Blessing and Exchange of Rings
Lighting of the Unity Candle "Just the Way You Are," Ayre,
           by Purcell

Final Blessing
Recessional   "Trumpet Tune," by Purcell

This program was for a nuptial mass with communion:

WEDDING CEREMONY

Seating of Mothers   "Ave Maria," by J.S. Bach/
           Gounod

Processional
 Wedding Party   Canon in D, by Pachelbel
 Entrance of Bride   "Bridal March Chorus," by
           Wagner

Lighting of Parents' Candle "How Beautiful," by Paris
Liturgy of the Word
 First Reading   Genesis 2: 18–24
 Responsorial Psalm "On Eagle's Wings," by Joncas
 Second Reading   I Corinthians, 12: 31–13: 13
Gospel Acclamation   Celtic
Gospel Reading   John, 15: 9–12
Rite of Marriage
 Vows of Marriage
 Blessing & Exchanging of Rings
 Lighting of Unity Candle "One Hand, One Heart,"
           by Bernstein

Presentation of the Gifts "In This Very Room," by
           Harris

Communion   "How Beautiful," by Paris
Recessional   "Wedding March," by
           Mendelssohn

Another Catholic wedding in which coins and a cord were part of the ceremony used the following program:

THE WEDDING CEREMONY

Entrance of Mothers	"Jesu, Joy of Man's Desiring," J. S. Bach
Processional	Canon in D, by Pachelbel
Entrance of Bride and Father	"The Prince of Denmark's March," by Clarke
Opening Prayer	Father _____, Officiant

LITURGY OF THE WORD

First Reading	The Treasure of Love, read by _____
Responsorial Psalm	Psalm 148: 1–2, 3–4, 9–10, 11–12ab, 13c–14a (response is "Alleluia")
Second Reading	Colossians 3: 12–17 read by _____
Homily	

RITE OF MARRIAGE

Exchange of Vows	
Parents' Consent	
Blessing and Exchange of Rings	
Unity Candle	
Coins	presented by _____
Cord	sponsored by _____
Final Blessing	
Recessional	Finale from *Water Music,* by George Frideric Handel

The next program is from a Protestant ceremony:

The Marriage Celebration

Lighting of the Candles
(names of two lighters)

Processional
"Air," by Handel
"Trumpet Tune," by Henry Purcell

Gathering Prayer
Reverend _____

1st Reading
(name of reader)

2nd Reading
(name of reader)

"All I Ask of You," by Webber

Exchange of Vows

Exchange of Rings

Lighting of Unity Candle
"Love Is the Sunlite," by Busarow

Prayer of Blessing

Pronouncement

Final Benediction

Recessional
Trumpet Voluntary, by Clarke

"Wedding March," by Mendelssohn

Another Protestant ceremony, in the same church but with a different officiant, used this program:

THE WEDDING CELEBRATION

Prelude
Seating of Grandparents
Seating of Groom's Parents
Seating of Bride's Mother
Lighting of Parents' Candles
Processional of Wedding Party
Processional of Bride
Order of Marriage
    The Gathering
    A Prayer for the Bride and Groom
    Scripture Reading—I Corinthians 13: 1–13
    The Pledge of Intention
    The Vows
    The Exchange of Rings
    The Pronouncement of Marriage
The Lord's Prayer
Lighting of the Unity Candle
The Benediction
Introduction of Mr. and Mrs. _____
Recessional

The following is the program for a civil ceremony performed by a judge:

THE WEDDING CEREMONY

Prelude

Seating of Groom's Grandmother

Seating of Groom's Parents

Seating of Bride's Mother

Processional
Lèvres (Gustavson)

Entrance of Bride and Father
Liebestraum No. 3 (Liszt)

Welcome
Judge _____

Reading
(name of reader)

Ceremony

Exchange of Vows

Exchange of Rings

Pronouncement

Introduction of Mr. and Mrs. _____

Recessional
Wedding March (Mendelssohn)

Any format is possible. Some of our couples have used legal-size paper (8½ × 14) and made trifolds. Several have had a lot to share with their guests and ended up with multiple pages, fastened together with staples at the fold or ribbons.

Remember, programs take a great deal of time to put together, but, fortunately, this is a task you can do way in advance. As soon as you know the order of your ceremony and have chosen your music, you should start. We do not suggest you leave this until the last minute. We have been to quite a few rehearsals in which the groom has come running up with programs "hot off the press."

14

DETAILS, DETAILS, DETAILS

TYING THE LOOSE ENDS TOGETHER FOR A FUN AND ORGANIZED WEDDING DAY

THIS CHAPTER DESCRIBES a myriad of details—some seeming very mundane and others very important—that need to be addressed in putting together a wedding. Of course, not every wedding will need everything we mention. The biggest suggestion we would make is not to let these details overwhelm you. Tackle each job efficiently, and don't leave details to the last minute, which is what really triggers pre-wedding stress.

Also, don't be shy in asking for help: use a professional coordinator or volunteer and/or a couple of hired hands to ease the load. In this chapter we also discuss at length how these helpful people can handle various details to assure a smooth-running and enjoyable wedding day. Note we do not say "perfect," since no wedding comes without a little glitch here or there. We simply strive to keep those little glitches insignificant trifles, not huge disasters.

Using a Coordinator (or Two)

As we have stressed throughout our book, we feel very strongly that on your wedding day, you should have only two things to think about: getting married and enjoying yourselves. If you have organized your day well, the details can be turned over to others, and you can feel confident that everything will run smoothly. We suggest you ask one or even better, two people to coordinate your ceremony and reception.

A staff person at your ceremony site might tell you, "You don't need any help. We have a lady who will get everyone down the aisle." That lady, however, is only concerned about dripless candles and giving the organist the cues. Similarly, the manager at your reception location or even the DJ might insist, "We take care of everything." This is not always the case. We recently arrived at a reception location to find the florist standing around waiting for the cake to be delivered. The staff at this reception hall knew nothing about the cake. We made a quick call to the bakery and were told the cake had already been delivered that morning to the reception hall. The crew that worked earlier in the day had taken delivery of the cake and refrigerated it, but they neglected to let the evening staff know of its whereabouts. No one was taking the initiative to solve the problem. And what help would the DJ have been in this case? This is a perfect example of why all couples should request the assistance of a coordinator for the day.

As we said at the start of this chapter, things can go wrong even with the most perfectly planned day. Weddings, like life itself, are rarely predictable. We have heard about or witnessed almost everything. We have patched bald spots on cakes where the summer heat caused the frosting to run off the cake. We have taken our canine ring bearer for a last-minute rest stop before it was his turn to go down the aisle. We have righted fallen topiaries and rearranged floral arrangements. We have carried Kleenex and decongestant for a groomsman with a cold. We have doctored a ring bearer who scuffed his knees after falling outside the church. We have used our cellular phone to give a lost vendor last-minute directions. We have mended the hem for a mother of a bride when the back of her dress caught on her shoes as she got out of a car. We have even run after a limousine that was circling the block because the maid of honor had left the groom's ring inside. None of these things were planned or on anyone's list of things to do. They just needed to be handled, and a coordinator is the perfect person for such a job.

HOW TO CHOOSE YOUR COORDINATOR

Who is the ideal person? Most important, your coordinator should be someone who has a real interest in you and your wedding, such as a sister or best friend. If the person is a volunteer whom otherwise wouldn't be invited to your wedding (i.e., not a relative or close friend), you should include him or her on your guest list now. It helps if they are organized and energetic by nature, and they should be willing to take on responsibility—no shrinking violets! A person who's married and has gone through the wedding process him- or herself is useful (but not necessary), since such a coordinator might anticipate small, necessary details based on their own experience that you hadn't foreseen.

> ### Wedding Day Reflections
>
> We are really glad that we asked for help. It made the wedding extra special because friends chipped in to assist. For example, it ended up being very hot on our wedding day, and we called someone at noon before our 4:00 P.M. ceremony to ask them if they could rent some industrial fans for the reception tent. This definitely made a big difference in the temperature, and they were happy to help.
>
> —Pam and Rick

The person or persons you have chosen to be your coordinator should be aware of the whole picture—not just the flowers (that is the florist's responsibility), not just the cake (the bakery will handle it), not just the ceremony music (the organist knows the music), but the whole picture. The coordinators are taking on a great deal of responsibility. It is not desirable or even fair to ask them to also do any decorating or table setting and so forth. They need to be free to take charge of the entire day and address unforeseen things that will come up. That is why we feel a coordinator should be a take-charge person, someone who is up for a challenge.

TWO IS BETTER THAN ONE

We suggest that you use two coordinators. One person can handle everything, but it is a very long day for them. If you have two volunteers, one can coordinate the ceremony and the other handle the reception, or they can work throughout the entire wedding as a team, as we do.

PREPPING THE COORDINATORS FOR THEIR BIG DAY

Set aside some time to meet with your coordinators, giving each a copy of the vendor list (discussed later) and a schedule for the day (described in the next chapter). Take the time to go over these information sheets so they know who all the players are and where they should be and when. Identify all the things your coordinators are expected to be responsible for and oversee.

To help simplify their duties at both the ceremony and reception, we have our brides prepare two separate bags; large department store shopping bags with handles work well. In one of the bags, place everything that is needed at the ceremony site: programs, the ring pillow, the unity candle, guest book and pen, extra maps left over from your invitations, the marriage license, and anything else you'll need. The other bag contains the items that need to be taken to the reception: the cake knife or knives, toasting goblets, place cards, a basket for the gift cards, a roll of tape to attach cards to gifts, favors, and disposable cameras for guest tables. Review the contents of the bags with your coordinators so there are no questions. They should have custody of the bags several days before the wedding or, at the

---

Wedding Day Reflections

The smallest of the details will go unnoticed by everybody but you. We were driving ourselves crazy in the days before our wedding looking for the perfect serving platters for appetizers and the perfect pearl buttons for the back of my dress. We did not find either and were quite disappointed; however, now we realize that no one noticed but us that we had inexpensive serving trays or that my dress lacked decorative buttons near the zipper. Remember to keep everything in perspective.

—Jennifer and Peter

latest, at the rehearsal. The ceremony bag should be taken to the rehearsal. The reception bag contents are not needed until the wedding day.

At this informational meeting also let each coordinator know the names of your attendants and the order they will be standing at the altar. Both coordinators should attend the rehearsal to assist where possible and to acquaint themselves with all the relatives and other participants.

AT THE CEREMONY The wedding day typically starts for the coordinators when the flowers are delivered and the photographer arrives for the first pictures. This is usually an hour and a half before the ceremony. Coordinators' duties may include some or all of those listed here, or even more depending on your particular wedding. Be sure you have communicated all of the details with your coordinators.

◆ Pin on boutonnieres and corsages as the families and groomsmen arrive.

◆ While pictures are being taken, put out the guest book and pen, arrange the programs, give the marriage license to the officiant (if it wasn't left with him or her at the rehearsal), and see that the ring bearer isn't sweeping the floor with the pillow.

◆ Direct people to the restrooms (an inevitable question people will ask).

◆ Know what flowers the florist is bringing and what decorating (if any) he or she will be doing.

◆ Know whether there are pew bows and who is delivering and/or placing them.

◆ Know who the musicians are and what selections they will be playing.

◆ If children are handing out programs, make sure they are positioned at the door.

♦ If there is a guest book attendant, show that person where to stand.

♦ Make sure the couple and their attendants are out of sight when the first guests arrive.

♦ Make sure the ushers are ready to seat guests a half hour before the ceremony, and help them with any seating questions they might have.

♦ Inform musicians of guests arriving so they may start playing the prelude music.

♦ Check in with the bride and her attendants and make sure they are comfortable and just about ready.

♦ Confirm that candles are lit at the appropriate time.

♦ A few minutes before the ceremony time, close the guest book and ask latecomers to please seat themselves as the ceremony is about to begin.

♦ Give the musicians the cue that the ceremony is starting and the chosen selections should begin.

♦ Assemble grandparents' seating, and organize accordingly with the ushers who are seating them.

♦ Complete the same for the seating of the groom's parents and the bride's mother.

♦ Gather the attendants and line them up for their processional. As the bride and her father go through the doors, coordinators close the doors behind them.

♦ At this point the coordinators have the luxury of taking two minutes to say "Good job!" before getting back to work tending to details.

If your coordinators are working as a team, we suggest that now they split up, with one leaving for the reception while the other stays at the ceremony location. If you have one coordinator, he or she should leave for the reception now.

If a coordinator is staying at the ceremony location when pictures are taken afterward at the altar, that person should oversee these tasks:

- Make sure that everyone needed for the pictures is there.
- Ask the bride and groom if they would like a drink of water.
- Gather up any programs left behind, the unity candle, and other items to be put back in the bag for safekeeping and taken to the reception. (The guest book attendant will have taken the guest book with her to the reception earlier.)

After pictures are done and making sure nothing is left behind, this coordinator may now join the other at the reception with a feeling of a job well done. If you have one coordinator and this person leaves for the reception right after the processional, someone will need to pick up any items left behind. Ask a bridesmaid or two if they would please take care of this for you, put the items in the bag, and take the bag with them to the reception.

AT THE RECEPTION Again, be sure your coordinators each have a copy of the vendor list in case they need to call anyone. (This is why it is best for one person to be at the reception site early.) The coordinators' responsibilities at the reception might include some or all of the items listed here:

- Surveying the room and making sure everything is laid out the way you have requested. (You will have told them the room layout and what linens are being used.)

- Knowing what the centerpieces are and who will be placing them on the tables.

- Placing items from the reception bag in the appropriate spots.

- Putting the place cards at the correct tables.

♦ Making sure the DJ or musicians are ready to play at the designated time.

♦ As the guests arrive, making sure they are comfortable and seeing that drinks are available for them.

♦ As the wedding party arrives after pictures are taken at the ceremony site, taking their bouquets and placing them on the head table and cake table.

♦ Knowing when the food is to be served and the time for the toast.

♦ If the coordinators are invited guests, they should take time to sit, relax, and visit with friends and family over dinner.

♦ Letting the bride and groom know that they have a few more minutes to visit with guests and then there will be the toast, followed by the cake cutting and the first dance, and guiding them through each.

♦ Confirming that a microphone is available (the DJ or bandleader will have one) for the best man. Asking the maid of honor whether she also wishes to give a toast.

♦ Making sure the champagne is poured for the toast, just before the best man is given the microphone.

♦ Placing a wet napkin on a plate on the cake table for sticky fingers.

♦ Instructing the bride and groom on how to hold the knife when cutting the cake (the photographer may do this instead).

♦ Knowing whether the bride wants the top layer of the cake cut or saved.

♦ Knowing where the throwaway bouquet is, and letting the DJ or bandleader know when it will be thrown.

♦ While guests are dancing, securely taping all cards to the gifts (this saves much grief when it comes to writing thank-you notes).

♦ Distributing any checks to vendors that need to be paid on the day of the wedding.

◆ Gathering up the toasting goblets and cake knives, at least wiping them clean if not washing them, returning them to their boxes, and putting them in the bag. Collecting the disposable cameras and returning them to the bag also. Placing this bag at the gift table. (Someone else will be assigned to take the gifts after the reception along with the bags.)

The coordinators' job is over! Now they may sit down and relax or join in the dancing. (This is not appropriate for a hired, professional coordinator.)

As illustrated, many details unfold "behind the scenes" at a wedding that you, as the wedding couple, cannot possibly oversee. Your coordinators allow you, as well as your families and attendants, to do your job: enjoy this very special day.

Using a Helper (or Two)

As you've no doubt already realized, an amazing number of "little" things need to be done on the day of the wedding. Several of our couples, as they have gotten closer to their wedding day, have expressed concern about how all such jobs were going to get accomplished. An extra hand or two, to complement your coordinators' role and do some of the more physical tasks, can be an immense help for minimal cost—or for free, if friends volunteer for the job. Your coordinator, after all, cannot be in two places at once, let alone the *several* places that might demand last-minute attention on the wedding day itself.

Following is an example of necessary tasks one couple compiled for their volunteer coordinator:

1. Who will pick up the rental items?
2 Who will set up the chairs and arch at the ceremony location?
3. Who will put the extension cord from the community center to the lawn for the harpist?

4. Who will take the wine, beer, and soft drinks from the bride's home to the reception area?
5. Who will get ice at the last minute?
6. Who will take the gifts, extension cord, and any unused drinks home after the reception?
7. Who will return all the rentals?

These were all somewhat physical jobs, and after reviewing them, this couple decided to hire two young men to handle the details. The groom, a high school teacher, asked two of his students, Mark and Deron, whether they would like a job on his wedding day; the young men were delighted to earn some extra money. The groom borrowed his brother's pickup truck, and the helpers used it for all the errands. Mark and Deron had a list of the rental items they were picking up (these were prepaid) and a layout of how the chairs and arches were to be placed. After getting the ceremony site set up, Mark went to the bride's home and loaded up the drinks, the extension cord, and large freezer chests and took them to the clubhouse. Because this was a public facility, Deron stayed behind to make sure nothing was disturbed. When Mark returned, the boys unloaded the drinks at the community center. Deron placed the extension cord, while Mark left to buy ice. They both put the ice in the four chests, one for ice to be used in drinks and the others for keeping drinks cold. By then the caterers had arrived, so the young men were free to leave for a while. They returned at the end of the reception and loaded up all rentals, and then returned to the community center to pick up the leftover drinks, the ice chests, and the extension cord. They did a very nice job of taking care of everything just as it had been laid out for them, and each was happy to receive $50 at the end of the evening.

Another couple hired one young man to deliver the table centerpieces to the reception site. After the ceremony he removed pew bows at the church because their church required everything be immediately removed, and he took the altar arrangements from the church to the reception. After the reception, the couple wished to donate their altar arrangements to the local hospitals' burn center, so this helper transported the flowers there and then dropped the gifts off at the couple's home.

In our example in the upcoming sidebar "Prepping the Helpers," the bride has been very specific. Aunt Sue and Lisa know where they are to be and when, what things they are to get, what they are to do with the items, and within what time frame. Let your coordinators have a copy of helpers' schedules also. Of course, decorating for the reception preferably takes place earlier in the day, but this is only possible if you have access to the room. In our example, these relatives volunteered to miss the ceremony and joined the reception later.

Wedding Day Reflections

W e are glad we did not have the added stress of leaving for our honeymoon the day after our wedding. We were completely exhausted and were thankful we did not have to rush anywhere to catch a plane. Flying out Monday allowed us to arrive at our destination well rested.

—Kim and Matt

HELP AT THE FINALE

At the end of the evening, many things will need to be removed from the reception location: unopened beverages, the cake top, cake stands, floral arrangement baskets or urns, the two ceremony and reception bags, gift packages, and the basket containing wedding cards that didn't accompany gifts. Let helpers assigned to these details know where the items are to be taken and whether someone will be at that location to let them in or whether they need a key. If now is the time to remove decorations, break down tables and chairs, and so forth, at your reception location, this is another job for extra help.

Taking the time to think all these things out in advance helps ensure that your day will go smoothly. Again, we can't stress enough the importance of having someone else handle the assorted details. Even if you must hire helpers, this is money well spent; it buys you the confidence to be able to relax and enjoy your wedding day.

Prepping the Helpers

❧

Meet with anyone you use as helpers and lay out what needs to be done and how you want it handled. Provide them with their own schedule for the tasks for which they are responsible. Be specific as to time, location, what their duties are, and how you want them done. Aunt Sue and Cousin Lisa, for example, have volunteered to attach the pew bows at the church and will also decorate at the reception. A schedule for them might look like this:

11:00 A.M.   Stop by Tamara's house and pick up the following:
               Ivy—to be attached to all bows
               22 bows
               10 centerpieces

11:25 A.M.   At church:
               12 pew bows—on the first three pews attach on each side and
               then skip every third row
               2 bows—attach to two candelabra

12:15 P.M.   Must be done at church—leave for Community Center

12:30 P.M.   Arrive at Community Center
               4 bows—gather up cloth and attach to cake table
               4 bows—spaced evenly on front of head table
               10 centerpieces—place one on each guest table

1:30 P.M.   Must be done

Vendor List

MAKE a list of all the people who will be helping with your wedding, whether paid or volunteer. List all participants—such as staff at the ceremony and reception sites, bakery, and florist, the musicians, chauffeur, and so forth—and include the names and phone numbers of your contacts. You will use this list continually in the weeks up to your wedding, but, just as important, your coordinator(s) will have this information at their fingertips on the wedding day in case they need to contact anyone.

> ### *Wedding Day Reflections*
>
> W*e were glad that we were determined to enjoy the day no matter what went wrong. And we did, even though it rained a few hours before the outdoor ceremony."*
>
> —Karen and Mark

Vendor and Helper Follow-Up

SEVERAL times during the months before your wedding, we strongly urge you to contact all providers of wedding services, whether paid or volunteer. Call them to find out what remains to be done. Are there decisions still to be made, are there any monies due, and when should you meet next?

MIKE AND CANDY'S STORY

Mike and Candy, a client couple of ours, were very ho-hum about getting things accomplished. Three weeks before their wedding they still had not decided on a cake, despite our prodding. (This was one of our grooms who pulled the programs hot off the press the day of the rehearsal!) We met with them ten days before their wedding to review everything, including vendors and scheduling. Mike commented that he had been put in charge of choosing the cake and had had his fill of tasting. He assured us they had finally chosen a bakery and he had ordered the cake. The owners of the bakery they chose were on vacation until the day before the wedding, so we made a note to call upon their return. We wanted to let them know the final delivery time for the cake. When we called to say, "You can have access to the building at 5:00 P.M., and the florist will be standing by to decorate your cake," we received a moment of complete silence, heard paper shuffling, and were asked to hold a moment. The bakery owner came back on the line to say, "Yes, that couple was in and did quite a bit of tasting and told us what they liked, but they didn't give us any money as a deposit, and we didn't hear from them before we left on vacation. I just checked with my staff, and they didn't get a call, either. We thought they had chosen another bakery." A quick call to Mike got "I was sure they knew we wanted their cake. We told them what we wanted." But he hadn't completed the order form, nor had he given them a deposit. If we hadn't called as a courtesy to let the baker know when the cake could be delivered, there wouldn't have been a cake! Be sure to take care of actual orders, deposits, and subsequent dollars due. *Follow up!*

Stay on top of your payment schedule to budget your money outflow. Keep notes in each appropriate file of your conversations with a vendor, jotting down the date and name of the person with whom you spoke. We also suggest sending letters like the samples presented here, one to a professional and one to a volunteer, during your planning:

Mr. DJ
101 Disc Drive
Music City, California 12345

Dear Mr. DJ,

Thank you for meeting with us last Tuesday. This letter is to confirm our wedding date of June 15, 1999, where you will provide the music at our reception at the Community Center, 1310 J Street, from 1:30 to 5:30 at the cost of $375 for the first three hours and $75 for each additional hour.

I am enclosing our deposit of $100, with the balance being due the evening of our reception.

We will contact you several weeks before our wedding date to review the schedule for the evening and our choices of music for the first dance and so forth. Thank you.

Sincerely,
[signature]
Sandy Rosenbaum

Dear Uncle Mike,

Thank you so much for offering to drive your beautiful car for our wedding on Saturday, June 15. As you and I discussed, we will want you to take my dad and me from our house to the church at 11:30 for pictures (the ceremony is at 1:00) and then take Matt and me from the church to the reception after pictures are taken (close to 2:00). Of course, you and Aunt Betty are invited to both the ceremony and reception.

Thank you so much for offering us the use of your car and yourself as our chauffeur. You are helping make our wedding very special.

Much love,
Kim

If you make any changes to your plans, be it date, time, location, or service, be sure every person is notified in writing.

WHAT TO COMMUNICATE TO VENDORS

When you call your photographer to check in, ask what time he or she plans to start taking pictures on your wedding day. Also ask about getting an engagement picture taken, if you want one. The photographer will want to meet with you prior to the big day to discuss what pictures will be taken, where, and when. Review your schedule at that time and make any changes necessary.

When you follow up with your DJ, give him or her your choices for the first dance, father's or parents' dance, and whether you want a bouquet and garter toss or any other special extra.

?

What do I have to do to change my last name?

If you are going to change your last name to the groom's, inform the following entities: Department of Motor Vehicles, Social Security office, banks, and your employer's human resources office. Have a certified copy of your marriage license as proof.

You will need to let the caterer (whether a facility, an outside caterer, or family and friends) know your final menu choices and keep them apprised of guest count changes.

Follow up with your bakery to reaffirm the time the cake will be delivered at the reception. Pass this information on to your florist in another quick call, if he or she will be decorating the cake with fresh blooms. Also verify with your florist the drop-off time of floral arrangements at the ceremony and reception sites and whether he or she will transport flowers from the ceremony to the reception for you.

Finally, verify any monies due to your vendors. Make out the checks for vendors that are to be paid on the wedding day. Place these in envelopes and give them to your coordinators for distribution.

Marriage License

THE only thing you really must have to get married is a marriage license! We can't begin to tell you how many couples give this step very little thought. Because each state has different policies, we suggest you call a few months before your wedding to find out your state's requirements. Your local county clerk's office or marriage license bureau can give you information about costs and whether an appointment is necessary. Find out what forms of identification are acceptable. Inquire whether a medical exam or a blood test is required also. You may need to produce proof of divorce or annulment if you were previously married.

Some licenses are valid statewide, whereas others are valid only in the county or township issued. Some licenses expire after sixty days and some after ninety days. Many states require the license be issued at least twenty-four hours in advance.

About a month before the ceremony, we suggest you have an appointment at the county offices and make it into a fun afternoon outing. In all the hubbub of the planning, getting your marriage license is something that only the two of you can and must do together. Make an occasion of it.

Name Change

IF you will take your groom's surname after your marriage, you will need to have your name changed on a number of documents, such as your driver's license, social security card, insurance policies, voter's registration, passport, bank accounts, and employer's records. Call or send for the necessary forms to make this change. Some agencies require a copy of your marriage certificate before the change can be recorded.

Hotel Accommodations

FOR your out-of-town guests, it is a most gracious gesture to let them know of conveniently located hotels that are reasonably priced, clean, and comfortable. Some hotels have complimentary airport shuttles that might alleviate their having the expense of a car rental or your having to arrange other transportation. Several of our couples also have made reservations for get-togethers at the hotel the morning after the wedding for breakfast or brunch.

Hotels will let you reserve a block of rooms for your guests at a slightly reduced rate. Contact the hotel you are considering to ask what arrangements can be made. Hotel staff will ask how many rooms you think your guests will need. You may have a different number for Friday (the rehearsal evening) and Saturday (the actual wedding day), say, five rooms for Friday and twelve rooms for Saturday. They will hold these rooms under your names (e.g., the Jones/Smith wedding) usually until two weeks before the wedding, when they release them to the general public.

Let your guests know you have reserved a block of rooms at a hotel, providing the address and telephone number, preferably a toll-free number. This information should be included as an insert enclosed with your invitations, so this task is again something that can and should be done well in advance.

Bridal Registry

ANOTHER thing that should be completed by the time invitations are sent out is registering for gifts. Most department stores have a bridal registry, which sometimes includes a salesperson to accompany you as you choose your silver, dishes, glassware, pots and pans, cutlery, bed linens, towels, and other housewares. No longer are you limited to registering only for these traditional items, however. An amazing array of stores is jumping on the bridal registry bandwagon. We had one couple register at a home building supply store, for example. They had jointly purchased an older home that needed much renovation, and they registered for lights (both indoor and out), faucets for both the kitchen and bathrooms, closet shelving, miniblinds, doorknobs, and fireplace tools. They even had a wheelbarrow and crowbar on their list! Another couple, who were real outdoor enthusiasts, registered at a sporting goods store. Their list included a pup tent, rock-climbing gear, and his-and-her headlamps for their camping trips.

Remember, information regarding where you are registered is passed on by friends and family, if a guest inquires. It should *not* be included with your invitation.

> ## ?
>
> *We know we should register, but we already have sheets and towels. Where should we go?*
>
> *Some fun places to register include these stores (some may not be in your local area):*
>
> | | | |
> |---|---|---|
> | *Home Depot* | *Linens and Things* | *Pier One* |
> | *Recreational Equipment, Inc. (REI)* | *Macy's* | *J. C. Penney's* |
> | *Pools, Patios and Things* | *Crate and Barrel* | *Pottery Barn* |
> | *Eddie Bauer Home* | *Williams & Sonoma* | *Ikea* |

Reminder About Decorations

WE discussed decorations in detail in chapter 9, "Decorations," so let us simply remind you here to work on your decorations for your ceremony and reception as you go along. Deciding what you want in advance allows you time to find the "makings" on sale. It is also much more fun to create decorations leisurely in the evenings or at a few assembly parties than to madly try to put things together at the last minute.

Necessary Accessories

YOU may need to make, borrow, or purchase varied items for your wedding, and, again, we suggest you start looking for them in advance so you have time to find what you want at good prices. For the most part, items in wedding stores are priced higher than the same item found outside the "wedding industry." A little comparison shopping is always a great idea.

RING PILLOW

If you are using a ring bearer, tradition has him carrying a ring pillow. You can buy ready-made satin and lace creations, but this item is very easily made. Because of the unpredictability of young ring bearers, we suggest you attach small plastic gold rings to the pillow rather than your actual rings. Have the best man hold your real rings in his pocket.

DANNY AND ALLISON'S STORY

Okay, are you ready to hear the story of the canine ring bearer? When we arrived at the home of Danny and Allison to discuss coordinating their wedding, above their fireplace, hanging in a place of honor, was a very large professional portrait of their dog, a shepherd mix. This should have given us an idea of things to come, but at that point, we were clueless. Over the months of planning we got to know their dog, Aussie, fairly well. He eventually stopped barking at us (thanks to our giving him the mandatory liver treats) but was still held tightly on his leash to keep him from jumping all over us. In one of our planning sessions we were talking about their wedding party and asked whether they were having a flower girl or a ring bearer. Very straight-faced, the couple replied, "Oh, yes. Aussie will be the ring bearer." We both had rather startled looks on our faces. Aussie just stared at us from across the room. We realized they weren't joking. Alison made a beautiful "ring pillow" for Aussie that was actually more like a saddle. On their wedding day, Aussie was led down the aisle by the bride's brother (who also was a bit intimidated by the dog). The dog was handed off to us after the exchange of rings, and we, in turn, quickly handed Aussie off to his trainer (who had been paid extra money to be in attendance for the evening). The trainer was waiting at an exterior door (with a pocketful of liver treats) and kept Aussie entertained until he was called to come back in for pictures. We never had imagined a dog in a wedding party! We must admit though, Aussie is quite high on our "well-behaved ring bearer's list." He is certainly the most memorable!

GUEST BOOK

Several of our brides have bought inexpensive nonwedding guest books and covered them with material to match their chosen decor. The books were beautiful and very personalized.

A popular alternative to signing a guest book has become signing the matting around a special picture. One couple, for instance, had an 11 × 14" engagement picture of themselves in very casual dress on their "guest book" table, and the guests signed the matting. This personalized photo would then be framed to hang in their new home. Recently a couple had a matte for their guests to sign that held a drawing of a bride and groom done by the groom's five-year-old nephew. Their photographer took a picture of all their guests, and that photograph eventually would replace the child's stick-figure drawing. This couple also had very inexpensive cotton gloves on the table for each guest to put on when signing so as not to leave any oil from their hands on the matte.

Another couple used a tablecloth on their guest book table as their "guest book." The guests were to sign this cloth with the provided laundry marking pen, enjoying plenty of room for adding lengthier good wishes, also. The couple said they would bring this cloth out on each anniversary.

> **?**
>
> ### Should the real rings be put on the ring bearer's pillow?
>
> We suggest having the ring bearer carry a pillow with two inexpensive symbolic rings instead of the actual bands. We have heard horror stories of rings falling off the pillow and bridesmaids on hands and knees in the church foyer searching desperately on the wildly patterned carpet for them. Fortunately, in all stories, the rings were recovered; however, we believe the wedding bands are always safer in the best man's pocket.

Yet another idea is to have a friend stationed at the reception door to take a Polaroid picture of guests as they arrive. These pictures may be immediately double-stick-taped to pages in a book (two to a page), and the guests then sign on the page opposite their picture.

It is not necessary to buy the fancy plumed pen you see in all wedding stores. An ordinary pen with a nice tip works beautifully. Try various ones to find the one you like. We also suggest you have a backup pen available to your guests.

TOASTING GOBLETS

If you need to buy them at all, you don't have to spend a fortune on toasting goblets. Choose a pair you both find pleasing. Several of our couples have purchased two champagne flutes in the same pattern as the wineglasses they registered for. Another couple bought two glasses at a great price from a factory outlet store. Perhaps you already own an elegant set of glassware; simply tie a pretty ribbon on the stem to dress them up for pictures. Other couples follow the "something borrowed" tradition and use the same goblets their parents had used at their own wedding.

CAKE KNIFE

A cake knife is used infrequently in everyday life, so it seems an unnecessary expense to purchase one (or a set). Does your mother, grandmother, aunt, cousin, friend, or neighbor have one you may use on your wedding day? This might be the only time you would ever use it. The cake knife, too, can be easily decorated with a bow tied to the handle for pictures.

BRIDAL PURSE

If you are having a money or honeymoon dance at your reception, you should have a bridal purse for your "bounty." This accessory is very easy to make yourself. Simply sew up pretty material to make a bag with outside dimensions of approximately five inches high by seven inches wide. Sew a seam along the top with a drawstring inside that's long enough to tie and hang over your arm as you dance with the "contributors."

GARTER

A plain garter can be purchased very inexpensively at a craft store and then decorated with lace and a blue ribbon (for your something blue) if you choose.

DISPOSABLE CAMERAS

Disposable cameras for your guests' use at your reception are a fun, inexpensive way to supplement the more formal pictures taken by your photographer. The drugstores' camera departments or large discount stores often have these cameras on sale.

GIFTS FOR ATTENDANTS

Gifts for your attendants are a token of thanks for participating in your special day; they are usually given at the rehearsal dinner during the evening's festivities or at a pre-wedding party. Whatever you choose is just fine. Traditional presents for the best man and groomsmen include engraved beer mugs, key chains, money clips, or pen sets. Our grooms have been more imaginative with their gifts, choosing items such as Swiss army knives, fanny packs, and small pieces of sports equipment. Gifts for bridesmaids and your honor attendant are usually necklaces or earrings the attendants will wear on your wedding day. One bride gave dressy black, beaded purses that her attendants carried, while another gave each an engraved bookmark. Again, whatever you feel would be an appreciated gift is fine.

Pre-Wedding Parties

MANY wedding-related parties will be held for you in the months before the wedding, which is one of the reasons we suggest not waiting until the last minute to address wedding details. The closer you get to your wedding date, the busier your social life will become. You will want to be well organized and relaxed enough concerning the nitty-gritty details so you can enjoy these fun times, too.

SHOWERS

Showers often have themes such as lingerie, time of day, or kitchen and involve game playing. Bridal attendants, friends, or sometimes coworkers are usually in charge of giving the bridal shower. This sort of party, where gifts are expected, should properly not be given by the immediate family of either the bride or groom (i.e., mothers or sisters).

Also quite popular today are couples' showers. These usually end up being barbecues in a friend's backyard or casual parties with small gifts for the home or one larger gift from all in attendance.

Sending thank-you notes immediately for gifts received at showers will help keep you on top of the big job of thank-you's after the wedding. Remember not to use stationery with your married name or monogram before the wedding.

BRIDESMAIDS' LUNCHEON

Traditionally, the bride has hosted a luncheon for her bridesmaids to give them an opportunity to get to know each other. Today, however, sometimes this is just not practical in our busy lives or when friends and family live far away. A casual get-together after the final dress fittings is a possibility. If the attendants are arriving from many different locations, just being together for several hours before the rehearsal would be nice so your attendants get a chance to meet and spend a little time with each other.

BACHELOR PARTIES

Bachelor parties tend to conjure up images of bawdy, slightly risqué bashes. In the case of our grooms, however, bachelor parties are more than merely drinking fests. They have been fifty-mile bike rides, weekend camping trips, a day spent deep-sea fishing, and even a climb up Mount Whitney.

We urge couples to plan time for a bachelor party, no matter what form it takes, several weeks before the wedding, not a day or two before. No one should be recovering from a wild party or invigorating sporting activity on the day of his or her wedding.

BACHELORETTE PARTIES

Not to be left out, the ladies are also having their night on the town. While some might go to dinner and a dance club afterward, others are planning weekends away. A cabin was loaned to one of our brides and her attendants for a weekend. The attendants planned the meals and got all the food together. They swam, hiked, rented a *Father of the Bride* video, planned their hairdo's for the wedding, practiced doing their makeup, and gave each other manicures and pedicures. The bride said it was a great weekend and a relaxing way to get away from the wedding preparations.

REHEARSAL DINNER

Normally the groom's family hosts the dinner following the rehearsal. This can be any format they choose, from very formal affairs to backyard barbecues. The following people should be invited to the rehearsal dinner: the parents of the bride, grandparents of both the bride and groom, all attendants and their spouses or significant others, the ring bearer and flower girl and their parents, the readers, anyone else who is asked to participate in the wedding, and honored guests who have already arrived from out of town, such as aunts and uncles.

One dinner that sounded like great fun was a barbecue at a park complete with a volleyball game. The groom's mother had read a story in a wedding book that told of having T-shirts made for the

> **?**
>
> *When is the best time to have the bachelor or bachelorette party?*
>
> The best time for these parties is a few or even several weeks before the wedding, on a weekend that is convenient for the bride or groom, and a time when all or most of the wedding party can attend. A celebration of this sort is not a good idea the night before the wedding! No one wants the puffy eyes of sleep deprivation to be obvious in their wedding photos.

attendants with their titles and names on each. She knew the cost for that idea would be formidable so came up with a great substitute. She bought a spool of wide white ribbon and red fabric paint and made "Miss America"–style sashes saying the person's name and role (e.g., "Mariko—Bride," "Toby—Best Man"). The sashes were a big hit—a fun touch that really helped break the ice. At the end of the evening even those who had just met felt like old friends.

> ### Wedding Day Reflections
>
> We hosted the rehearsal dinner in our backyard. We served previously frozen lasagnas and made it an informal picnic, which was a nice contrast to the more formal proceedings that took place the next day.
>
> —Nicqueline and Skip

A rehearsal dinner usually features toasts, the first being proposed by the groom's father (as the host), then a toast by the bride's father including a thank-you to the groom's parents for the nice evening. This is often the occasion, too, when you give your gifts to the attendants. Try to make your rehearsal dinner an early evening, because you all have a big day the next morning!

Beauty Care

OPEN any bridal magazine and you will see articles about spending a day or two before your wedding at a pampering health spa. The plain truth is, we have yet to meet a bride with two extra days to while away wallowing in mud. Spending an afternoon at a makeup counter in a department store is a much more realistic outing. This is a wonderful place to get wedding-day makeup suggestions. Salespeople there will happily give you a complimentary make-over consultation. Of course they hope, too, that you will buy some of their products, but you'll have fun learning what a makeup expert suggests for you.

If you decide to have your hair done, take the time to visit several hair salons, if you don't have a regular stylist, until you find someone who can give you the look you want. Take your headpiece and veil with you. If you are going to do your hair yourself or have the help of one of your friends, take the time to practice. When getting your hair done, don't forget to wear a button-front blouse so you don't muss your new hairdo pulling your shirt over your head.

Visiting a beauty school is a great way to afford manicures for the whole wedding party. Having your nails done the day before the wedding seems to work best. If you do have scheduled nail and/or hair appointments, be sure to reconfirm times.

Clothing Check-Up

BE sure to follow up with your tuxedo store and confirm that all men have been in for their fittings or have mailed in the cards with their measurements. We suggest that ring bearers not be measured until about two weeks before the wedding as young boys grow quickly.

Don't forget to have your fittings with your bridal gown. Take the shoes and undergarments you will wear under the gown to each fitting. Make sure your attendants are getting fitted, too, or arrangements are in order for last-minute fittings for the out-of-towners. Check on accessories for yourself, the mothers, and your attendants. No later than early in the week preceding the wedding you should have nylons, nail polish, slips, and any other accessories you'll need.

If you wish to leave your reception in a different outfit than your wedding attire, you will also need to plan your "going-away" outfits. Some couples leave in dressy attire, while others wear very casual clothes; this choice is completely up to you. Just be sure to have these outfits ready to take with you when you leave your home

> ### *Professionally Speaking*
>
>
> **W**hen *choosing a wedding-day hairstyle, take into account the style of your dress. Having hair up is fancier than having it down, yet keep the style simple so it does not detract from your face.*
>
> —Wendelyn Duncan
> Wendelyn's Hair Design

on the wedding day. Your outfit on a hanger, with shoes and accessories in a plastic bag hanging from the hanger, keeps everything together nicely.

If you are leaving for a honeymoon right after the reception, plan your wardrobes and gather all else you need to bring along (e.g., cash, traveler's checks, toiletries) no less than a few days ahead of your wedding. Don't save your packing for the few tired moments between your wedding day and honeymoon.

Also remember to eat while preparing for your wedding day. Countless brides and grooms have forgotten this important point or felt too nervous for even a light snack, only to feel truly weak in the knees later. For this reason, we also carry ammonia inhalants with us, just in case someone becomes faint.

Items to Throw at the End of the Ceremony

RICE used to be thrown at weddings as a symbol of fertility, but most churches and reception facilities no longer permit it because it makes for slippery footing and is not good for birds. Birdseed is usually an accepted substitution, but many places don't permit it, either; if they do, you are sometimes responsible for cleaning it up.

Several of our brides have had rose petals available for tossing at their garden weddings. Also popular are miniature, decorated bottles of bubble solution so that guests can blow bubbles as the couple leaves the ceremony site.

Emergency Kit

Invariably, on the day of the wedding, someone in your family or wedding party will need or have forgotten something. For this very reason, we recommend assembling a small kit like the one we take with us to all weddings. It's a plastic box containing the following items:

- **Hair**   Brush, comb, mirror, hair spray, bobby pins.
- **Personal**   Toothbrush, toothpaste, deodorant, breath mints, hand lotion, aspirin, eye drops, handkerchief, packet of tissues, handy wipes, nail file.
- **Clothing**   Needle and thread (white, ivory, and maids' and mothers' dress colors), baby powder (helps cover up stains on the bridal gown), stain remover, fabric glue and white tape (for hems), safety and straight pins, scissors (for loose threads), extra pair of pantyhose for bride and one for attendants, clear nail polish (for runs), earring backs.
- **Miscellaneous**   Tape, note pad, Post-It's, pen (these come in handy if you have to leave a note for someone who is running late).

15

THE FINISHING TOUCHES

Scheduling and Rehearsing the Details

Most of the decisions have been made, everything has been ordered, your coordinators and other helpers have been assigned their duties, and now it is time to put it all together. All the things you have accomplished over the last few months need to be organized into schedules and then practiced in the rehearsal. In this chapter we will lead you through some of the finishing touches that help make your day beautiful, memorable, and problem-free. Everything in this chapter should be completed a minimum of a week before the big day.

Preliminary Schedule

For your wedding day to proceed smoothly, everyone—including the wedding party, the vendors, the coordinators, and the volunteers—needs to know where they are to be and when. To figure out the logistics of your day, you need to prepare a schedule. Start by talking with your contacts at the ceremony and reception locations:

• When is the earliest we may have access to the ceremony location (to dress, to decorate, for pictures, etc.)?

261

♦ When is the earliest we may have access to the reception location (for rental delivery, to decorate, food and cake delivery, etc.)?

For illustrative purposes, say the ceremony will be 1:00 P.M. Photographers usually begin taking pictures of the wedding party an hour and a half before the ceremony, but ask yours specifically what time he or she plans to start. The florist needs to have all bouquets and personal flowers to the church before the pictures are taken. In our example the ceremony is a Protestant ceremony, and the pastor estimates it will last a half hour. The guests will leave for the reception shortly after the ceremony ends, and the reception site is close by so the caterer should expect the first guests not long thereafter. Finally, let's say you want music playing when your guests arrive at the reception. Your preliminary schedule should look something like this:

Saturday, June 15

11:15 A.M.	Florist delivers flowers to church
11:30 A.M.	Photographer arrives to take pictures
1:00 P.M.	Ceremony begins
1:30 P.M.	Ceremony ends
	DJ ready to play music at reception
	Catering staff ready
1:45 P.M.	Guests arrive at reception

Fine-tune your schedule until all the people on your vendor list (described in chapter 14, "Details, Details, Details") appear on it. Double-check your files so you don't forget anyone. If everything seems to be in order and you can complete your final schedule, you may make the last calls to everyone on your vendor list, except for the caterers. (You'll need a final guest count before contacting the caterer.) Tell everyone involved where they are to be and when. Are they still waiting for something from you? Do you have any changes or additions (such as telling the florist you need two more boutonnieres, or letting the DJ know you want him to be sure to play "YMCA")? Verify the final payments. Prepare and mail any checks that are due.

Also, let each person involved with your wedding know you have coordinators for the day. Tell them their names, that they are knowledgeable about your day, and that they should deal directly with them—not you—with any questions or concerns on your wedding day.

Guest Count

ALMOST every wedding includes the glitch of guests who do not respond by the requested date. If your caterer needs a final guest count and you still have not heard from someone (or several someones), you may need to phone these people. We suggest you call and just let them know, "We need to give the caterer the final count. We hope you are able to come." A more direct approach is to ask, "Are you coming?"

Once you have contacted these people, you can tally the numbers in the upper right-hand corner of your 3 × 5 cards in the "Acceptances" category for the number of your guests who have said they would attend. At weddings we have been involved with, an average of 5% to 6% of the guests have responded affirmatively but then do not actually attend, for one reason or another. Therefore, some of our couples actually subtract 5% before giving their guaranteed count to the caterer. Your final payment will be based on that figure, and you don't want to pay for several guests who won't be there. Remember, though, that the reverse will be true also: you will be expected to pay for any guests who show up unexpectedly beyond those who had been tallied into your final guest count.

Guest Appeal

W*e attended a reception where it was obvious no one was in charge of the schedule. The guests had been mingling in "cocktail hour style" for three hours and were getting anxious to do something else. The DJ finally asked the mother of the bride if they were still planning on having dancing. The answer was yes, but the room was only rented for thirty more minutes with no possibility of extension. Many of the guests were really looking forward to dancing, but by the time we danced to four songs, we all were being asked to leave by the management.*

—Nancy Van Huff, wedding guest

Once you have determined your final count, you are ready to call the caterer. An invoice will be prepared, and that amount is usually due a week before the reception.

Details Regarding Attendants

You should discuss several details with your attendants. Let them know what time the rehearsal is and where. At least an hour should be allowed for the rehearsal. If you know one of your attendants is habitually tardy, tell that person to be there a half an hour earlier than the real start time.

Let both bridesmaids and groomsmen know the appropriate clothing for all functions they will be attending. The groomsmen should pick up their tuxedos the day before the wedding. It is fun if the men all meet at the tuxedo store at the same time. Be sure each man tries on the *entire* outfit, including both shoes (we actually had a groomsman who received two left shoes). If each man is not returning the tux to the store himself, be sure he knows to whom he should give the tux to return it.

Discuss with your attendants how the two of you want them to stand at the altar. Don't wait to decide at the rehearsal. The best man and maid of honor always stand next to the groom and bride. The easiest "lineup" after that is by height, but this is, of course, something you may determine yourselves. A chart with this information should be prepared and given to your coordinators ahead of time, the officiant at the rehearsal, and the staff at the ceremony site on your wedding day. See Figure 15.1 for an example of an altar setup.

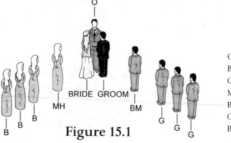

O – OFFICIANT
BRIDE
GROOM
MH - MAID OF HONOR
BM - BEST MAN
G – GROOMSMAN
B – BRIDESMAID

Figure 15.1

Decide what groomsmen will seat the grandparents and parents. If there are any potentially awkward or difficult situations, discuss the family dynamics with your fiancé ahead of time and then pass this information to the groomsmen and ushers. Don't wait until the rehearsal to work out ceremony seating arrangements for anyone. Traditionally, the parents of the bride are both seated in the front row. If they are divorced and either has remarried, the bride's mother is still seated in the front row and is joined by her new spouse, parents, or other close family members. The bride's father is now seated in the second row with his new spouse, parents, or family members. The grandparents could be moved back to the third row, if not seated with their son or daughter. The scenario is the same on the groom's side. We have had divorced parents with very amicable relationships who have chosen to sit together.

Also, figure out which family members are to be in the other reserved rows at the church. Let these people know that they are to be seated in the third row, left side, or wherever you have determined, and ask them to tell the groomsmen when being seated. (At the same time, you can tell them whether they have reserved seats at your reception.) Remember to let your coordinators know all seating arrangements before the rehearsal.

Remind the best man that he will give a toast at the reception, and ask your maid of honor whether she would also like to give a toast. Give your best man an envelope with the cash honorarium for the officiant. He will give the envelope to the officiant before the ceremony.

The Rehearsal

IF at all possible, we suggest that everyone be done with all the wedding preparations two days before the wedding. This goal will let you be rested and relaxed going into the rehearsal, which is a very special time itself. The most important people in both of your lives are all together to rehearse for your wedding day. How exciting!

If you have not already given the ceremony and reception bags to your coordinators, take them with you to the rehearsal so you will not have to worry about them the day of the wedding. Don't forget the marriage license if your officiant has requested that it be brought to the rehearsal. If a bouquet was made from ribbons from your showers, bring that too. You can use it to practice passing off the bouquet to your maid of honor.

Depending on the officiant, some conduct the entire rehearsal, some only review parts of the ceremony, while others don't even attend the rehearsal. The officiants who do not attend say they will guide the participants through the ceremony on the wedding day and that the rehearsal is primarily for members of the wedding party to know the order they will follow in the processional and where they will stand during the ceremony. Know how your officiant wishes to handle the rehearsal. If he or she will not be attending, then you and your coordinators may need to rehearse how to rehearse!

If your church has a particular protocol for rehearsals, you will

Who Should Be Invited to the Rehearsal?

❧

Those who should attend the rehearsal are as follows:

- ◆ All attendants.
- ◆ Both sets of parents (the groom's parents may have responsibilities for the rehearsal dinner that day and may not be able to attend).
- ◆ The readers.
- ◆ Candle lighters.
- ◆ Any other participants in the ceremony.
- ◆ If you are having a videographer, often they attend the rehearsal to plan camera angles. Photographers don't usually attend. The organist/musicians and the soloist rarely attend.

need to follow it. We always defer to the officiants. If a church hostess is provided, she will know how the officiant or the church wants things done. We give the officiant (and the church hostess) the sheet showing the names and the order the couple wants for their attendants, and ask them whether they would like any assistance from us. We have gotten answers ranging from "How wonderful! I would really appreciate it if you would take care of where everyone stands and the procession. Then I'll walk them through the ceremony" to "This is my church, and nobody is going to come in here and tell me how to run a rehearsal." The latter comment was from an Irish priest who obviously doesn't like coordinators. We must admit, he did a great job of running the rehearsal by himself! (He did let us line up the bridesmaids and the bride and her father in the foyer and hold the doors open for their entrances.) We were "friends" with him by the time the reception rolled around, however; with half a smile he said we'd been "a help."

A SAMPLE REHEARSAL

In this example, we are assuming that the officiant is not conducting the rehearsal, and you will be relying on your coordinators. Any variation of this sample is, of course, a possibility. We feel the easiest, least confusing way to start a rehearsal is to line up the attendants at the altar in the order they will be standing during the ceremony, and then practice how they will get there. The officiant stands facing the guests; the attendants are lined up (as shown in Figure 15.2) with the bride and groom, in the center, directly in front of the officiant:

O – OFFICIANT
BRIDE
GROOM
MH - MAID OF HONOR
BM - BEST MAN
G – GROOMSMAN
B – BRIDESMAID

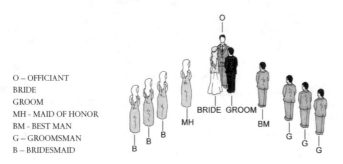

Figure 15.2

We then have the bride, her father, and the bridesmaids adjourn to the foyer and ask them to wait for further instructions. If there are two coordinators, one can work with the women and one can work with the men. A coordinator working solo should practice first with the men, since they traditionally are the first of the bridal party to enter the church.

The men enter the church. The officiant, followed by the groom, his best man, and then the groomsmen, come out from the front of the church on the right side. The officiant stands facing the guests. If you have a large wedding party (more than six), rather than having all the men enter looking like they were filing in for a police lineup, we suggest the groomsmen come down the aisle in pairs. The officiant, groom, and best man would still come in from the right. Then the groomsmen would come down the aisle, immediately preceding the bridesmaids. The groomsman walking in on the right would be the farthest right at the altar, the groomsman walking in on the left would be the second in from the right, and so forth. See Figure 15.3 and Figure 15.4 for an example of what the groomsmen's processional would look like which shows how they will end up at the altar.

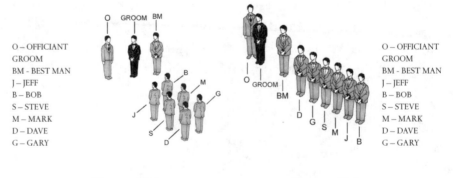

O – OFFICIANT
GROOM
BM - BEST MAN
J – JEFF
B – BOB
S – STEVE
M – MARK
D – DAVE
G – GARY

O – OFFICIANT
GROOM
BM - BEST MAN
J – JEFF
B – BOB
S – STEVE
M – MARK
D – DAVE
G – GARY

Figure 15.3   **Figure 15.4**

While we have the men's attention, we suggest they stand looking down the aisle until the bride is at the altar and then they all turn inward. We also suggest they stand in what we refer to as "fig-leaf style"—that is, arms clasped in front of them where a fig leaf would be most advantageously put. If their arms are clasped behind their backs, their jackets gape open. We also ask them not to put their hands in their pockets. We ask the men to wait at the altar, and we go to the back of the church and practice the processional.

Now it is time for the bridesmaids to enter. Line the bridesmaids up in the correct order by calling each name. We show them how to hold their bouquets, with forearms resting on their hips. This stance deters them from their natural tendency to hold the bouquets too high, as if they are trying to hide. The bridesmaid farthest from the bride at the altar is the first one in line. We are sure to tell her how important her job is as she will set the pace for the others and assure her she will be given a cue to begin. Again, if you have a large wedding party, you might want to pair up the bridesmaids for the processional. This would be done the same as for the groomsmen, but the bridesmaid walking in on the left would be the farthest left at the altar, the one walking in on the right would be the second in from the left, and so forth. See Figure 15.5 for an example of what the bridesmaids' processional would look like.

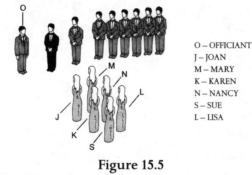

O – OFFICIANT
J – JOAN
M – MARY
K – KAREN
N – NANCY
S – SUE
L – LISA

Figure 15.5

The maid of honor is next. Walking by herself, she is followed by the flower girl and/or ring bearer. After they are all at the altar, the music changes and the bride and her father enter, the bride on her father's left arm. As they reach the altar, the groom and the bride's father shake hands, the father puts the bride's right hand in the groom's left hand, and usually the couple moves a little forward.

Depending on whether the father is "giving away" the bride, he will stand there until asked the question, or he will take his place in the front row immediately. We caution the father of the bride to be aware of the train on the bride's dress. It may be necessary for him to back up a little and step around it.

A variation on the father escorting the bride down the aisle has been used in several of our weddings. In one wedding, the bride wanted both her parents to escort her, as in Jewish ceremonies. They both stood at the altar and answered, "We do," when the officiant asked, "Who gives this woman?" At another wedding, the bride's two sons from a previous marriage escorted her. Another bride had been raised by a single mother and chose her to escort her down the aisle.

See Figure 15.6 for an example of what the altar lineup will look like after the processional.

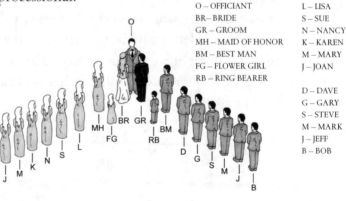

O – OFFICIANT
BR – BRIDE
GR – GROOM
MH – MAID OF HONOR
BM – BEST MAN
FG – FLOWER GIRL
RB – RING BEARER

L – LISA
S – SUE
N – NANCY
K – KAREN
M – MARY
J – JOAN

D – DAVE
G – GARY
S – STEVE
M – MARK
J – JEFF
B – BOB

Figure 15.6

Ceremonies held in locations other than a church setting may be conducted similarly. If you're having a Jewish ceremony, everyone comes down the aisle, led by the rabbi, then the groomsmen (singly or in pairs), the best man, the groom with his parents, the bridesmaids (singly or in pairs), the maid of honor, and lastly, the bride with her parents. All will remain standing at the huppah, the bride and groom in the center and the parents standing on the outer edge.

If the officiant is present, he or she will now briefly go through the ceremony. If the ceremony is lengthy, as in a nuptial mass, the attendants will be directed to take their seats, both in the rehearsal and at the actual ceremony. If a flower girl and a ring bearer are participating, we suggest they take a seat with their parents for the ceremony. Their parents should be seated along the aisle or other location where the children can easily find them. Any readers should know their cues, and they also should sit at the end of an aisle so they have easy access to the altar. The maid of honor should know when to pass her bouquet to the bridesmaid next to her so that she may hold the bride's bouquet. We tell all the bridesmaids that if necessary, keep handing the bouquets down so the maid of honor has her hands free to adjust the train or whatever else she might need two hands for.

After the officiant has gone through the ceremony, practice your recessional. At the end of the ceremony, we suggest the flower girl and ring bearer return to their spot at the altar. The bride and groom are introduced and head down the aisle, followed by the flower girl and ring bearer, the maid of honor and best man, and each bridesmaid paired up with a groomsman. If there are an odd number of attendants, the last three should exit together (see Figure 15.7 for an example; if there are more groomsmen than bridesmaids, this setup can be reversed.).

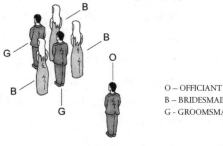

O – OFFICIANT
B – BRIDESMAID
G - GROOMSMAN

Figure 15.7

As everyone practices the recessional, direct the wedding party to exit the church, go around to another entrance, and return immediately to the altar area for pictures.

We now practice seating the grandparents and parents. We know which groomsman, or usher, is seating whom and practice with each. The groom's grandparents are seated first. The designated groomsman extends his right arm to the grandmother. The grandfather follows behind. Instruct the groomsman to be aware if the grandfather can keep pace and adjust his steps accordingly. They are taken to the second row on the right side. After the groom's grandparents are seated, seat the bride's grandparents on the left side. Then the groom's parents are seated. Again, the groomsman extends his right arm to the mother and the father follows behind. We think it is best if the mother is directly on the aisle when seated in her pew as she is better able to see all that is going on. Then it is time for the entrance of the bride's mother. She is escorted alone to the first pew on the left side. The groomsmen who seated both the grandparents and parents will now take their place with the rest of the men for their entrance. Tell the mother of the bride that after the bridesmaids have entered, the music will change for the processional of her daughter and husband. At the first strains of the music, she should stand and turn toward the back. This will be the signal for the guests to stand also.

Instruct the groomsmen, or ushers, on how to seat guests. They should approach guests and extend their right arm (crook their elbow). If they are to seat a man and a woman, they extend their arm to the woman and the man follows behind. If there are two women, they extend their arm to the elder of the two. The guests will probably say the bride's side (left) or the groom's side (right). If you know that one side will have more guests than the other, the groomsmen can tell them, "We are seating on both sides today." The groomsmen should know how many rows are reserved on each side. The guests in the reserved rows need to be told ahead of time so they can tell the groomsmen where they are to be seated.

While you have the attention of all the parents and grandparents, explain their recessional. After the last bridesmaid and groomsman has walked past, the bride's parents should rise and exit their pew, followed by the groom's parents, then the bride's grandparents, then the groom's grandparents, and so on. It is a nice touch if there is a single parent or grandparent for them to be matched up as the attendants were. We did a wedding where the groom's father had recently passed away. Instead of the bride's parents exiting and the groom's mother exiting by herself, the bride's parents went across the aisle to the groom's mother. The bride's father extended his left arm to her and with his wife on his right arm, the three recessed together.

After the last grandparents have exited, each row of guests is then free to leave. Several of our more formal weddings have chosen to have two groomsmen return to "bow out" the guests. The groomsmen recessed with the other attendants and then hurried from the back of the church down the two side aisles to the center just in time to stand at the end of a pew on either side of the aisle. They moved slowly up the aisle indicating that the next row should exit—a very nice touch.

If candles are to be lit, practice with the candle lighters. During the ceremony, the candles are lit just before the grandparents are seated. The altar candles are lit first, then the candelabra. The candle lighters should watch each other and stay together. They walk back up the aisle.

If the guest book attendant is in attendance, show her where the book will be and where she should stand. Suggest she leave the church for the reception immediately after the ceremony ends. This way she can set up the book before the other guests arrive at the reception.

The coordinator or participants may want to go through the practice again, but probably not—they have a dinner party to attend! If everyone is comfortable after the first run, then you are done. We remind everyone what time, and where, they will be expected the next day.

16

THE DAY YOU'VE BEEN WAITING FOR

MAKING YOUR DREAM COME TRUE

THE DAY THAT seemed so far away when you first started planning is actually here! Your wedding day will consist of many activities and emotions; some will be a blur, and some will be etched in your mind forever. From the excitement of the early-day preparations, through the seriousness of the ceremony, to the celebration of your marriage surrounded by family and friends, your day will be truly wonderful. In this chapter we describe what a "typical" wedding day might be like.

Conquering Stress Before You Start the Big Day

YOU will be amazed at how quickly this day will fly by. It's easy to get lost in the chaos of emotions, appointments, anxiety, and every detail in between, but remember, this is your wedding day. This should be the happiest day of your life—not a day you're dreading. Stop throughout the day and put yourself in the moment. Remind yourself what you're doing, take a moment to breathe, and force yourself to smile when you imagine walking down the aisle to the person you will spend eternity with.

The Day Begins

ON the morning of your wedding, gather the things together that you will need for your day: your bridal outfit, going-away clothes, and luggage for your honeymoon if you're leaving after the reception. If you are going to the hairdresser, don't forget to wear a button-front shirt and to take your headpiece with you. Plan to eat early in the day. Also have food available for everyone in the wedding party to eat as they are dressing.

When leaving the place where you dressed for the ceremony, make sure everyone has what they need. It is easy to leave a bow tie, belt, or earrings behind. We actually had a group of attendants who had gone to great length to leave a car at the reception location. They had put purses and cameras in the trunk (items they wanted at the reception). The attendants dressed at home. A limousine picked everyone up and took them to the church and later on to the reception. It was only then that they realized they had left the keys to the carefully thought-out and well-placed car at the home where they dressed.

While ideally you all should be dressing in a relaxed manner, keep your eye on the clock. You want to be ready for the pictures. Make sure the mothers, fathers, and others are aware of the time also. We had one father of the bride who escaped to watch football in the safety of his den as the rest of his house was overrun with girls, gowns, and curling irons. When it was time to leave for the church, we all had to wonder, "Where's Dad?" He had completely lost track of time, was happily watching the game, and wasn't even dressed yet. We quickly gathered his things together and he arrived at the church in his jeans and hurriedly had to dress there.

> ### *Wedding Day Reflections*
>
> *Our biggest fear about our wedding day was that it would pass too quickly. We made a promise to each other beforehand to pause a few times together and take in the scene.*
>
> —Suzanne and Russell

At the Ceremony

ONCE everyone is at the ceremony location, whether or not pictures have already been taken, you no longer need to be aware of time. The day will just happen. Your wedding coordinator will make sure the couple, their families, and the wedding party are guided through most of the rest of the day.

Because you have rehearsed, you know how the ceremony will go. Immediately after the ceremony you will lead the recessional from the altar, exit, and take a circuitous route, ending at the altar for pictures. All people who are to be included in these pictures should be back at the altar so the pictures can be finished in short order. Once the photos are finished, the families and your attendants are free to leave for the reception. At this point some of our photographers like to stop at a park or other outside location for romantics. Whether you stop for pictures or ride directly to the reception, this is a perfect chance for the two of you to have a bit of time all to yourselves. Enjoy and savor it.

> **?**
>
> ***Where do I put my engagement ring when I walk down the aisle?***
>
> We suggest wearing your engagement ring on your right hand. It is customary to wear your wedding band "closest to your heart," so the band is slipped on first. After the ceremony is over, you may move your engagement ring to your wedding finger. If your bands have been soldered together before the ceremony, the best man should carry them.

Let's Party!

AT the reception, your DJ or bandleader may announce your arrival, if you would like. If you are having a receiving line, it should be formed as soon as you arrive at the reception. Because the bride's mother is the official hostess, she stands at the beginning of the line. The groom's father is next, followed by the groom's mother, the bride's father, the bride, and finally the groom.

After the guests have had a chance to visit with each other, the meal will be served. You and your attendants will be at the head table or whatever arrangement you have chosen. The families will be close by at reserved tables. If you are having a buffet, the DJ or bandleader can use the microphone to direct one table at a time to come up so your guests aren't standing in line for any length of time. After the two of you have finished eating, if you did not have a receiving line, this is a good time to walk around and visit with the guests at each table.

When the guests are finished with their meal, the toast is given. This usually takes place at the head table or near the cake table. Your best man will propose the first toast; the maid of honor usually chooses to give a toast also. When the toast is being given to you, the guests raise their glasses in your honor, but you do not raise yours. After the honor attendants have given their toasts, other guests may choose to add their good wishes, too.

The cake cutting comes next. You will stand behind the cake, the bride will hold the cake knife, and the groom's right hand will be placed over hers. Together you cut a slice and put it on a small plate. Carefully feed each other a piece and wipe your sticky hands on the wet napkin provided. If you choose, you could serve a plate of cake to each of your parents. The staff will cut and serve the remainder of the cake.

Now you are ready for the first dance. The DJ or bandleader will know your selection and will have the lights dimmed as you dance in each other's arms. There are variations on how the first dance is done. Some couples wish to have the first song all to themselves, while others prefer to have their parents and/or attendants join in. The second dance is usually reserved for the bride and her father, but, again, vari-

---

Wedding Day Reflections

S*tay together as a couple when moving around the room and greeting guests. This way you know that each of you will meet and/or talk to everyone invited.*

—Carrie and Brian

ations are possible; all parents may be included, for instance. Do whatever you like. If you decide to have a bouquet and garter toss, that will be done a little later but while most of your guests are still there.

The formalities are now over, and you have the rest of the reception to visit and dance with your guests. Receptions are celebrations of the love and happiness that have brought family and friends together today. Enjoy!

A Wedding-Day Sample Schedule

WE are going to use a sample couple, Matt and Kim, as a first example to show how their day developed. The activities of the bride and groom are shown in bold. From this schedule you can see how much goes on around the couple and how valuable extra help can be.

Saturday, June 12, 1999—1:00 P.M. Ceremony

8:00 A.M.	**Bride—Hair appointment**
	Mom cuts ivy in backyard; ivy to pail in garage
9:00 A.M.	Bill and Jim (hired help) pick up rental tables and chairs, set up at Community Center
9:30 A.M.	**Bride back home**
9:45 A.M.	Attendants arrive at bride's home to dress
10:30 A.M.	Men meet at groom's parents home to dress
10:45 A.M.	Uncle Mike arrives to drive bride and dad to church
11:00 A.M.	**Bride and dad leave for church**
	Mother and attendants drive two cars to church
	Aunt Sue and Lisa (volunteer decorators) to bride's home to pick up bows, ivy, etc.
	Caterer and staff arrive at Community Center
11:15 A.M.	Florist delivers bouquets and personal flowers to church
	Coordinator arrives at church
	Bride, her parents, and attendants arrive at church
	Flower girl arrives (with her parents)

Coordinator pins on mom's corsage and father's boutonniere

11:30 A.M.   **Photographer arrives and takes pictures of bride, her parents, and her attendants**

Aunt Sue and Lisa arrive and decorate church

Coordinator puts out guest book, pen, programs, and unity candle

11:45 A.M.   **Groom, his parents, and his groomsmen arrive at church**

Coordinator pins on mom's corsage and all men's boutonnieres

Ring bearer arrives (with his parents)

12:00 P.M.   **Pictures of bride's side finished; they are now in parlor until called for processional**

Coordinator asks if they need anything

Photographer ready to take pictures of groom, his parents, and groomsmen

Aunt Sue and Lisa ask coordinator quickest way to Community Center; coordinator shows them on map

Coordinator gives ring bearer his pillow for pictures

12:15 P.M.   Aunt Sue and Lisa leave for Community Center

Bridesmaid asks coordinator if she has a needle and thread

Coordinator does quick fix on bride's mother's hem

12:30 P.M.   Photographer done with pictures

Groom and best man to room to wait with Pastor Johnson— remind best man to give honorarium to Pastor Johnson; does he have the ring?

Ring bearer asks coordinator where bathroom is; she shows him and rescues ring pillow

Men ready to seat guests; they ask coordinator which arm to extend; she explains it's arm opposite his boutonniere. She reminds them the first three rows on each side are reserved.

Program distributors arrive, ask coordinator where programs are; she shows them where to stand

Organist starts playing

Guest book attendant ready with guest book

Quick check on bride, attendants, and families—does maid of
    honor have ring?

Candle lighters a little late arriving; coordinator hands them the
    lighters, reminds them to do the candles on the altar first,
    then the candelabra

12:50 P.M.   Tells families that the grandparents should be ready to be
    seated, then the parents

12:55 P.M.   Guest book attendant closes guest book; coordinator advises
    guests, "The ceremony is about to begin. We will have the
    guest book at the reception for signing."

Coordinator tells groomsmen to stop seating guests. Those
    groomsmen who aren't seating parents or grandparents
    should join Pastor Johnson and groom.

Tells guests to please seat themselves

Coordinator lines up grandparents and parents, adjust
    grandpa's bow tie

12:55 P.M.   Seating of groom's grandparents by Gary

12:57 P.M.   Seating of bride's grandparents by Dave

1:00 P.M.   Seating of groom's parents by Gary

DJ arrives and sets up at Community Center

Cake delivered to Community Center

1:02 P.M.   Seating of bride's mother by Dave

Dave and Gary join other men

Attendants lined up; coordinator give ring bearer back the
    pillow, reminds bridesmaids to hold bouquets lower

1:04 P.M.   **Pastor Johnson, groom, and groomsmen come out at front of
    church**

1:06 P.M.   Processional of attendants

Fluff the bride's train

1:08 P.M.   **Processional of bride and her father**

Ceremony begins

Coordinator has two minutes to collapse and then hurries
    over to Community Center

1:15 P.M.   Aunt Sue and Lisa were lost and just now arrive at Community Center

DJ helps them carry in things

Coordinator helps Lisa put bows on cake table and places cake knife and toasting goblets

Coordinator puts place cards on reserved table

Coordinator puts tape and basket for cards on gift table

1:30 P.M.   **Ceremony ends**

Pictures taken at altar

DJ ready to play quiet music

Bill and Jim arrive with ice

1:40 P.M.   Guest book attendant arrives at Community Center and sets out book and pen

1:45 P.M.   Guests arrive at Community Center

Drinks and light hors d'oeuvres served

Uncle Mike pulls fancy old car up in front of church

Two bridesmaids gather up unity candle and programs, put in bag, and take with them to reception

2:00 P.M.   Bridal party leaves church for reception

Matt and Kim ride in car to reception

2:15 P.M.   **Bridal party arrives at reception**

Coordinator takes bridesmaids' bouquets and places them on the head table and cake table

2:30 P.M.   DJ announces buffet; bride and groom should be first in line

Guests eat; coordinator should, also

3:00 P.M.   **Bride and groom finished eating; they visit with guests at tables**

3:20 P.M.   Coordinator will let bride and groom know that the toast will be soon

Coordinator reminds the best man and maid of honor of toast

Coordinator reminds the caterer to get champagne poured

Coordinator dampens napkin and places on cake table

3:30 P.M.   DJ announces time for toasts

Best man takes microphone and gives toast

                Maid of honor gives toast

3:45 P.M.   **Bride and groom to cake table**

                Coordinator shows them how to hold the cake knife;
                    photographer readjusts

                Coordinator reminds catering staff to save top layer of cake

4:00 P.M.   **First dance**

                Parents' dance

                All guests dance

                Coordinator gives DJ his check

                Coordinator tapes cards to gifts

                Coordinator and date dance to a few songs

4:30 P.M.   **Bouquet and garter toss;** coordinator finds bouquet

                She gathers up toasting goblets, cake knives, pillars for cake,
                    guest book

                Groomsmen ask coordinator if she has white shoe polish so
                    they can write on the getaway car; she is pleased to say no

5:15 P.M.   DJ announces last song

5:30 P.M.   **Bride and groom leave in decorated car** (with no writing on
                  windows)

                Families still standing around talking: "Wasn't it a perfect day?"

                "Everything went so smoothly."

                "It was just wonderful."

                "We are so glad you could come."

                "It was so nice to get to sit and talk with you."

                Bill and Jim load up gifts, bags of goodies, leftover drinks, and
                    cake top and take to bride's parent's home

                Bill and Jim return to community center to load up chairs
                    and tables

                Coordinator smiles and heads to her home (to take off her
                    shoes)

We hope you have an idea from this schedule what transpires on a wedding day. The next schedules are actual ones used in two of our bride's weddings. The first schedule is for an 11:30 A.M. ceremony held in the beautiful courtyard of a bed-and-breakfast. This was followed by a brunch reception with dancing inside the inn.

Thursday, August 18

        Liquor delivered to location

Friday, August 19

        Men pick up and try on tuxes

        Rental company delivers arch

6:00 P.M.   Rehearsal

        Rehearsal dinner

        Bride and attendants staying at bed-and-breakfast

Saturday, August 20

        Bed-and-breakfast sets up ceremony area

9:30 A.M.   Florist arrives

Decorate arch	Pew bows
Aisle runner	Personal flowers
Decorate cake	Centerpieces

        Videographer arrives

10:00 A.M.   Photographers arrive

        Bride, attendants, and her family ready for pictures

        Bakery delivers cake

10:30 A.M.   Groom, groomsmen, and family arrive for pictures

        Musicians arrive and set up

11:00 A.M.   Groomsmen ready to seat guests

        Musicians play

        Judge arrives

        DJ arrives and sets up

11:22 A.M.   Close up guest book

11:25 A.M.   Seating of groom's grandparents

11:27 A.M.   Seating of bride's stepgrandmother

11:29 A.M.   Seating of bride's grandmother

11:31 A.M.   Seating of groom's parents

11:33 A.M.   Seating of bride's stepmother

11:35 A.M.	Seating of bride's mother
11:37 A.M.	Judge and groomsmen come out
11:39 A.M.	Processional
11:42 A.M.	Ceremony begins
12:00 P.M.	Ceremony ends
	Two groomsmen bow out guests
	DJ plays soft music inside bed-and-breakfast
	Guests proceed inside for drinks
	Pictures of wedding party and families taken
12:30 P.M.	Buffet
1:30 P.M.	Toasts by best man, maid of honor, father of bride, and judge
1:45 P.M.	Cake cutting
2:00 P.M.	First dance—bride and groom
	Second dance—first half, bride and her father
	second half, wedding party
3:00 P.M.	Photographer departs
3:45 P.M.	Bouquet toss
3:55 P.M.	Garter toss
4:30 P.M.	Limousine arrives
4:45 P.M.	Bride and groom depart
	Guests depart
	Maid of honor will take gifts, toasting goblets, etc., to bride and groom's home
	Best man's wife will return cake stand to bakery

The following schedule was used for a 4:00 P.M. ceremony in a lovely old church. The reception with dinner and dancing was held in the beautiful lobby of a historic building.

Friday, January 15

10:00 A.M.	Topiary trees delivered to reception site (lobby) and stored in back room
1:00 P.M.	Bridesmaids, mothers, and fathers decorate topiaries

2:00 P.M.	Check in at hotel
3:00 P.M.	Men to pick up tuxedos
4:00 P.M.	Ladies to bridal store to pick up five dresses
5:00 P.M.	Everyone to hotel to dress for evening
6:00 P.M.	Rehearsal
7:00 P.M.	Rehearsal dinner

Saturday, January 16

9:00 A.M.	Rental company delivers tables and chairs to lobby
	Hair stylist and manicurist arrives at hotel to "do" women
12:00 P.M.	Caterer arrives at lobby
1:00 P.M.	Men gather in best man's room at hotel to dress
2:00 P.M.	Florist delivers personal flowers to hotel
2:15 P.M.	Rental company delivers pew candles to church
	Florist delivers flowers to church
	Friend puts out programs, guest book, and attaches pew bows
2:30 P.M.	Photographer arrives at hotel to take pictures of bride, bridesmaids, and family
2:45 P.M.	Groom, his family, and groomsmen arrive at church
	Friend puts on their corsages and boutonnieres
3:00 P.M.	Photographer arrives at church to take groom's side pictures
3:30 P.M.	Women ready to leave hotel for church
	Horse and carriage arrives at church
	Friends decorate carriage
	Groomsmen ready to seat guests
	Organ starts playing
3:45 P.M.	Candle lighters light candelabras
	Cake set up at reception by bakery staff
	Friend decorates head table at reception
3:55 P.M.	Close up guest book
	Seating of groom's grandparents
	Seating of bride's grandmother
4:00 P.M.	Seating of groom's parents
	Seating of bride's mother

	Mothers light parents' candles
4:08 P.M.	Minister, groom, and best man enter from side
	Bridesmaids and groomsmen down aisle
	Matron of honor down aisle
	Mother of bride stands to signal all guests to stand
	Trumpet plays
	Bride and father down aisle
	Ceremony begins
4:15 P.M.	DJ arrives at reception
	Bartenders arrive at reception
4:30 P.M.	Bells rung
	Recessional
	Pictures in sanctuary
	Guest book attendant leaves for reception
4:45 P.M.	Guests arrive at reception
	Hors d'oeuvres and drinks available
5:00 P.M.	Friend takes down pew candles and loads in truck
	Husband of matron of honor takes altar flowers to reception
	Wedding party leaves church in cars
	Bride and groom leave in horse and carriage
5:10 P.M.	Wedding party and families arrive at reception
5:30 P.M.	Bride and groom arrive at reception
	DJ announces bride and groom
5:45 P.M.	Salad served
6:00 P.M.	Dinner served
7:00 P.M.	Toasts by best man and matron of honor
7:15 P.M.	Cake cutting
7:30 P.M.	First dance
8:15 P.M.	Garter and bouquet toss
8:30 P.M.	Photographer departs
10:30 P.M.	Last dance
10:45 P.M.	Bride and groom depart
	Friend takes cake pillars, champagne glasses, cake knife, guest book, tape, gifts, and candleholders from head table.

These schedules represent just a few of the endless forms a wedding can take. Your special day will evolve into its own set of unique memories. More than anything, we wish you a simply elegant wedding that launches a lifetime of happiness for you. Good luck!

BRIDE'S CHECKLIST FOR WEDDING DAY

____ Be sure to eat!

____ Hair appointment; take headpiece, and wear a top that buttons.

____ Gather your bridal outfit, your going-away clothes, and luggage for honeymoon.

____ Allow yourself plenty of time to leisurely dress and apply makeup.

____ Make sure you have the rings before proceeding to the ceremony.

____ Relax! You have worked hard preparing for this day. Enjoy!

APPENDIX

CAKES

Cake Decorating Workstation, $21.99
Jenny Harris and Sara Carter
Price Stern Sloan
ISBN: 0-8431-7973-2

The Wedding Cake Book, $35
Dede Wilson
Macmillan
ISBN: 0-02-861234-5

CALLIGRAPHY

Calligraphy, $16.99
Don Marsh
North Light Books
ISBN: 0-89134-666-X

CEREMONIES

African-American Wedding Readings, $24.95
Tamara Nikuradse
Dutton Publishing
ISBN: 0-525-94403-6

The Catholic Wedding Book, $19.95
Molly K. Stein and William C. Graham
Paulist Press
ISBN: 0-8091-2956-6

Everything Jewish Wedding Book, $12
Helen Latner
Adams Media Corporation
ISBN: 1-55850-801-5

For as Long as We Both Shall Live, $12
Roger Fritts
Avon Books
ISBN: 0-380-76928-X

Interfaith Wedding Ceremonies: Samples and Sources, $19.95
Joan C. Hawxhurst
Dovetail Publishing
ISBN: 0-9651284-1-5

Into the Garden: Poetry and Prose on Love and Marriage, $13
Robert Hass and Stephen Mitchell
Harper Perennial
ISBN: 0-06-016919-2

Weddings by Design, $14
Richard Leviton
Harper San Francisco
ISBN: 0-06-2501007-X

Weddings from the Heart: Ceremonies for an Unforgettable Wedding, $14.95
Daphne Rose Kingma

Conair Press
ISBN: 0-943233-21-6

DECORATIONS

Tabletops, $24
Barbara Mulo Ohrbach
Clarkson Potter
ISBN: 0-517-70332-7

Twenty Wonderful Weddings and How to Craft Them, $19.95
Barbara Finwall and Nancy Javier
A Leisure Arts Publication
ISBN: 1-57486-090-9

DETAILS

The Beautiful Bride, $12
Mitchell Behr
A Perigree Book, The Berkley Publishing Group
ISBN: 0-399-52373-1

ETIQUETTE

Emily Post on Weddings, $7.95
Elizabeth L. Post
Harper Perennial
ISBN: 0-06-274008-3

FLOWERS

Bridal Flowers, $25.95
Maria McBride-Mellinger
Little, Brown and Company
ISBN: 0-8212-1917-0

The Complete Book of Wedding Flowers, $16.95
Shirley Monckton
Cassell Publishing
ISBN: 0-304-34565-2

The Flower Arranging Expert, $12.95
Dr. D. G. Hessayon
Expert Books
ISBN: 0-903505-41-X

Wedding Flowers, $24.95
Fiona Barnett
Simon and Schuster
ISBN: 0-671-72834-2

Wedding Flowers, $26.95
Shane Connolly
Trafalgar Square Publishing
ISBN: 1-57076-108-6

FOOD AND DRINK

The Buffet Book, $29.95
Carole Peck
Viking Press
ISBN: 0-670-86516-8

Catering Like a Pro, $19.95
Francine Halvorsen
Willy Press
ISBN: 0-471-006882

Fast and Fabulous Hors D'oeuvres, $17.95
Michelle Braden
Macmillan
ISBN: 0-02009185-0

Guide to Great Wine Values, $10 and under, $9.95
Wine Spectator's Press
ISBN: 1-881659-41-0

WEDDING ATTENDANTS

I'm in the Wedding Too, $14.99
Caroline Plaisted
Dutton Children's Books
ISBN: 0-525-45752-6

WEDDING ATTIRE

Sew a Beautiful Wedding, $8.95
Gail Brown and Karen Horton Dillon
Palmer/Petsch Publishing
ISBN: 0-935278-05-02

Sewing for Special Occasions, $15.95
Singer Sewing Reference Library
ISBN: 0-86573-287-6

"I Do" Veils—So Can You!, $19.95
Claudia Lynch
Harpagon Productions
ISBN: 0-9650813-6-2

TRAVEL INFORMATION

Consulate or embassy for the country of
    your choice
Travel agencies

HOW TO FIND LOCATIONS

[City name] Convention and Visitors
    Bureau
[City name] Chamber of Commerce
[City or county name] Local and Regional
    Park Districts
[City or county name] Park and Recreation
    Departments
Local wedding magazine (on display at
    bridal gown stores or bridal fairs)

MARRIAGE LICENSE

[County name] Clerk's Office
[City or county name] Marriage License
    Bureau

WEB SITES

www.accuweather.com—local weather
    including five-day forecast

www.ultimatewedding.com/songs—
    database of songs to choose from for
    ceremonies and receptions

www.usabridal.com—features bridal
    gowns and where to purchase them,
    as well as online bridal catalogs

www.usno.navy.mil—sunset time for
    any day of the year

www.weddingsourcebook.com/page75.
    html—wedding etiquette questions
    and answers

www.weather.com—current weather
    across the United States, including
    current temperature and five-day
    forecast

www.yourstorybookwedding.com—
    information from wedding coordinat-
    ing professionals for brides and
    grooms to be

RECOMMENDED READING

Bride's Guide to Emotional Survival, Rita Bigel-
Casher, C.S.W., Ph.D (Prima Publishing)

What to Do After You Say "I Do", Marcus
Jacob Goldman and Lori J. Goldman
(Prima Publishing)

INDEX

❧ NOTES ❧

❧ Notes ❧

❧ Notes ❧

❧ Notes ❧

❧ Notes ❧

❧ Notes ❧

The Perfect Wedding Is About Elegance—
Not How Much You Spend

You don't have to spend a fortune to have the beautiful wedding you've always wanted. In this complete wedding planner, bridal expert Sharon Naylor shows you step-by-step how to plan your dream wedding and still have money left over to enjoy a fabulous honeymoon or put a down payment on a house!

ISBN 0-7615-3597-7 / Paperback / 368 pages / U.S. $16.95 / Can. $25.95

Modern-Day Weddings with Grace and Style

Wedding ceremonies are still about love and romance, a special moment that creates a beautiful and everlasting union. But not everything related to weddings stays the same over the years. Etiquette evolves, rules change. With the help of this book, you can stay on top of it all and learn how to combine timeless wedding traditions with the latest trends and social styles.

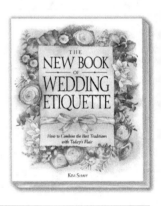

ISBN 0-7615-2541-6 / Paperback / 312 pages / U.S. $16.95 / Can. $25.95

The Ultimate Planner for the Ultimate Honeymoon

On your honeymoon, would you like to swim with the dolphins in the Bahamas? Enjoy a breathtaking Alaskan cruise? Whatever your romantic getaway dream, you'll find it inside—along with practical and innovative ideas, new travel trends, budget breakdowns, and the top 10 honeymoon spots in several categories of style and location across the globe. This must-have guide provides everything you need for your once-in-a-lifetime honeymoon.

ISBN 0-7615-3731-7 / Paperback / 384 pages / U.S. $16.95 / Can. $25.95